The Condition
of Jewish Belief

The Condition
of Jewish Belief

A Symposium
Compiled by the Editors
of *Commentary* Magazine

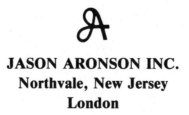

JASON ARONSON INC.
Northvale, New Jersey
London

The material in this book originally appeared in *Commentary* magazine,
August 1966, Volume 42, Number 2.

Library of Congress Cataloging-in-Publication Data

The Condition of Jewish belief.
    1. Judaism—Doctrines.   2. Judaism—United
States.   I. Commentary (New York, N. Y.)
BM601.C63   1989   296   88-33345
ISBN 0-87668-863-6

Manufactured in the United States of America. Jason Aronson Inc. offers
books and cassettes. For information and catalog write to Jason Aronson Inc.,
230 Livingston Street, Northvale, New Jersey 07647.

CONTENTS

PREFACE

It is almost a quarter of a century since *Commentary* magazine presented a symposium entitled the "State of Jewish Belief" and alas! a quarter of the symposiasts are no longer in the land of the living. May their souls be bound in the bundle of life.

Why the symposium, and why then?

In 1966 Vatican II, Catholicism's own Reformation, was still news, commanding the attention of many previously indifferent to religion generally but more particularly to theology. Equally arresting were reports, here and abroad, about Protestant prelates and theologians delivering themselves of sentiments that sounded rather lacking in piety, not to say downright atheistic. (To paraphrase the second couplet of a clerihew of W. H. Auden's, "That was not the trade/For which they were paid.") The editors of *Commentary* wanted to know what Jewish theologians would say.

Looking back, we can see that the Zeitgeist not only helped to bring the symposium into existence but also influenced the choice of questions to be asked. To our eyes, *now,* two questions were conspicuously absent: concerning the Holocaust and concerning Israel. Why did the editors fail to ask them then—for that matter, why did I fail to note then what I am noting now—and why did so many of the symposiasts fail to raise them? After all, the memorialization of the Holocaust is today so hallowed among Jews as to discourage any suggestion, however modulated and respectful, that an overemphasis on victimization can be unwholesome and counterproductive. And when it comes to Israel, American Jews today are accused of having made Israel the sole content of our Judaism.

Theologically, the Holocaust would come under the head of theodicy or of *haster panim*—God's hiding His face, or absenting Himself—and Israel would come under the head of God in history, or of messianism. I have heard Christian theologians say that what strikes them in dialogue is how Jews characteristically treat those aspects of theology as if there were no other.

First, Holocaust. That is our name for Hitler's murder of the Six Million. A generation ago the name was not yet standard. People tended instead to use synecdoche: "Auschwitz," for instance, or "crematoria." A commonly accepted name was lacking because a commonly accepted recognition of the need to come to terms with the unnamed thing was lacking.

Second, Israel. The State of Israel was established in 1948, but not until 1967 and the Six Day War did Israel seem to become real and precious to most of us—mortally imperiled, and in the end, gloriously victorious.

From Gerson Cohen we learn that historically it has taken Jews a full generation to admit to full consciousness, as by chronicles and threnodies, the calamity of the generation earlier. Calamities we have had in plenty, but only one re-establishment of a State of Israel. Acknowledgment of blessing appears to be as subject to a one-generation delay as acknowledgment of curse.

I have been stressing the symposium's limitations: its debt to a Zeitgeist, with all that that connotes of mere temporality, and its inattention to the Holocaust and Israel. That is not the note on which I wish to end.

What symposium—even Plato's—has been unaffected by time and circumstance? Yet some symposia are of more enduring worth than others. This one is published anew because it merits renewed reading and study.

M. H.
Erev Sukkot 5749
September 1988

INTRODUCTION

Milton Himmelfarb

Contributing Editor of Commentary *magazine.*

⟨ One of the ironies surrounding all the discussion which has recently been taking place over the "death of God" is that, in many intellectual circles at least, God has not been so alive since Nietzsche wrote His obituary almost a century ago. The editors of *Commentary* were curious to know whether this might also be true among Jews, especially since so much of the talk about Jews in past decades has been about Jewishness—that is, Jewish identity, understood historically and sociologically—rather than about Judaism, the system of belief and practice to which Jews are presumably obligated. Accordingly, a list of questions was submitted to some 55 rabbis (not all of whom, however, have congregations). Thirty-eight responses were received: 15 Reform, 12 Conservative, 11 Orthodox. They appear in this book in alphabetical order.

Why were these rabbis invited and not others? These seemed likely, by the consensus of colleagues or by their own reputations. Why slightly more Reform respondents than Orthodox or Conservative? That is how the acceptances came out.

So much for the statistics. Reading the responses, one sees that the true division is between Orthodox and non-Orthodox. Cover the identifications of the non-Orthodox and what they write will not usually give you a clue to a Reform or a Conservative affiliation: few call themselves Reform, none Conservative. (Yet when a Conservative wants to pray in a synagogue and has no Conservative synagogue to go to, he is much more apt to go to an Orthodox than a Reform one—especially if he is a rabbi.) Of the 27 non-Orthodox, I come up with this census: more or less classical (or serene) Reform, 4 or 5—including a borderline case whose affiliation is Conservative; Reconstructionists, 6 or 7—including one who takes his lead not from Dewey but from Sartre and Camus; disciples of Franz Rosenzweig—15 to 17, mostly youngish. The single greatest influence on the religious thought of North American Jewry, therefore, is a German Jew—a layman, not a rabbi—who died before Hitler took power and who came to Judaism from the very portals of the Church. Obviously we have not given Nahum Glatzer and Schocken Books anything like the thanks we owe them for telling us about Rosenzweig in English. Obviously, also, since even his name is unknown to most of us, the rabbis have not spoken about him loudly enough.

Any other group of non-Orthodox North American rabbis would probably show a similar distribution, but it is uncertain that the Orthodox respondents in this symposium are equally representative of the Orthodox rabbinate. The uncertainty does not derive from the ratio here of so-called modern Orthodox rabbis to other rabbis; modern Orthodoxy is not a theological category, it is a sociological one. Nor does the uncertainty derive from the absence of some of Yeshiva University's young critics of Orthodoxy from within, since their criticism basically is of strategy and style. It derives, rather, from something that is hinted at in one of the more uncompromising responses below. To be able to write English passably well; to have earned a doctorate in English literature, or analytical philosophy, or biology; above all, to teach those subjects—for Orthodox Jews of a certain kind, such interests and achievements and occupations are, if not sinful, capable of inciting to sin. At the very least, the old-school Orthodox say, a man who studies Milton or Mendel or Wittgenstein is guilty of *bittul Torah*, the transgression of wasting on frivolities the time he could give to studying Torah. Of course this is not an unchallenged Orthodox doctrine, or rather, attitude; but of course, equally, this symposium cannot adequately represent those whose doctrine or attitude it is. Still, some of the eleven Orthodox respondents here are in a certain measure spokesmen for Orthodoxy of this traditional East European type. They may even think of themselves as sacrificially risking the world's slow stain in order to shield the purity of those whose study of Torah is never diluted or diminished by the study of anything else.

Two or three give this impression. One is wild, not easily

classifiable. The rest stand in the tradition of another German Jew, this one of the nineteenth century, Samson Raphael Hirsch. For him a guiding principle was *Torah 'im derekh eretz*, Torah together with secular studies. Thus he irritated the modernizers, for whom Torah was outmoded, and the old-fashioned, for whom secular studies were unclean. I say that most of the Orthodox rabbis here stand in Hirsch's tradition —though some would prefer to say they are the disciples of Elijah Gaon of Vilna—because Hirsch was not only Rabbi Hirsch, he was also Dr. Hirsch. That was why the Polish and Lithuanian rabbis regarded him as a bad example for their own people, though no doubt useful enough for the fallen-away Jews of the West.

Hirsch and Rosenzweig, Germans. All modern Jews—insofar as they are modern, or even post-modern—walk in the footsteps of German-speaking Jewry, the pioneers of Jewish modernity. Besides Hirsch and Rosenzweig, there are Mendelssohn and Heine and Zunz and Frankel and Hess and Herzl and Freud and Kafka and Baeck and Buber. Most of us, children or grandchildren of Jews from Eastern Europe, have inherited a dislike of German Jewry. We still chuckle when we remember Chaim Weizmann's *mot*, that the German Jews combined the best elements of both cultures, having all the modesty of Jews and all the charm of Germans. It is time we did the handsome thing and acknowledged our debt.

What has been Buber's influence on Jewish thought in America? From the evidence of these statements, hardly any. That is strange and needs explaining. Buber was the first Jewish religious thinker since Maimonides eight centuries ago who was able to influence Christian theology, and his thought might therefore have been expected to benefit among Jews not only from its own merit but also from its prestige among Christians. Yet as between Buber and Rosenzweig, close associates in the 1920's, it is Rosenzweig, fated to die young and ignored by Christians, who dominates non-Orthodox Jewish theology; and it is Buber, who died full of years and honored in Christian theology, whose influence on Jews is relatively slight. Some Jews read his books on Hasidism, more flocked to his lectures, and a few respected his work for rapprochement between Arabs and Jews. That is about all.

Buber was for encounter and openness, not for law. His opposition to *halakha* as the enemy of openness and spontaneity made him unusable for the Orthodox, of course; but also for the non-Orthodox who affirm the principle of *halakha* (though not the *halakhot* specifically) on either Rosenzweigian or Reconstructionist grounds. Classical Reformers, while not put off by Buber's anti-halakhism, can be made uncomfortable by his talk about encounters between God and man. Reformers of this type like to say that "the essence of Judaism" is contained in Micah 6: 8: ". . . what does the Lord require of you/but to do justice, and to love kindness [*or* mercy], /and to walk humbly with your God?" When they use their own language, the essence is apt to be worded in some such way as this: ". . . a religion [that] affirms ethical monotheism, rejects idolatry, makes central the sanctity of man and the significance of the task of bringing about a just society . . . is a true religion." The part about walking humbly with your God tends to get lost.

What impression does this symposium give of the present state of Jewish religious thought? In general, that there is far less theological ferment than among the Christians and that there are few new ideas about Judaism. Mordecai M. Kaplan's system was all but complete thirty years ago, Rosenzweig's forty years ago, Hirsch's a hundred years ago. What is a novelty to some Christians is, as many of the rabbis here remind us, old-hat to Jews. The Anglo-American "death of God" corresponds in a way to the slogan—and title of a book—that preceded the worker-priest movement in French Catholicism in the 1940's: France, missionary territory. This was short-hand for the discovery that France, once the Eldest Daughter of the Church, had become so dechristianized that it had to be won back for Christianity almost as if it were *in partibus infidelium*. With Jews, the large-scale defections and indifferences go back before that, and before Nietzsche and Feuerbach, to when we were first becoming modern. From this point of view, at least, Spinoza was the first modern Jew.

Those modern Jews who want to be religious, including rabbis, have such a long familiarity with modernity-godlessness that they are less apt to be shocked by it, for good or for ill, than the Christian clerical "country boys," as one of the rabbis below calls them. Biblical criticism, for instance. Most of the non-Orthodox (and perhaps a few Orthodox, too, privately) would say what Rosenzweig said: Wellhausen may be right, and the Torah may be composed of four independent documents, J, E, D, and P, brought together by R; only for me, R does not mean Redactor, as for Wellhausen; for me it means *Rabbenu*, our master, or teacher, or rabbi. Living in tension with modernity, embracing and repelling it, doubting and believing—these are old experiences for religious modern Jews.

On the whole, therefore, the relative absence of newness was to be expected, together with the dominant intellectual, if not emotional, calm. After all, Judaism is rather old. Intellectually—if it is decent to make such a distinction—even the crematoria are not qualitatively new. Before Hitler the Jews knew Hadrian and Chmelnitzki and how many others. Intellectually, Auschwitz should shake the secular humanist at least as much as the theist.

In any case, theology is not the same as religion or faith, and Jews have normally theologized less than Christians. It was not Jews but Christians who, to use an old illustration, massacred each other for an iota: is the Son *homoousios* with the Father, of the same substance, or *homoiousios*, of like substance? Even when bloodless, Christian theologizing has often led an independent life of its own, with no effect on deed or creed but serving ultimately as little more than raw material for dissertations in *Dogmengeschichte* or some other branch of intellectual history.

The typical Jewish attitude is embodied in an old story about a German Jew who had returned to Judaism and was lecturing on prayer one afternoon at an Agudath Israel convention. (Naturally, the title of his lecture was "A Prolegomenon to a Preliminary Approach to the Philosophy of Prayer, Ontologically Considered.") After he had been talking for some time, his auditors began to drift out in twos and threes, until he was all but alone with the fidgeting chairman. "Have I offended them?" "No," said the chairman, "they're leaving to say the afternoon prayer."

That is how I feel, but when others say it to me, in defense of the minimal theological activity in our rabbinical seminaries, I become suspicious. I am not a follower of Buber, but once, when everybody at one seminary was sneering at

Buber-*mayses* (a pun on the Yiddish *bobbe-mayses*, old wives' tales), I almost wanted to enlist on Buber's side. They were obviously sneering at the theological enterprise itself and rabbis should know that a sneer is no refutation. Historically, some Jewries were more theological than others. The more advanced the culture they lived in and the more vigorous its philosophical life, the more they had to theologize. Medieval Spanish Judaism was more theological than Franco-German Judaism, Maimonides more than Rashi. In those terms, we live in Spanish and not Franco-German conditions, and we too need theology. How much? More, I would say, than we are getting.

THE QUESTIONS

1. In what sense do you believe the Torah to be divine revelation? Are all 613 commandments equally binding on the believing Jew? If not, how is he to decide which to observe? What status would you accord to ritual commandments lacking in ethical or doctrinal content (e.g., the prohibition against clothing made of linen and wool)?

2. In what sense do you believe that the Jews are the chosen people of God? How do you answer the charge that this doctrine is the model from which various theories of national and racial superiority have been derived?

3. Is Judaism the one true religion, or is it one of several true religions? Does Judaism still have something distinctive—as it once had monotheism—to contribute to the world? In the ethical sphere, the sphere of ben adam la-chavero, *what distinguishes the believing Jew from the believing Christian, Moslem, or Buddhist—or, for that matter, from the unbelieving Jew and the secular humanist?*

4. Does Judaism as a religion entail any particular political viewpoint? Can a man be a good Jew and yet, say, support racial segregation? Can a man be a good Jew and be a Communist? A Fascist?

5. Does the so-called "God is dead" question which has been agitating Christian theologians have any relevance to Judaism? What aspects of modern thought do you think pose the most serious challenge to Jewish belief?

Jacob B. Agus

Rabbi of Beth-El congregation (Conservative)
in Baltimore, Maryland.

ℂ (1) A great sage of the Talmud maintained that of all the 613 commandments in the Torah, only two were spoken by God, as it were, while the other 611 commandments were articulated by Moses. These two commandments, which constitute the divine core of revelation, are the first and the second of the Ten Commandments—"I am the Lord Thy God who has taken thee out from the land of Egypt, from the house of bondage" and "Thou shalt have no other gods beside Me."

This seminal observation is, as Maimonides noted, an excellent introduction to the meaning of revelation in Judaism.

The word of God in the heart of man is not an auditory hallucination, but a power, a deposit of energy, a momentary upsurge toward a higher level of being. So, all of Scripture speaks of the divine word as the power of creation in the universe. Our contemporary science concurs in recognizing freedom as the vertical dimension of evolution from the amoeba to the human, and from the primitive to the prophet or the philosopher. This divine pulsation consists of a rhythmic thrust and retreat. In its forward movement, the divine word is articulated in a new vision of freedom, the import of the first commandment. As Philo pointed out, freedom is the "divine image" in man. Now, the embryonic feeling of freedom is expressed either in the quest of the intellect, or in the judgment of conscience, or in the aesthetic drive of productivity. In these three dimensions, man creates freely by asserting an identity between his own spirit and the universal laws of being.

This outgoing flow of the tide of spirit is followed by an ebb which is expressed in the second commandment—namely, submission to the One God. From the psychological viewpoint, this retreat takes one of two forms—either submission to a communal pattern of worship, or a personal mystical surrender to the divine Being. The collective tradition symbolizes this passive phase of the divine word, when the recipient feels himself embraced and fixed within a divine design, "chosen" and "covenanted."

The active and passive phases of divine revelation are, to my mind, two facets of the same phenomenon. So, the word of God is revealed within us when we join in worship no less than when we seek to articulate its meaning by way of intellectual concepts, ethical undertakings, or imaginative constructions. The human response to the word is necessarily of this two-sided form—"*na'aseh venishma*," we shall do and we shall listen.

The account of the divine revelation at Sinai therefore represents not a historical event, but a paradigmatic image of the perennial course of revelation. Whatever it is that actually happened in the wilderness of Sinai is of great historical interest. But historical events should be studied by the appropriate methods of inquiry. I follow the researches of scholars in this domain with avid fascination, but the scientific reconstruction of the steps whereby the primitive religion of the Semitic nomads became the Jewish religion is not directly relevant to my understanding of the character of divine revelation.

The human spirit, in its alternation from worship to free creativity and back again, is the self-revelation of the universal spirit. This process cannot be complete, or exclusive, or unique. It is an ongoing movement in the culture of a people as in the life of an individual. The entire panoply of religion and the diverse fields of culture are "the commentary," as Hillel put it.

The "original sin" of man consists in the tendency to stop the impetus of this creative undulation of man's spiritual life. In the phase of self-surrender to the inherited tradition, which is the congealed lava of previous deposits of faith, man may come to believe that he already possesses the fullness of the divine word. He has eaten of the tree of knowledge. It is now a concrete possession, ingested in his bowels, as it were. If he is to grow and evolve, the divine word must expel him from his fool's paradise. Out in the dark and the cold, he knows that somehow God has both embraced and rejected him; it is his destiny to regain his "lost paradise," by laboring with the sweat of his brow. Through his productive work, he can become "a partner to the Holy One, blessed is He, in the work of creation."

While dogmatism halts the flow of revelation at its phase of surrender to the all-embracing mystery, idolatry stops it at one of the way stations along the three currents of freedom. There is the idolatry of the intellect, in the arrogant affirmation of man's own self-sufficiency; idolatrous too is the self-righteousness of those who love one or more aspects of the infinite; but worst of all is the self-idolization of a community, the public life of which has been enriched by works of beauty and power.

When the three expressions of freedom are cherished together as independent values, without any relation to a Supreme Being, a secular humanism results, which is the better half of a dynamic faith. Yet, by itself, it poses the danger of alienation—man comes to feel adrift and rudderless, an easy prey to the diverse storms of mass hysteria. To be truly human, we must seek that which is more than human; otherwise, we come to idolize fragments of our protean and dynamic self. Our intellectual, ethical, and productive faculties tend to separate in practice, each producing its own categories and criteria. But, in the depth of our soul, they fuse together. In utter "truthfulness," *Wahrhaftigkeit*, as Hermann Cohen put it, we cannot but feel that our quest for reality must partake of the three realms of being—the rational, the ethical, and the aesthetic. And as this outgoing flow of spirit ebbs, we feel the glow of holiness, the awareness of being part of a grand design, in which our being is completed and also transcended. This is the meaning of Moses's injunction—"complete shall ye be, *with* the Lord, thy God."

On this view, the Torah, or the sacred tradition, mediates to us the spirit of holiness, and it builds up within us the power and dedication to ideal ends. Since revelation can no more be verbal than God can be a physical being, we must regard literalism or fundamentalism as the disease of religion. We acknowledge sadly that Judaism has been afflicted by this disease at various times, but we maintain that the tradition has never been either monolithic or inflexible. During the biblical period the prophets encountered massive resistance; the Sadducees restricted revelation to the written Torah, as other groups were to restrict it later to the biblical canon, to the Talmud, or to the Shulhan Arukh. But a succession of movements of self-renewal redeemed Judaism from the danger of fossilization—prophetism, the Pharisaic movement, the Philonic tradition, the rise of medieval rationalism, the emergence of Hasidism, and the gradual growth of the modernist movements—Reform, Conservative, and nonliteralist traditionalism.

I believe that the nonrationalist components of our tradition are essential to the symbolical structure of the faith. We can sense the feeling of holiness only in an atmosphere which reflects the transcendent mystery of our existence as individuals and as a community. Thus, I value highly the texture of worship, the various laws of so-called "sanctification," from circumcision to the dietary regulations. But these regulations are not literally ordained by God; therefore, they are subject to change in accord with the best judgment of the organized community. Whether the religious authorities should tacitly allow certain practices to become obsolete, or whether they should openly and officially disavow certain dogmas and rites, is a question of tactics. I happen to prefer the second alternative, as a rule.

The measuring rod is not only doctrinal content, or ethical validity, or aesthetic fitness, but also the need of maintaining the integral texture of the tradition as a whole. In religion, no law or practice may be judged in isolation from the general context of the life of faith.

(2) I consider that the traditional doctrine of the chosen people should be frankly and radically reinterpreted. If ever we hold an ecumenical "Jerusalem Council," this revision should be officially carried out. It is not enough to resort to the usual homiletical devices—the Jews were chosen for service, not for lordship; they were given greater responsibilities; they were to consider themselves aristocrats of the spirit, endowed with the ardor of *noblesse oblige*; they were in the actual unfolding of their historic destiny the "Suffering Servant" of humanity.

These apologetic turns and twists are totally inadequate, so long as they leave untouched the central core of the doctrine, the metaphysical uniqueness of the Jew. All the nations which in the nineteenth century claimed special divine missions were inclined to interpret their "white man's burden" in similarly grandiloquent terms. And in all the dogmatic faiths of the Western world, the whole of mankind was believed to be sustained by the merit of the "elect."

The doctrine of "chosenness" is too deeply embedded in the Jewish tradition to be ignored. Also, the feelings of "chosenness" are renewed perennially by two factors—the religious experience of individuals and the ethnic or historic consciousness of our community.

As a component of faith, the feeling of being "covenanted" should be generalized: every person should find a vocation and dedicate himself to it. So, too, the pride of belonging to a historic people should be universalized. All men should take pride in the noble achievements of their respective peoples, scrutinize their national failings, and guard against their collective weaknesses, even as we Jews are bidden to do.

As the doctrine is reinterpreted, we say that we ought to be a chosen people, as *example*, not as *exception*. We call upon all faiths so to universalize their sense of being covenanted as to recognize that other faiths offer similarly holy, even if not identical, doctrines and commitments. Perhaps we may induce other religions to follow our example and renounce their claims to exclusive possession of the "keys of the kingdom." In the same way, we call upon all nations to utilize their respective potentials for the benefit of all men. So, in our day, we demand of America that it act as a chosen nation. Its power and its idealism can and ought to be used for the advancement of all mankind. The American Negro is at present "chosen," in a similar potential and ethical sense, to serve as the spearhead for the elimination of poverty.

The pretense that this interpretation was always upheld in Judaism serves only to confuse our own people and to perplex the general scholar. The following sentence was part of the official formula for the admission of converts to Judaism —"Know that the World to Come is only for the righteous, and they are Israel. That which you see, Israel is in trouble in this world, it is a hidden good for them." (Yevamot 47a. Maimonides, Hilkhot Issurei Biah 14, 4. Shulhan Arukh, Yoreh Deah 268.)

The difference between this concept and the one herein

outlined is obvious. In any *aggiornamento* of our own, the revision of the ethnocentric impetus in our tradition should be the first item on the agenda.

(3) Rejecting the incubus of "sacred ethnicism," we find the elements of religious humanism in our Jewish heritage. I am frankly selective in my approach to the tradition. My philosophy and practice are influenced by my participation in Western thought, and properly so.

Within the Christian community, I find currents of religious humanism, which, apart from their ritualistic and dogmatic expressions, are similar to my own views. But the philosophical parallelism of ideas and sentiments does not diminish the deep gulf between the two faiths, consisting of the historic panoply of symbols, dogmas, rites, and institutions. Frequently, the same terms denote effectively different meanings in the two faiths. In many ways, the two faiths assume opposite and complementary orientations toward the divine mystery. But there is also an objective, shared domain of philosophy, social concern, historical consciousness, and cultural values. A religion can remain relevant and vital only if it confronts the challenge of this objective realm, which is the common universe of discourse of Jews and Christians. Hence the supreme, positive value to both faiths of their meaningful confrontation in an ongoing dialogue. But we cannot lightly bridge our differences, or aim at a mutually acceptable compromise. We must remember that we cannot jump out of history any more than we can stop the world and get off.

I do not maintain that Judaism contains certain ideas that are peculiar to itself. All ideas are communicable. In the course of time, they circulate freely in the intellectual marketplace. But as a historical creation, Judaism possesses a certain strong individuality, compounded out of a multitude of tangible and intangible factors. It is not unique, in a cosmic sense, for all historical religions are similarly distinguished by their own individual characters. All of us, as human beings, differ from one another, but when our sentiments and ideas are analyzed, we discover that in their component parts all men are alike.

I consider that the myth of Jewish metaphysical uniqueness is not a harmless superstition; it lies at the base of mythologi-

cal anti-Semitism. For the unspoken axiom of this complex
of malice and fantasy is that the Jew differs from all other
human beings in a deep, cosmic way, not merely in the way
all men differ from one another. It is this "metamyth," as I
call it, that made it possible for millions to believe the kind
of canards concerning Jews that they would have instantly
rejected in the case of other people.

Does this mean that there is no special value in our life
as Jews? There is value in the life of all communities *if* they
utilize their collective existence for the ends of God and
man. Our communal institutions are conceived and structured
to serve these ideals. Moreover, our faith and destiny are
historically involved in the central ideals of Western civilization, for good and for ill. There was no surge of freedom
that did not project us to the forefront; there was no tide
of popular passion and pride that did not vent its fury upon
us. Our fate as well as our faith have placed us at the cross-
roads of history.

(4) As a religious-cultural tradition, Judaism cannot be
identified with any social economic system. In a Communist
society, it would foster loyalty to the existing system, even
while it would encourage the inviolate freedom of the individual in matters of conscience. As a faith, Judaism opposes
the ideology of historical materialism; as the historical culture
of a minority, it resists the leveling process of a monolithic
society. But once the ideal of individual freedom is accepted,
it becomes possible to synthesize socialism with religion.

I believe that the antireligious belligerency of the Soviet
government is not essential to the healthy functioning of
Soviet society. In part, their atheist propaganda is anachronistic; in part, it is a component of their global attack against
the ideological substructure of the West. But when they mel-
low to the point of accepting genuine coexistence with the
West, the Communists will also moderate their opposition to
religion.

The plight of the Jewish religion in Soviet Russia is due
to the atheistic ideology of the government; the tragedy of
the individual Jews is due to the emergent nationalism of the
Russian peoples. On neither score is there reason to lose hope.

Fascism comes in two forms. It amounts to an absolutizing

either of the state, or of the nation. It would homogenize
society in the interest of economic efficiency or of national
greatness. The Jew, as a man of faith, cannot but oppose its
moral nihilism; as a member of a scattered minority, he must
resist its all-leveling, egalitarian impetus.

Judaism, as an old, historic faith, incorporated racist ideas
at diverse times, permitting slavery to thrive for many centuries. But the dynamic aspiration inherent in our millennial
experience as well as in our faith is certainly directed toward the goal of eliminating all forms of exploitation and
injustice. Accordingly, we should do our level best to eliminate the venom of segregation from American society. At the
same time, our long history makes us sensitive to the horrors
of artificial integration and enforced egalitarianism. In the
Great Society, there should be room for the organized sub-
groups to maintain social enclaves which provide fellowship
and a sense of domesticity. Also, the principle of equal opportunity for individuals cannot but be compromised in any
endeavor to give all groups their proper share of the preferred positions of the nation.

(5) The "God is dead" upheaval in Protestant circles is,
as I see it, right insofar as it is a reaction and a protest,
wrong insofar as it is a principle. The new theologians remind us that faith is a pointing to the ultimate mystery, not
a possession of it.

From the Jewish viewpoint, Christianity has been overly
"theological," making salvation dependent upon the right
opinions concerning the nature of God, the identity of the
Savior, and the meaning of salvation. Bishop Pike's assertion
that the Christian dogmas of the Virgin Birth, the Trinity,
and the Incarnation impede the essential message of religion
instead of helping it is altogether in line with the traditional
attitude of Judaism: "Would they left me alone, but kept
my Torah."

However, the atheistic theologians throw the baby out along
with the bathwater. In their eagerness to explore the implications of faith in God, they would deny its reality. They
serve a useful function as critics, not as teachers of religion.

What are the dangers to Judaism or the Jews that we can
glimpse on the horizon? I consider that the well-being of our
community depends on the maintenance of a relatively stable

equilibrium among all sorts of extremist movements. There may be reversions to fanaticism, along nationalistic, rather than religious, lines. A new wave of "know-nothingism" may arise when our nation recoils in disgust from its contemporary infatuation with crusading globalism. There is no reason to expect that future patrioteers will be any more tolerant of Jewish extra-American loyalties than the demagogues of the past were. In a way, the posture of "Israel-centrism" built into the structure of our worldwide philanthropy makes us more vulnerable to attack from this quarter than our former stance as a homeless and scattered people.

At the opposite extreme from nationalist or religious romanticism, a deep and wide-ranging nihilism may result from the fragmentation of ideals and pursuits in our society. Since religion is the meeting ground of three wholes—the whole of personality, the whole of existence, the totality of values—it is affected by every disintegrating movement. When the human personality is dissected into dehumanized fragments for the purpose of analysis, it becomes ever more difficult to regain the feeling of the mystery of man as "the image of God." When the bounds of existence expand to the point where intelligibility is completely lost, we can no longer sense the hope of "God becoming One and His Name One." When philosophers come to feel that the task of teaching an integrated philosophy of life is too much for them, then the gates are opened wide to cynicism and despair.

It may seem that the extremes of moral nihilism and romantic fanaticism are poles apart. But Hitler brought them together, for they are psychologically very close.

Our destiny is, for better or worse, tied up with the causes of individual dignity and social sanity.

Bernard J. Bamberger

*Rabbi of Temple Shaaray Tefila (Reform)
in New York City.*

❏ I am a Reform Jew by inheritance and conviction. That is to say, I am (1) committed to a positive religious view-

point that is (2) rooted in Jewish experience and (3) combined with intellectual and moral freedom. "

The phrase "positive religious viewpoint" needs further
explaining. Reform Jews do not, and need not, agree on all
matters of theology. I do not question the legitimacy, or the
positive religious character, of views held by Reform Jews or
others, even when I am not fully in accord with them. Indeed, those Christians who are currently publicizing the death
of God regard their position as affirmatively religious, and
they are probably justified in doing so. (Incidentally, I find
it ironic that Nietzsche's *mot* should suddenly become stylish
eighty years later!)

What the death-of-God school seems to be driving at is
first, the proposition that only scientific knowledge is true
knowledge; and second, that the scheme of scientific knowledge seems to provide no room for a traditional God-concept.
The second statement seems plausible, the first is open to
serious doubt.

For the scientific method precludes from the very start any
consideration of the factors of purpose or value. A scientific
hypothesis is an attempt to explain certain phenomena in
terms essentially mechanistic. To account for these phenomena
by saying that they were created for a certain purpose, or
that they are inherently good, noble, beautiful, etc., would
be to depart from scientific method.

Now the practical results of scientific research are exceedingly impressive, and (with some qualifications) I am duly
grateful for them. But this does not mean that science can
help us to deal with problems of life's ultimate meaning,
aims, and values—since these factors were eliminated in advance. Yet values and purposes are the most important things
in human life. The self, with its hopes and fears, its standards
and aims, may not be objectively observable and measurable,
but it is the one reality with which we all start. A scientist
dedicating himself to the impartial study of nature, an atheist
rejecting beliefs that would be pleasant because he cannot
compromise his intellectual integrity—all these express a concern with values which are outside the scope of scientific
treatment.

Indeed, not all natural phenomena are equally adaptable
to the exact measurement and controlled experiment that sci-

entific procedure requires. Research on problems of hearing is more advanced than research on the sense of smell, because it has proved difficult to fit odors into a mathematically controllable system. Yet no one suggests that perfumes are less "real" than melodies.

The area of purpose and value, the most vital area of our experience, seems beyond quantitative analysis and mechanistic explanation. We must deal with it as best we can, using the less precise tools of speculation and faith. I do not see how man can be radically alien to the world. His body is admittedly part of nature; how can his consciousness, with its intellectual, aesthetic, and moral content, be mere illusion, epiphenomenon? I hold to the faith—which I cannot prove, but which does not seem to me unreasonable—that there is a cosmic root out of which man's values grow. I believe that man's strivings, above all his ethical strivings, are not irrelevant to the universe. I believe man has some kinship with ultimate reality. Or, in more traditional language —though no language is adequate—I believe in God as a living power.

This faith is part of my Jewish heritage. Perhaps the most profound idea suggested by the *Shema* is this: that the source of our human values and the source of cosmic order are one and the same. The Bible affirms that God is both creator and lawgiver; He is to be served by obeying a law that is suffused with moral purpose. Implicit in the divine unity, likewise, is the conclusion that mankind must and shall become one.

The teachings of the Bible—the one and holy God, the sensitivity to human need and social obligation, the vision of world peace—evoke wonder and awe. How did it happen that the seers of the small people of Israel should have perceived so much that was both new and profound? The rediscovery of the literatures of Egypt, Babylon, and the rest—ancient Israel's neighbors and conquerors—has served only to heighten the mystery. The not infrequent parallels to the Bible which these literatures offer, far from reducing the extent of the Hebraic contribution, only underscore the spiritual uniqueness of Israel. The subsequent career of the Jewish people, rooted in the biblical heritage; the continued spiritual and intellectual development; the will to survive against overwhelming force; the involvement in so many of the crises of human history—all these add to one's sense of amazement. But more than that: the unique experiences of Jewry, it seems to me, impose special religious and moral obligations on the Jew. As a Negro student once said to me, "Jews should know better."

To recognize the facts of Jewish history and the responsibilities they impose upon the Jew does not seem to me arrogant. The suggestion that our doctrine of the "chosen people" has provided a pattern and rationale for aggressive militaristic nations is, frankly, rubbish: Did the Assyrians and the Romans, or even the modern Japanese, get their notions of conquest and loot from reading the nineteenth chapter of Exodus? The idea of pushing other people around, unfortunately, does not have to be learned.

I believe, to resume, that God *is*, and that the experience of Israel has been an experience of His revelation. But I cannot believe that He has revealed Himself only in Israel; and I do not see how any revelation can come to man except through man. This applies to the great insights attained by the philosophers, scientists, poets, and prophets of many peoples; it applies also to Hebrew Scripture and tradition. Despite my reverence for the Bible, I find in it not only evidence of divine inspiration, but also of human fallibility. What prevents me from according absolute authority to the Torah is not primarily the discovery by modern scholars that the Pentateuch is a composite work and largely post-Mosaic; it is the unmistakable fact that the Torah contains some elements which are intellectually untenable and some that are morally indefensible. It is no longer possible to allegorize what is irrational and explain away what is unethical. I do not believe any revelation, however genuine, is absolute and final. But the recognition of human deficiencies in the Torah does not require me to reject it altogether. It contains much that is sublime and challenging; and even the survivals of primitive thinking serve a purpose: they enable us to measure the grandeur of the spiritual achievement which the Bible records.

The commandments of Scripture and tradition, ethical and social, as well as ceremonial, are not to be adopted blindly. They must be considered thoughtfully and reverently. Only on the basis of genuine understanding can the individual make the decision as to which of the commandments he can and should obey, which should be modified, and which he may (or even should) discard. In arriving at such judgments, he may well be guided by the opinion of informed and committed members of his own religious community, and he will not lightly disregard the consensus. But as a free person, he must assume the responsibility of the ultimate choice.

Experience seems to indicate that the regular and intelligent observance of tradition and rite enriches the spiritual life of adults and children alike. Reform Judaism, which at the start challenged the Orthodox doctrine that the ceremonial law is no less divine and binding than the ethical imperatives, today tends to encourage more observance, especially in the home. But even more urgent is the problem of applying to present-day situations the great moral principles proclaimed by the prophets. To respond as believing Jews to the challenge of war, poverty, and racial injustice is today the great *mitzvah*. But a deep concern with social morality in no way conflicts with the cultivation of personal piety, including custom and ritual.

To what extent are the theological and ethical teachings of Judaism distinctive in today's world? This question seems to me not at all urgent, and indeed not very meaningful. Western culture has been profoundly influenced by the Hebrew Bible; it has also, without knowing it, absorbed much of Pharisaic Judaism, as transmitted by the New Testament. It is not surprising, then, that Christians share many of our beliefs, and that Jewish moral standards are accepted even by persons who do not consider themselves religious. This does not make these values any the less Jewish, or any the less compelling to us. (I remember a kindly Christian lady who asked me if we Jews have the Psalms *too*.)

Judaism remains significantly different from historical Christianity, if only by rejecting much that Christianity added. And, if some liberal Christian groups approximate our theological position, that would seem to be a problem for them: since they share the Jewish outlook, why don't they become Jews? For us this is hardly a problem. I deny that Judaism would be improved by divesting it of its distinctively Jewish elements. On the contrary, it would lose immeasurably by severing its essential connection with the life and experience of the Jewish people. Much of its power lies in the fact that it is not an abstraction, that to be a Jew is not merely to assent to a creed, that the Jew must identify himself with a varied and inspiring past and with all Jews in the world today, whatever they believe or practice, even if they renounce belief and practice.

To the born Jew, this means that he may select from the total Jewish heritage what he is able to believe and to do; but to be or not to be a Jew is not really within his choice. For to repudiate his identity is to deny part of himself. On the other hand, I have found that prospective converts to Judaism are often greatly attracted by its specifically Hebraic and traditional elements. Judaism appears to them as something organic and alive, in contrast to some other liberal religions, which appear somewhat colorless and "synthetic."

What I have written will appear theologically naïve to some persons of Jewish origin and sympathies; to others it will seem hopelessly inadequate because it does not accept the divine origin and absolute authority of the entire Torah. Realizing this, I myself am bound to avoid dogmatic definitions as to who is and who is not a Jew. If someone regards himself as an affirmative Jew, I shall be reluctant to deny his claim, however appalled I may be by his notions about Judaism. To me, the notion of white supremacy, for example, is a repudiation of a central truth of Judaism—the oneness of mankind. To me, Communism appears completely incompatible with Judaism, not only because of its explicit rejection of religion, but because it denies the rights of the individual conscience. But then, some of my fellow Jews hold that one who rejects *kashruth* has rejected essential Judaism, and others hold that one who does not migrate to the State of Israel really cares nothing about Jewish survival. I shall then vigorously oppose racialism and Communism and try to keep them from influencing the actions of the organized Jewish community—just as my Orthodox and Zionist friends will work for what they believe is good and oppose what they believe is wrong. But I shall not be willing to read out of Jewish life any persons who want to be a part of it.

In short, I reject all the absolutisms. In politics, the ex-

should at all times and in every situation show obvious ethical or doctrinal content. To fulfill even the ritual commandments is to do the will of God. Doing the will of God represents for the Jew the only possible contact between himself and God outside the actual revelational experience —which theoretically is a constant possibility, though actually it occurs very seldom. Contrary to the entire antinomian Pauline tradition, Christian or emulated by Jews, the doing of the will of God is, for the authentic Jew, a deeply inspirational and highly ennobling experience. It is an intensely religious experience, which keeps religion itself alive. Since for the religious Jew all ethics and doctrine are anchored in Judaism, the ritual commandments, which are one of the sources of Judaic inspiration, are never without ethical or doctrinal relevance. Judaism is neither ethics nor doctrine, but a life of obedience to God out of awe, and of submission to Him out of love; within this life ethics and doctrine, too, have their place.

But if this is the case, would not any commandment of God, because it expresses His will, have the same religious significance or effect? The answer to this old theological question is Yes; no matter what the contents of the commandments were, man would still be obligated to submit to the will of God and obey them. But it so happened that God revealed and commanded this Torah and not another one, because of His concern for man. As to the meaning of the commandments, even those that apparently have neither ethical nor doctrinal content, one must—as always—refer to the oral tradition, as well as to the continually developing philosophy and theology of Judaism. One may explain the ritual commandments according to Saddia's hedonism, or according to Yehuda Halevi's quasi-mysticism; according to Maimonides's rationalism, or Kabbalistic mysticism, or according to some more sophisticated modern religious philosophy or theology. The commandments, however, remain unchangeably binding.

(2) It is not possible to answer this question without saying a few words about the nature of Judaism. Judaism is not a religion of mere faith, but of a faith that leads to the realizing deed. In Judaism one is damned or saved by one's

way of life. A religion of mere faith is a religion of the soul; a religion which is a way of life is a religion of the whole man. Faith is always private; the way of life, which demands the comprehensive deed, is always public. An act of faith concerns only the individual soul and its God; a deed, because of its public quality, concerns other people. And the more comprehensive the deed, the more it concerns others and affects them. In fact, a way of life which comprehends life in all its manifestations is not realizable by the individual, but only by a group, a people, a community that makes its realization a communal responsibility. Such a way of life, a religion of the all-comprehensive deed, is Judaism. Judaism had to become the religion of a people, if it was to be at all. It is for this reason that in my book, *God, Man and History*, discussing the subject of the chosen people, I made the statement that God did not choose the Jews, but the people that God chose became the Jewish people as a result of their taking upon themselves the task and responsibility for the realization of Judaism.

On numerous occasions the Bible itself warns the Jews against every form of national or racial conceit. If Jews at times do indulge in a sense of national or racial superiority, this is not a consequence of the religious concept of having been chosen by God. Rather, it derives from the historic experience of Israel, based on the treatment Israel has received at the hands of other nations and religions. Bearing in mind that experience, often it was hardly possible for a Jew not to be convinced of his own moral, ethical, and religious superiority. Any other group's theories of racial or national superiority which are based on the same kind of historic experience of suffering and martyrdom at the hands of others are no less justified.

(3) Judaism is the one true religion—for the Jew. As for the rest of mankind, Judaism teaches that the righteous of all the nations have a share in the world to come.

Judaism did not *once* contribute monotheism to the world, as this question assumes; it is still being contributed. Monotheism is not yet the possession of the overwhelming majority of mankind. It is not even a reality in the kingdom of Christianity. This is not merely a matter of dogma and its theological interpretation; it is a question which fundamentally affects one's interpretation and evaluation of the whole of existence. The God of monotheism, who tolerates no mediator between Himself and man, is not the deity that by its very nature necessitates a mediator. Man, too, is understood by monotheism in a manner vitally different from the way he is seen by Christianity. The man of monotheism can only confront God without a mediator; in Christianity, man cannot confront God except by way of the mediator. From the point of view of Jewish monotheism, God's relation to man and the world is essentially different from the relation which is affirmed by Christianity. The entire position and purpose of man in the monotheistic scheme of things is greatly different from the Christian interpretation. Nor is monotheistic messianism, Christian messianism.

From the Jewish point of view, the only non-Jewish monotheistic religion is Islam. But neither has Islam accepted Jewish monotheism. Allah who rules by fate is not the God of Israel; nor is Islamic man, who is ruled by divine fate, the man of Jewish monotheism. Here, too, the ramifications of Jewish monotheism reach into every area of human existence. As ever before, Jewish monotheism is still in the possession of Israel alone. Nor can this ever be otherwise. Even if all mankind should accept Jewish monotheism, Jewish monotheism would still remain in Jewish hands. According to Judaism, Jews do not simply happen to be monotheists, but rather monotheists are of necessity Jews.

Because of the special quality of Judaic monotheism and its ramifications, which comprehend all of life, the believing Jew's ethics are also distinctive. The quality of obligation in Jewish ethics is absolute. But absoluteness of obligation may be derived only from the will of God that wills the good. The unbelieving Jew or the secular humanist adheres to an ethic that derives from man or society. Consequently, such ethics must forever remain relativistic. Secularist ethics possess neither universal nor absolute validity. The Nazi criminals pleaded correctly that they acted in accordance with the valid law of their state.

As to Christian ethics, one should remember that it is questionable whether Christianity is universal rather than totalitarian. The very concept that human salvation may be

achieved only through faith in Jesus destroys the idea of a
universal mankind. It divides humanity into the redeemed
and the unredeemed. The unredeemed, given over to original sin, can do little good in this world; only the redeemed
are free from the morally and ethically crippling burden of
original sin. Thus, from the Christian point of view, Christian ethics is superior to the ethics of the unredeemed.
Christian charity toward the non-Christian always proves
Christianity's superiority; it always carries within itself an
attitude of condescension. A Christian is kind *even* to the
unredeemed. Because of the Christian premise, Christian
humility is inverted pride. Monotheistic ethics is universal.
The one and only God is the father of the one and only
mankind. Man, as God's creature, is capable of goodness
and, therefore, responsible for his actions.

Again, man's position of responsibility within Jewish
monotheism equips the ethical law with greater seriousness
than it is able to have within a religious system in which a
fated destiny is bound to water down the concept of human
responsibility. As to Buddhism or Hinduism, it is questionable whether they are not amoral and altogether lacking in
ethical seriousness. According to the Bhagavad-Gita, the
truly wise mourn neither for the living nor for the dead. In
the world of Maya nothing may be taken too seriously.
Reality, what truly matters, is to be found not in this world,
nor in individual existence. But there is no ethics in the All.

(4) Taking "racial segregation" to mean what is meant by
it in contemporary parlance in the United States, I would say
that one cannot be a good Jew and support it. It should, however, be understood that such a statement by itself is rather
far from being a program for the solution of the very real
problems involved in the conditions of the Negro citizens of
this country.

I believe that dialectical materialism is not the only possible philosophy of Communism. A communistic form of
social organization need be neither antireligious nor atheistic, just as capitalism is not of necessity God-fearing and
nonmaterialistic. There are sufficient historical examples to
prove the point. One cannot be a good Jew and a Marxian
Communist. But one may be a Communist without being a

Marxian materialist. A religious communism is not a contradiction in terms. I cannot, however, see how one can be a good Jew and a Fascist.

(5) The "God is dead" question is a direct outgrowth of the Christian promise to man. Christianity promised redemption through a self-sacrificial act of God. The sacrifice was made, but all historical experience has gone to show that the promise has not been kept. Mankind has remained unredeemed. The question's relevance to Judaism I see in the fact that among the untold abominations of human history, the murder of six million Jews in the heart of Christian Europe has been one of the most abominable. For me this fact proves that *that* God is indeed dead. The theological meaning of the concentration camps and the crematoria is that the guilt of man has never been taken from him through any divine self-sacrifice. But for the non-Jew, too, man's historical experience, especially in the twentieth century, has shown that the God who, according to Christian teaching came into the world for the specific purpose of human salvation, was nowhere when salvation was most needed.

Man has been let down by the God who made the promise. This is essentially a Christian dilemma. The God of Israel never made such a promise. On the contrary. His plan for mankind has never been revealed. Whatever the divine plan, there was never any doubt left that according to the God of Israel man himself had to play an important part in his own salvation. While Israel's martyrdom in our generation does raise serious theological questions for the Jew, what happened does not belie a divine promise and is explainable in terms of human responsibility.

The "God is dead" theology, too, could emerge only from the womb of Christianity. Jewish monotheism is an "either-or" proposition. Either God or no God; if God is dead, then He was never alive. If God is dead, then He can have no theology. If He is dead, why bother at all? But one can understand how within Christianity the mediator may "theologically" survive the death of God. The ground for such a "theology" was prepared centuries ago by Marcion. "God is dead" has no relevance to Judaism directly. From the Jewish point of view it is the not altogether unexpected

Christian version of the old pagan cry about the death of Pan.

The most serious challenge to Judaism is not modern thought but "modernism" as such. But modernism is an attitude, not a thought. It has been brought about by affluence and the increase in the means of living, which in themselves seem to guarantee security to man. Man has become rich in means, and the rich in means never seem to be in great need of ends. At the same time, the future of man is so dark and impenetrable that the very complexity of the problem induces man to throw up his hands and adopt a philosophy of *carpe diem*. It is not modern thought which poses the challenge to Jewish belief, but the absence of a genuine inclination on the part of most Jews to think seriously about human experience and the human condition in our times, and to do so from a position of rootedness in their own historic tradition.

Eugene B. Borowitz

*Professor of education and Jewish religious thought
at Hebrew Union College-Jewish Institute of
Religion in New York City (Reform).*

❡ I confess I cannot answer the questions put to me. In part, that is because in today's world it is no longer clear what might constitute an answer. What will do: A Whiteheadian resolution of God with science? A linguistic analysis of Covenant? A phenomenology of *mitzvah*? A poem so moving, a deed so luminous, conviction so inescapable? Hardly. Every response begets another question or two; every answer fathers new doubts in the believer no less than in the man who says he has no faith. The more significantly human our questions are these days, the less anyone seems able to give relatively firm and unshifting answers to them. That, probably, is why the only literature that thrives today is criticism, though with the continuing decrease of positive voices, the critics must spend much of their time criticizing other critics.

Another reason answers do not come easily is the nature of Judaism. *Moshe Rabbenu* never claimed to be the theological answer man. That role, of course, was left to Elijah, but only when he came to announce the advent of the Messiah. Judaism, finding stability in law and community, could maintain great theological openness without losing its identity. While answering many questions firmly, our tradition ignored some and left a good many others open for debate, divergence, and hopeful waiting.

That older dynamic of integrity was badly shaken by the Jewish Emancipation. Worse, since the Emancipation began, Jews have never been able to arrive at a new theological equilibrium. Every time it seemed as if a satisfactory Jewish intellectual adjustment to this radically new social circumstance might be achieved, the cultural milieu itself underwent major transformation. German philosophical idealism, Zionist nationalism, Reconstructionist naturalism, Buberian existentialism—all spoke to a world which disappeared virtually the moment those doctrines were elaborated. How can you adjust your Judaism to a culture that will not stand still? The Emancipation has not meant a revolution in Jewish life but a series of revolutions—and the end is not yet in sight.

Finally, and most important, how shall we speak when the passions on both sides of the conversation regularly turn answers into charges and questions into refutations? One cannot try to speak for Judaism without being plunged into great anxiety. The Jewish community appears so perfidious and out for such tawdry gain. Every indicator seems to say that this precious Jewish heritage may soon be squandered away by an unthinking generation or two. No wonder that such explanations as can be offered quickly turn to moralizing and denunciation, often made the more inaudible by the tone of assured sanctity in which they are sounded. Yet even where the words proceed simply, they are often not heard. We listen only in order to rebut. We attend only to determine which of our armory of retorts will be most devastating. What shall we hit them with most damagingly— religious wars, David Hume, the Grand Inquisitor, or the bourgeois nature of the synagogue? The depth of the defenses is understandable. To believe, even to begin to

believe, would mean to change our lives, probably fundamentally. Moses Herzog discovered that painfully but with
some ultimate satisfaction—though we do not follow him
far enough to see what he makes of his new/old Jewish
rootedness.

The stakes are great on both sides and that generally leads
to the ludicrous situation where those who cannot speak
directly are talking to those who refuse to hear. Yet we must
do what we can, and I begin with these words on our special
problem of communication because I am convinced that how
we talk to one another is as important as what is said.

Let me begin with an assertion that itself could form the
focus of a lengthy discussion. Today, only religious faith,
only Judaism or Christianity, can provide the basis for a
social (and therefore personal) ethic worthy of the name.
The man who values high intellectuality, social responsibility,
compassion for the underprivileged, and justice for the powerless, the man who insists that self-fulfillment must simultaneously mean devotion to mankind's ennoblement, finds
those values increasingly without foundation in today's world.
Individuals may still care, but "hot" concern is odd in a society
intent on "playing it cool." What contemporary social institution can be counted on to give Western man a strong sense
of moral direction? The university? The mass media? The
corporation? The country club? The laboratory? The
couch? The debate over the end of ideology hinges on the
recognition that no general support for social-ethical values
is now available to us. To hope that selective involvement
and situational response can long be relied upon to produce
effective social-ethical results seems most unrealistic to me.
It is an effort to secure the present by living off the inherited
religious and philosophic capital of other generations. It may
work for a while but already the shortage of resources to
draw upon is becoming clear.

If we are to affirm our sense of social ethics we must do
so through some sort of religious faith. That does not make
religion true, only useful. But I believe that the reverse is
also real; that men who know, not in a detached or technical
way, but in a very intimate and personal way, that these
social concerns are not just individual caprice but are fundamental to the universe itself—such men are already religious.

They already have faith in a ground beyond themselves which mandates and authorizes their personal and social ethics no matter what vulgarities and degradations the culture around them cultivates and celebrates. Their commitment, their faith is so close to what the Jewish tradition knew as God that, from my point of view, the critical point of acknowledgment has definitely been passed. From there we move on to the lesser, though significant, questions of conceptions, envisagements, relationships.

That is why I am not deeply troubled by the death-of-God theology. It has thus far exploited every religious man's ambivalence by its sensationalistic negation from within. It has not yet had to face the positive question of the grounding of moral values. Such statements as have appeared indicate that this movement will not be able to evade the relationship of God to value noted above. Thus, van Buren insists he is only working at language "games"; Hamilton founds his ethics in the man Jesus, but can't say why Jesus should be anyone's ideal; and Altizer agrees with Nietzsche that we should welcome moral nihilism as necessary to progress— that, after Hitler and Hiroshima. For a change, Judaism has been through a modern experience before Protestantism and the results of our investment in secular Zionist ideology, humanist modern Hebrew literature, ethical culture, and salvation by socialism can well indicate the ultimate sterility of this line of thought. (I permit myself this brevity since I have treated this group of thinkers in detail in "Death of God Theology," *Judaism*, Winter 1966.)

The key intellectual problem of our time, then, is not science or technology but meaning; or to put it in Camus' affecting way, hope. Man's mind and man's society cannot provide either, for both rest on the reality of moral values. These need to be grounded in something transcending man himself. So somewhere at the core of his being, each man must make up his mind as to whether there is meaning and hope for life or not. Intellectuality alone cannot resolve so existential an issue, though reasoning may open one to decision. What is ultimately required is faith. I have profound respect for those men who deny general meaning yet in the face of the plague manage to commit their lives to the decency of fighting it. I also believe a great many men live in faith but do not wish to acknowledge it. Which means that the truly central religious issue is getting people to see the question and make their choice. Most of us prefer the modern style of building a worthy life by chasing diversion to avoid decision. The agnostic who glories in the righteousness of his indecision either hides from the faith he has or, in fact, has committed himself to a life of absurdity. To have the virtues of one's nonconvictions is hardly a living option in the face of life's demands for decision. The agnostic, and not the atheist, is the real hollow man.

What Judaism can contribute to the world is not, then, an idea or a concept—how strange such German idealistic philosophical constructions begin to sound! What Judaism can uniquely give the world is Jews, men, and, equally important, communities that live by their social, messianic hopes and try to effectuate them in day-to-day reality. That does not mean all Jews are noble or even that individual Jews are faithful all the time (one of the many things the Bible is quite frank about). It does not mean that Jewish commitment will quickly reveal answers to the problems of nuclear disarmament or feeding the world's hungry. What it does mean is that when this people is faithful to its God and its tradition, it produces an astonishingly high proportion of men and communities whose sense of interhuman responsibility is as great as anything mankind has ever known. No other human institution has yet shown the capability that Judaism has of transforming a statistically large number of individuals into socially motivated persons and groups. More important, Judaism has given Jews such a fundamental sense of the importance of the communal, linked to the human, linked to the personal, that the social concern has not vanished from among them even under the most trying circumstances, persecution and affluence alike.

To a great extent Christianity shares Judaism's social values and commitment. Believing in the same righteous God of history, the two faiths will often agree or act similarly as they face issues which their religious affirmations reveal as universally human. Still, if providing a foundation for personal and social value is the main virtue of religion today as seen from outside the circle of faith, then it is not the occasional identity of moral action but the question of its source which should most concern us. Here there is a subtle but substantial difference between the two faiths. Partially, it is the old issue of primacy for faith or works, and while that is in part a false distinction, the weighting of the response is decisive for determining the essential character of the ensuing life of faith. So when Jews stop believing all else they still have guilt about what they do or don't do. The responsible act remains critical as long as their Jewishness does not die. And when Christianity needs a sense of social passion it must largely turn to Israel's prophets to authorize and define it.

The nature of the hope is likewise significantly different. Where Judaism knows Exodus, Christianity has Easter. Judaism's trust is in the God who acts in this history. To Judaism, the terms "redemption" and "salvation" have as much to do with the here and now of the human situation as they have to do with eschatology. To my Jewish eyes, though Christianity affirms that God has acted for man in history, the hope He has given through the resurrection is that men can rise out of history. The *halakha* gives dignity to each act now, no matter how long the Messiah may tarry. Despite years of study, I have never been able to understand what significance there can be in Christianity to the acts done in the increasingly long interval between the first and the second coming.

The distinctive mood, then, of the Jewish religion is, of all things, hope. It is obviously not a simple trust that God will literally not suffer us to stumble. Egypt was our house of bondage for four centuries before it was the place of Exodus. And before Auschwitz and Treblinka, there was Assyrian genocide, Roman savagery, Crusader zeal, and Cossack brutality. Jewish hope is not to be dissociated from Jewish suffering. It is born in Jewish pain; that is why Jews have known how, religiously, to sigh—the impossible equivalent in a tranquil English to what the Yiddish feels as *krechtz*.

But Jewish tragedy is not the whole of God's truth nor even the most important truth. If one may say so, it is almost as if Judaism is not surprised when men are beasts. The Evil Desire precedes the Good by thirteen years according to tradition, and the non-Jewish world does not have the benefit of Torah with which to subdue it. Sodom and Gomorrah remain contemporary, a lesson we had forgotten. Is not much of our reaction to man's brutality to man in this century to be understood in terms of our shock at our self-disenchantment?

What surprises, astonishes, moves, determines the Jew is his realization, born of the experience of the Jewish people, that there is another, greater power moving through human events than man's brutality to man. The story of the survival of this improbable people is its chief testimony. The Jews have known not one but many Exoduses. All of them have been, if history has laws or repetitive patterns—miracles. Just by being here, then, the Jewish people is an evidence of hope. And when the Jewish people is faithful in practice to the God it knows has kept it alive despite the mammoth historical forces arrayed against it, it is an active force for hope.

Somehow the Jews know this, even today. Without anyone having to remind them of their pledged responsibility, against the reality of what they themselves had experienced of what it might mean to be a Jew, they rose up out of their concentration camps and, *lehavdil*, American apathy, to refuse Hitler his final victory. They insisted on continuing as Jews. That makes no sense. It happened. So, again, goes Jewish history, literally incredible, yet the real record of God and men shaping history.

Some will say this is a harsh, even cruel hope. It is indeed a far cry from Grossinger's, the East-European Jew's folk-paradise become reality. It does not promise much to the individual Jew or any given Jewish community, certainly not ease and security. Yet when Jews join in this people's millennial service and make it their own, they have a sense of purpose and meaning which personal failure cannot destroy and cultural retrogression cannot undermine. What they do not complete, they know the Jewish people will stubbornly work out. And though the Jewish people falter, God will see it through history, as tough and punishing a course as that may be. He has done so until now. He does so today. He will continue to do so until the Messiah comes.

That is not much to give for what is demanded in return— one's heart and soul and might. Yet it is the most precious thing a man or mankind itself could have in this troubled age. It is hope, realistic without being pessimistic, positive but not naïve. It will make God's kingdom possible despite the traumas history yet contains.

The man who shares Israel's historic hope will want to express it in his life as do other of his people, today as yesterday. The issue cannot be the 613 commandments. Characteristically, no one has ever clarified what Rabbi Simlai was talking about when he used that number and no one can keep them "all" today, e.g., the sacrifices. The question of Jewish practice in a time of radical social dislocation is more usefully one of the respective roles of God and man in revelation. If God gives, and that is all, change is limited to what He allows and man's dignity is, by modern standards, severely diminished. If only man creates—then, like a diet, the laws are too easily changed and the values tend to disappear. Neither the older orthodoxy nor the older liberalism will do. My understanding of revelation involves both man and God actively. Its best analogy is human relationship. The intense personal reality of a relationship demands that we express and fulfill it in action, but the person who knows this must find which acts will be appropriate to the relationship. Thus man fills in the content of the law— that is his honorable role—but he does so in response to the living presence of God who is the source and the criterion of the appropriateness of his action. In the case of the Jew, because the convenant relationship is historic and communal, the decision cannot be made in terms of what is purely personal and momentary. Tradition will play as much of a role as innovation.

We stand in a curious post-halakhic, pre-halakhic stage. The social context of the old law is shattered so that even if we were to restore personal assent to Israel's convenant, the old patterns of its observance could not fully be restored. Some seem, to my liberal mind, presently inappropriate to the reality of the relationship as best we know it. Yet, as a nucleus, perhaps a decisive one, of American Jews comes more and more to believe and practice, a new, general, community-wide standard of Jewish observance may well emerge (if the social milieu does not once again drastically change). Until then I am satisfied to let each Jew ask, mindful of other Jews and the tradition, what does God want of me, a member of His covenant people? I acknowledge that such a standard will perpetuate the present chaos of contemporary Jewish practice, but I trust that a renewed sense of the reality of the covenant will maximize concern and increase practice, eventually to socially identifiable proportions.

The man who seeks the reality of Israel's covenant with God should know that it is far less likely to be found in thinking about it than in trying to live by it. One commandment will do for a beginning, any one which seems to speak to him and which he can undertake in his search to clarify his association with his people and its God. A morning prayer, study of an anthology of rabbinic literature, the blessing over whiskey, the prohibition against gossip—he can begin anywhere. And when the inner embarrassment of doing a *mitzvah* as a *mitzvah* has been overcome, he can then see what the reality of covenanted existence might mean—and then hopefully go on to another *mitzvah*. Going back will be our best means of going forward.

All I have written sounds too assertive and dogmatic to me, for I know that I do not lack for doubts or difficulties with much of what I have said. What I do lack is space in which to discuss them. For I, too, long for the coming of Elijah and since he, much less the Messiah, may delay, it would be nice if in the interim we could sustain one another with that old, great Jewish virtue: talk.

Maurice N. Eisendrath

President of the Union of American Hebrew Congregations (Reform).

℃ (1) I do not believe that the totality of the Torah is the literal revelation of God to man. This does not mean that the concept of revelation itself is meaningless. Rather, it means that every single syllable of the Torah cannot be taken as literally revealed. There are several reasons for this conclusion. First, there is much in the Torah that is self-contradictory. Did God, for example, create man on the sixth day after all the splendors of heaven and earth had been brought into being and proclaimed "good, even very good," (Gen. 1:6), or at the very outset of that creative thrust when "no shrub of the field was yet on earth" (Gen. 2:5–7)? Then, too, there are innumerable passages that offend our ethical sense: for instance, the statement in Exodus which suggests that a slave is money to his owner, or the command to destroy utterly the Amalekites, including the women and children, as well as Samuel's condemnation of Saul for not following this vicious and vengeful command to the letter. Second, it is self-evident, especially as a consequence of biblical and archaeological research, that much in the Bible is directly the result of the history and the surroundings of Israel.

The contemporary concept of revelation should mean, therefore, that man, by his very nature, struggles to understand the divine, and that for us as Jews the most important record of that struggle is the Bible and our religious literature. As a result of this search, a number of incandescent ideas have flashed into the mind—or spirit—of man, not exclusively in Judaism, but preponderantly there. Such concepts as one God, one mankind, a messianic age, are more than the fruit of man's ratiocination. To me, they are the consequences of what may well be designated as inspiration, illumination, or, if you will, revelation. Above all, they cannot be neatly or scientifically delineated or systematized. I am led to believe, therefore, that the source of this revelation is that force, power, or being-beyond-all-else, the concept of which—or whom—we only grow to grasp from generation to generation. This concept and its concomitant demands vary from age to age. As our rabbis long ago pointed out, realization and revelation of the God of Abraham, Issac, and Jacob differed (since each came to God through his own experience) and advanced (since each added something new).

Besides, I do not believe that the question of the identical value of the 613 commandments is really a relevant question for our time. Not only did Saadia distinguish between the rational and dogmatic commandments, but he definitely claimed superiority for the rational. The Talmud, too, indicates a scale of values in terms of the dominant consideration of the saving of life. It also demonstrates under what conditions one should sanctify God's name. So I am within solid Jewish tradition, not only Reform, but even Orthodox, in distinguishing among the commandments.

It is incumbent upon us to observe those commandments which adumbrate the essence of Judaism or which can be related to such an essence. Obviously, one cannot in such a brief exposition define what that essence is. One can, however, assert that all the commandments which are corollary to Judaism's ethical monotheism—however that unity is currently interpreted—and to its consequent moral imperatives should be obeyed.

Those that are predicated solely on long-antiquated historic episodes or on exclusively particularistic or outmoded unethical and superstitious notions should be discarded. Reform Judaism has correctly maintained that Judaism is an evolving religion and that consequently there are aspects of Judaism one should accept and others that should be discarded, while in still other areas creative innovation is required. More important than the question of obsequious, abject obeisance to the totality of the 613 commandments is whether such responsible creativity is not essential to the viability and survival of Judaism.

(2) It was Hilaire Belloc, I believe, who quipped: "How odd/Of God/To choose/The Jews." To which a comtemporary wit has added: "It was/Because/His son/Was one." Wherefore one of our own more chauvinistic Jewish brothers calls upon us to: "Rejoice/The choice/Annoys/The Goys." Such arrogant *hauteur* regarding the "chosen people" I reject.

Per contra, any acceptable and decent concept of the chosen people must be understood in terms of what Zangwill called a "choosing people," in terms of a special responsibility, an *ol malchus shomayim* that the Jews have willingly assumed as a result of their historic and religious commitment. This is exemplified by the biblical dictum "And ye shall be unto Me a kingdom of priests and a holy nation."

Thus the Jews have taken upon themselves a singular stewardship as witnesses to the truth of ethical monotheism. As such, we have a mission to speak for justice and righteousness, not only because, as history has tragically demonstrated, we are the first victims of injustice, but rather because our Torah confronts us with a moral task which insists that we bring ever nearer the Kingdom of heaven on earth. This charge is incumbent upon us if we take our ethical and religious commitment seriously.

As I have interpreted the concept of chosenness—or choosingness—no doctrine of national or racial superiority can possibly be derived from it. In an era of venomous racial strife and inequity, in a time of the threat of total thermonuclear destruction of all that man—and God—have wrought, this witness to the ethical truths of Judaism becomes an agonizing responsibility, a responsibility which we shirk only at the expense of being untrue to our Jewish heritage.

(3) Jewish tradition has often indicated that "the righteous of all peoples have a place in the world to come." Anyone who, according to rabbinic exegesis, fulfills the seven commandments of the sons of Noah has satisfied the minimal moral and religious demands. However, the basis of Judaism is the rejection of idolatry. Thus, any religion which embraces idolatry is, in Judaism's sight, untrue. It is no accident that the rabbis conceived of Abraham as shattering the idols: such an abrogation of idolatry is the quintessence of monotheism. Ethical monotheism is not merely something that happened in the past. Rather, it is still essential—perhaps more exigent than ever. Our generation genuflects before more idols than any past generation. Nazism, Communism, the worship of any political leader as Big Brother, the absolute sovereignty of the state—all are idolatrous.

As in the days of Israel's prophets, unbridled worship of the nation, particularism unpurged by universalism, is idolatry and must be repudiated. It may even play the role of religion, but it is a false faith.

To the extent that a religion affirms ethical monotheism, rejects idolatry, makes central the sanctity of man and the significance of the task of bringing about a just society, it is a true religion. Different religions achieve this in greater or lesser degree in theory and practice. The task of Judaism is to bear witness to the Jewish faith and to make it concrete and relevant to our day.

It would require too much space to indicate why the ethical sphere does not suffice, and why transcendent areas are required to validate it. However, one can say that a believing Jew is distinguished from a nonbelieving Jew in several respects. A believing Jew is aware of and brings to bear in his life the teachings, ideals, values, and religious dimensions of *Judaism*. A nonbelieving Jew is merely aware of the accident of his having been born a Jew. He is alienated from his Judaism and although considered a Jew by the non-Jew, he finds the Jewish tradition with all its grandeur and pathos unintelligible. I doubt his staying power—and even more seriously that of "his children and his children's children unto the third and fourth generation."

The believing Jew has a faith to live by, a heritage to be proud of, a task and a challenge to be discharged. The non-believing Jew, since he jettisons his religion for the merely ethical (if even that), will deny himself those sources of religious experience and those elements of the Jewish faith which seek to answer the basic religious questions of man: What is the meaning and significance of my existence? Whence do I come and whither am I bound? *Why* is this "yoke of the Torah" placed upon me?

The nonbelieving Jew and the secular humanist can unite with the believing Jew in many ethical endeavors, but only the believing Jew can fuse such a universal ethic with what historically gave rise to it and abidingly nourishes and sustains it.

(4) As I have already indicated, Judaism entails a rejection of any political theory which maintains racial superiority or which justifies, as a necessary consequence of supporting it, the denial of the dignity and sacredness of man. I believe that Judaism demands the repudiation of totalitarianism under whatever guise. No, I do not believe "a man can be a *good* Jew"—and I doubt if he even deserves the precious designation "Jew" itself—if he cleaves to a totalitarianism of any breed or brand, which denies and denigrates the divine image in man and makes him a tool of the self-declared demigods and false gods of earth rather than the child of God, fashioned in His image and likeness, that unique blend of dust and divinity, of dust destined *for*

divinity, which the Psalmists rightly and rapturously believed him capable of becoming, "but little lower than the angels."

(5) Of course those "aspects of modern thought" which have led to the "God is dead" theology are relevant to Judaism. They challenge us gravely to reappraise all "sacred cows"—as Reform Judaism sought to do a century ago, but must now do again.

There are two aspects, however, to the "God is dead" debate. The first constitutes the belief that the God in the sky with the long white beard, the "cosmic bellhop," the messenger-boy God who is concerned with satisfying man's slightest whim, is dead. Such a God, being idolatrous, is better off dead and was actually never really alive. But there is a more profound sense to the phrase "God is dead"—the demise of all the values and structures which derived from the affirmation of the *living* God. Such a death sentence robs man of his capacity to integrate his experience so that he can believe in some fixed standards or philosophy of life. It was Heidegger who first interpreted Nietzsche's phrase to mean that all transcendent values have vanished. We can understand, even if we do not agree with, such a "transvaluation" of all values. The atrocities, the seeming meaninglessness of so much wanton destruction have critically challenged the simple belief in progress and the philosophy that all will be well in this "best of all possible worlds."

The real and far more dangerous deicides of our day, however, are not these theological nay-sayers, but rather all of us who so blasphemously breach the third commandment; who are so unforgivably guilty of the sin of *hillul Hashem*, so perverting the name of God by proclaiming His sovereignty and, at the same time, enslaving ourselves to every false god of our time: Mars and Moloch, Mammon and Baal, state and status, race and riches.

What actual blasphemy there is in the cry of "atheist" from the lips of many whose ears are deaf to God's decrees and whose hands are withheld from carrying out His will! Religion in America is less endangered by the occasional avowed atheist—even in the pulpit—than by those who profess His name in vain. And Judaism will be doomed, not by isolated God-denying preachers; it will be doomed by "the enemies within," by those who mumble their prayers mechanically in the synagogue and ignore God's teachings when they leave the sanctuary.

I believe that the truth of the death-of-God theology lies in the assertion that the God who does man's work is dead. But this leaves a genuine task for man and God. As long as man desired God to do man's work, he could not but be dissatisfied. But a genuine concept of God which sees God in terms of the ground and source of order and being, as the source of the ethical demands which challenge our lives, as the source of inspiration and holiness—this view in no way rejects man but makes God both meaningful and most truly alive.

A concomitant aspect of the Christian death-of-God theology is its commitment to Jesus. These theologians invert Santayana's "There is no God and Mary is His mother" by stating, "There is no God and Jesus is His son." But this is a sleight-of-hand—or mind—for the simple reason that Jesus *did* believe in God and if one truly commits oneself to Jesus and his faith and accepts Jesus as the symbol of man in the twentieth century, then one must also accept in some sense the faith that Jesus cherished. The process of demythologizing is arbitrarily limited to Jesus, the man. But what becomes of Jesus, the man, if he is simply the man who stakes his life on, and confronted death because of, his faith in God?

I believe that what may be termed practical atheism constitutes the most serious challenge to Jewish belief. Such atheism does not reject the concept of God theologically, but rather asserts that God and religion simply have no relation to, and no effect on, man's life. The problem of contemporary Judaism is to find a way for Judaism to know God in contemporary terms and to act as co-workers with Him in the "daily renewal of creation" and in the establishment of His kingdom of righteousness on His—and our—good earth in our time.

Ira Eisenstein

President of the Jewish Reconstructionist
Foundation and editor of The Reconstructionist.

❲ I believe Judaism to be the evolving religious civilization of the Jewish people. The origins of the Jewish people are lost in antiquity, but by the time it achieved self-consciousness it had already come to believe that it had been created by a special act of divine selection, that it had entered into a convenant with its God, Yahweh, who had given it a Law and a land, that it was destined to occupy that land so long as it obeyed the Law, and that by living in accordance with the will of Yahweh it would serve as a model for other nations, who worshiped false gods and led lives of immorality and violence.

From earliest times until the end of the eighteenth century, Jews believed that the Torah was divine revelation, that the Jewish people was God's "chosen people," and that all human history revolved around God's relations with Israel: God was either punishing Israel for her sins, and hence causing other nations to invade the land and exile the Jews, or God was rewarding Israel for obedience, and hence causing the nations to suffer defeat at Israel's hands. Since exile was, after the first century of the Christian era, the common lot of Jews, they assumed that they had not expiated their sins; but they believed that any day God might send the Messiah-king of the royal family of David to redeem them from *galut* and usher in the Sabbath of History, the messianic age. Then the dead would be resurrected, the final judgment would take place, and the righteous would enter into the world-to-come to enjoy their reward.

This entire syndrome of concepts has been shattered by modern historical science. Though traditionalists in our time continue to deny that any fundamental changes have taken place to undermine the validity of this version of Jewish history, I am convinced that the latter does not accurately describe what happened; nor are the prognostications of the future (the *eschaton*) based on any reliable evidence. Despite what the Torah claims for itself—and what some people still claim for it—I believe that it is a human document, reflecting the attempt of its authors to account for the history of the Jewish people, and for the moral and ethical insights which its geniuses acquired during the course of that history. It is "sacred literature" in the sense that Jews have always seen in it the source and the authority for that way of life and that view of history which gave meaning and direction to their lives.

I can understand why our ancestors believed the Torah (and its authoritative interpretations) to have been "divine revelation." For me, however, those concepts and values explicitly conveyed or implied in it which I can accept as valid represent *discovery*, partial and tentative glimpses into the true nature of human life. I find in the Torah adumbrations of ideas which I believe to be of enduring worth, and true insights into the unique laws which govern the relations of people and peoples.

Some of these ideas and values—that man is created in the image of the divine, that life is sacred, that man is his brother's keeper, that society must be ruled by law, that justice and compassion are the highest virtues, that moral responsibility is the most authentic form of ethics, that man must serve as a "partner to God" in perfecting this world, etc.—have exerted a tremendous influence upon Western civilization. I do not, however, infer from this fact that the Jews are the chosen people. I see no justification for ascribing metaphysical status to what is merely historical fact. Nor do I believe that the Jews are entrusted with any kind of "mission," in the sense of a preordained function in this world. I do, however, believe that Jews, as a people, have an opportunity to make a contribution to society which is uniquely their own.

Jews have a four-thousand-year history to draw upon. Those who know that history, make it part of their consciousness, and identify themselves with it should have (and I believe, on the whole, do have) a sensitivity to social evils which others might not have. They know what homelessness means, what exile, religious persecution, and political disability mean. They know what it means to suffer anxiety and frustration. They understand faith and hope and patience.

While Judaism does not "entail any particular political viewpoint," it knows from long experience that tyranny is incompatible with individual self-fulfillment or free cooperation. Jews intuitively sense (if they are Jewish Jews) that all Pharaohs are alike.

The question: "Can a man be a good Jew and yet support segregation . . . be a Communist? A Fascist?" calls for some careful definition of the term "good Jew." In my opinion, a good Jew is a person who strives to be a good person and who seeks to utilize the Jewish tradition to the maximum in achieving goodness. In other words, a good Jew is a functioning Jew, one who utilizes the literature, the history, the customs, folkways, and mores of Judaism to help bring out the best that is in him. A good Jew is one who seeks to be inspired by Jewish civilization as a means of eliciting his potentialities for moral responsibility. Obviously one cannot be a "good" person or a "good Jew" and still believe in racial inequality or totalitariansim.

Being a good Jew does not involve the observance of "all 613 commandments." A good Jew (an intelligent, well-informed, functioning Jew) distinguishes between ethical and ritual *mitzvot*. He selects, interprets, and adapts those ethical commands which seem to him to further justice, freedom, and peace; he sets the others aside as having been rendered obsolete by the growth of the human spirit. He selects, interprets, and adapts those rituals which function for him as a means of identifying himself with the Jewish people, past and present, and which best symbolize those ethical ideals to which he is committed. (If he finds in the prohibition of the use of *shatnez*—clothing made of linen and wool—a source of inspiration, he should certainly honor it. I happen to find it irrelevant.)

"Is Judaism the one true religion, or is it one of several true religions?" I believe that the question is wrongly framed. From my point of view, religions are the beliefs and practices which a group cherishes, through which it expresses its conception of salvation and the means by which that salvation is achieved. Obviously, in their own eyes, the members of any given group (church, nation, people, civilization) regard their beliefs and practices as the *true* way to salvation. If I had been born a Christian and had been brought up as one,

I would probably hold that my particular form of Christianity was the sole path to salvation.

But as a man of the mid-twentieth century, I must evaluate my Judaism and the religions of my neighbors by more objective criteria. I must ask whether my conception of salvation corresponds to the needs of human nature and of a humane society. A "true" religion is one offering a way of life which helps the individual and the group achieve maximum fulfillment. Whatever I find to be true in my Judaism ought to be applicable to any other group; and conversely, if I find a belief or a practice in the religion of another group which, to my mind, is worthy of emulation, I should, in all conscience, appropriate that belief or practice and seek to make it part of Judaism.

Indeed, this cross-fertilization of religions and cultures has been going on constantly. One need only observe the beliefs and practices of, let us say, the Yemenite Jews, to realize to what extent the Judaism of the West has absorbed ideas, values, and customs from the surrounding environment.

The question, then, may well be asked: If American civilization has already assimilated basic Jewish ideas and ideals, why struggle to maintain the survival of the Jewish people as a distinct entity? My answer has already been given in part: the unique experience of the Jewish people properly applied constitutes a reservoir of unique insights and sensitivities. But more, I believe that the Christian tradition and the secular humanistic tradition have distorted Jewish concepts and values, each in its own way. (These are the two major options on the American scene.)

Christianity has tended, on the whole, to move the center of gravity, so to speak, from this-worldly salvation to other-worldly salvation. While Judaism has also, in its traditional form, made the hereafter the ultimate goal, it has never rejected to the same extent the values of this earth. Christianity despaired of *tikkun olam*, the improvement of this world; Judaism demanded the constant effort to transform this world into an earthly paradise. Christianity held up as the model of holiness the man who assumed the vows of chastity and poverty; Judaism regarded sex and bodily satisfactions, properly channeled, as opportunities to carry out

God's will. Christianity insisted that salvation could not be attained except through an act of divine grace, miraculously bestowed; Judaism taught that the performance of *mitzvot* earns God's approval.

To be sure, it is necessary to reconstruct Judaism, too, if it is to function in the contemporary world; but the required changes can be (and are being) accomplished; they are rendered possible by the fact that the Jewish religion grows out of the ongoing experience of the Jewish people.

Peoplehood is the constant element in Jewish civilization. Within its context, religion evolves. In our time, two major adjustments need to be made: (a) Religion must be secularized, that is, it must take cognizance of the fact that modern man's major concern is to make this a better world. Speculation about the hereafter must be recognized for what it is: speculation. For Judaism to focus upon life in the here-and-now does not require revolutionary changes; it calls for a return to the this-worldly emphasis of the biblical period, a return which is rendered easier by the fact that Jews never abandoned it completely. (Incidentally, Christianity never had a this-worldly stage.)

(b) Religion today must be naturalistic, that is, people must regard themselves as able to experience the divine within the world as they know it. Today, miracles, revelations, visions, all theurgic manifestations are considered either figments of the imagination or products of febrile minds. Indeed, the whole so-called death-of-God question which has been agitating theologians recently is simply a restatement of the challenge to supernaturalism by naturalists. When they say "God is dead" they are merely using Nietzsche's famous remark to express the thought that the word "God" has become meaningless insofar as it is still associated with supernaturalism.

The implication, however, is that naturalism and God (religion) are inherently incompatible. I belong to a movement—Reconstructionism—which contends that there is no necessary conflict between naturalism and religion, just as there is no reason to believe that secularism, this-worldliness, is contrary to the spirit of religion.

The term "God" has always stood for the reality behind

the known universe which makes human salvation possible. In various ages, people have held different conceptions of salvation; and as their idea of salvation changed, their idea of God changed with it. In Judaism itself, an evolution is discernible. When the Israelites conceived of salvation as consisting in protection from enemies and in plenteous crops, God was for them the provider of these salvational goods. When the leaders taught that human life was not fulfilled without justice and righteousness, God was identified as the power that made for justice and righteousness. (We need not enter into polemics as to just when this occurred.)

In biblical times, the Israelites built a Tabernacle, believing that God would dwell therein. Later, God was conceived as the divine being who could not be contained by any house. Anthropomorphic terms were applied to God without hesitation in the Bible; by the time of Maimonides they had to be explained away.

God is not dead; anachronistic ways of conceiving of God are dead. New ways have to be devised, and are being devised by those who still believe that there is a power in the universe which, when mediated through man, manifests itself as conscience, as sensitivity to distinctions between right and wrong, as awareness of the discrepancies that exist between what is and what ought to be. It is here that humanism is deficient. Humanism concentrates—and properly so—upon the improvement of the individual and society; but it is not concerned with the larger question which troubles men and women more and more these days, namely, *whether life is so constituted that improvement is possible.*

Much of the despair in our time grows out of the haunting suspicion that man has reached the peak of his spiritual growth, and that there is no hope for any future development. Many people have lost their faith in the perfectibility of man—even in his ameliorability. The wars of this century, and especially the ghastly murder of six million Jews by the Nazis, have produced a vast and deep despair. To say that there is a God, but that He is in eclipse, is cold comfort; most seem to go further, and assert that there never was a God in the first place.

Whether it is my Jewish religious training, or the accumulated experience of generations of Jews operating in me unconsciously, I do not know; but I refuse to yield to this despair. For me the staggering problems of our time prove that men are moving forward, perhaps at a faster pace than ever before. Never, to my knowledge, have men been as aware as they are today that they are their brothers' keepers; never has the sense of worldwide interdependence been as strong as it is today. If, at this writing, we Americans are in the dilemma of Vietnam, it is because this generation has awakened to the fact (denied when Henry Wallace proclaimed it) that it *is* our business whether or not the Hottentots have a bottle of milk each day. If, in these United States, we speak of the Great Society, it is because some men truly believe that, while the potentialities for this-worldly salvation have not even begun to be realized, they *are* realizable.

Emil L. Fackenheim

Teacher of philosophy at the University of Toronto.

℃ The questions must be answered clearly, straightforwardly, and without evasion. But answers will inevitably seem evasive when no evasion is intended; complex and ambiguous when what is aimed at is clarity and simplicity; above all, they will seem far harsher and more dogmatic than their author actually is. Judaism is a spiritual life—dynamic, open, and whole. Answers to a questionnaire cannot capture that life but only open a door.

(1) The Torah reflects *actual events* of divine revelation, or incursions into human history, not a mistaken human belief in such incursions. But it is a *human* reflection of these events of incursion; the reception is shot through with appropriation and interpretation. Even a human listening to a human voice is inevitably an interpreting: this is *a fortiori* inevitable when the human "listening" is in faith and the "voice" heard is divine.

This rejects, on the one hand, the view that God dictated to Moses, a mere secretary. (Even orthodox tradition does

not reduce human reception to such extreme passivity. Why,
in that case, would there be any need for a Moses to receive
the Torah? And why, in that case, would the rabbis elicit
what is implicit in the Torah, instead of, in the style of fundamentalism, passively accepting its letter?) It rejects, on
the other hand, any liberal dissipation of the event of divine
incursion into "creative" human "insight," mistaken for
revelation by those who achieved it. (This rejected view
inevitably exalts the modern liberal above the ancient
authors of the Torah, if only because, unlike them, he
recognizes creative human insight for what it is. On any
such view, the modern liberal cannot *listen* to God through
the Torah. Nor can he truly listen to its ancient human
authors. His own standards are *a priori* superior, and the
Torah merely provides selective confirmation of his modern
insights.)

The view I have sketched implies that not all 613 commandments are equally binding. Shot through with *human*
appropriation and interpretation, both the Torah and the
subsequent tradition which is oral Torah inescapably reflect
the ages of their composition. But it also follows that it is
both naïve and un-Jewish to distill, as still binding, "eternal"
commandments from a complex composed of both eternal
and "time-bound" ones, the latter simply to be discarded.
(This is done by old-fashioned liberalism, with its rigid
distinction between the "principles" of prophetic ethics and
mere external "ceremonial" laws, a distinction which derives
its standards from external sources—Plato, Kant, Jefferson, and the like—and considers the standards by which it
judges to be superior to what is judged by them; this is an
inversion of the Jewish view in which a God speaking
through the Torah does the judging.) A modern Jew can
escape his own time-bound appropriating no more than
could his fathers; but his interpretation is Jewishly legitimate
only if it confronts, and listens to, the revelation reflected in
the Torah, which continues to be accessible only through
the ancient reflection which *is* the Torah. Our modern
appropriating is both possible and necessary because Sinai
is not an ancient event only: the Torah is given whenever
Israel receives it. But the act of present appropriation is

mediated through the original Sinai. It is this listening appropriation which creates historical continuity.

"Ritual commandments" ostensibly "lacking in ethical and doctrinal content" in fact display a religious meaning by their very presence in the Torah—that the ancient Jewish response to the divine challenge is a *total* response which encompasses all of life. If a modern Jew rejects a particular ancient response as invalid for him, he must do so not because his response to the divine challenge has been reduced to a mere compartment of life, but because the divine challenge demands of his life a different total response. Thus, new commandments are given even as ancient ones lose their reality.

(2) In revelation, the Divine meets the human: It does not remain in inaccessible transcendence. While meeting the finite human, It yet remains in divine infinity: the finite is not idolatrously deified. And It enters *into* the human situation: It does not force the human into a mystic surrender of its finitude. The Divine commands, and commands humans in their humanity.

But It cannot do so except by *singling out* particular humans in their particularity. A philosopher may rise above his particular situation to the perception of a timeless truth. Every prophet must remain *in* his situation, in which the divine word singles him out. And the same is true of the whole people Israel. A Jew may wish to abandon his belief in the chosen people (I would prefer: his covenant with God), and seek to transform, in the style of philosophy, his Judaism into a set of timeless universal truths to which he has risen. To do so, however, is to fragment the one reality of the covenant into two realities only accidentally connected: a Judaism reduced to purely universal principles, and a Jewish people reduced to a merely accidental particularity. To some this fragmentation is a modern necessity. To the believer in a singling-out revelation, it is a religious impossibility. To the believer, a Jewish self-understanding of Jewishness as a merely accidental manifestation of humanity-in-general, only accidentally having a special obligation to the "universal principles" of Judaism, is not a rise to a higher level of humanity. It is a betrayal of the Jewish position.

That the chosen-people concept has nothing in common with racism is shown by the traditional doctrine concerning converts, who become sons of Abraham. That it is diametrically opposed to racism—as well as to the religious tribalism which may be viewed as its ancient counterpart—follows from the being-singled-out which *is* the chosenness. Tribal deities, as finite as the tribes themselves, are bound to their respective tribes. Only an infinite and therefore universal God can single out the particular. Tribal deities behave by the standard of "my people, right or wrong," and modern racism makes the race itself divine. The God of Israel *judges* Israel's iniquities because He is no tribal deity but the God of all men: He who has singled out Israel, not for the sake of Israel only, but for the world.

In the light of the foregoing, the charge referred to in this question may be understood as reflecting a special form of religious anti-Semitism, which, having rejected a singling-out God, regards an Israel still singled out, and accepting itself as singled out, as an offense to its religious (or anti-religious) sensibilities. Such an anti-Semitism finds its extreme form in a racism which, rejecting the Judge, makes the master race judge of all things. Milder forms are shown by those Jewish assimilationists, or "liberals" of all kinds, who are scandalized by Jewish particularity, and those Christians (or pseudo-Christians) who contrast Christian "universalism" with "narrow" Jewish "particularism." Such a Christian view reflects a refusal to recognize that Christianity shares with Judaism the scandal of a singling-out God, and that the Jewish no less than the Christian God singles out the particular for purposes transcending the particular, i.e., nothing less than the world.

(3) If revelation is a reality, it follows that religious truth does not find primordial expression in propositions. Propositions merely reflect the relationship between a universal, singling-out God and the men singled out by Him. It is not therefore impossible that there can be more than one true religion; for the one God of all men may relate Himself differently to different men or groups of men. (The biblical

God does not relate Himself even to Abraham quite in the same way as He does to Abraham's descendants; and He who has led Israel out of Egypt has also led the Philistines out of Caphtor and the Cushites out of Cush.) Not all religions, however, can be true: idolatry, ancient and modern, is false. And some religions are only incompletely true. This is the believing Jew's best judgment, for example, concerning a high-minded agnostic humanism. He may view the agnostic as doing the will of God even though he recognizes no God; he may even view the agnostic as superior to less high-minded believers. This, however, is not tantamount to acknowledging the truth of agnosticism but only to acknowledging that there are fragments of truth within it.

Are there, then, any completely true religious alternatives to Judaism? It is no evasion to give only a partial answer to this question. The Bible, while in principle recognizing Gentile prophets, makes no real attempt to understand and judge their significance; for to do so would fall outside the scope of prophets sent to Israel. How non-Jews, and non-Jewish religions, may be singled out by Him whom the Jew knows as the God of Israel can be discovered by the Jew, if at all, only in dialogue with the testimony of these non-Jews and non-Jewish religions. Indeed, this discovery is what, from a Jewish standpoint, "dialogue" *means*. Hence it is not evasive to refuse to comment on such religions as Buddhism with which there has as yet been no Jewish dialogue, and to comment only inconclusively on Christianity and Islam, with which dialogue has hardly begun in earnest.

Abstractly, a true religion is one in which individual men or groups of men know themselves to be related, and responsible, to Him whom the Jew knows as the God of Israel. This much a Jew cannot deny of either Christianity or Islam. But by itself this is only an abstraction. Thus, those in earnest about Jewish-Christian dialogue cannot avoid the fact of conflicting—rather than merely different—testimony. To give a crucial example: by his faith, his actions, and indeed his whole existence, the Jew testifies to a world still unredeemed and yet destined to be redeemed. In this he testifies against the Christian faith in a redemption already actual, a faith splitting history in two through the event which has made redemption actual. Can the Christian take seriously history since the time of his Christ? Can he face those aspects of it—war, poverty, hate or, for that matter, the suffering of Israel—which to the Jew make history unredeemed and yet in need of being redeemed? For the sake of the God of both Israel and the church, the Jew cannot suppress such questions; or, if he must, it were better that dialogue be suspended, and replaced by an agreement to abide by a premessianic disagreement.

The foregoing implies a clear difference between the believing Jew and the unbeliever in the ethical sphere. Everything else being equal, what to the one is a two-term relation between him and his neighbor commanded by conscience, is to the other a three-term relation commanded by God. God is no mere external sanction behind the ethical commandment; if He were, the unbeliever would rightly dismiss Him as morally unnecessary and perhaps even impossible. His commanding presence *enters into* the relation, disclosing to the believer that the person with whom he is in relation is a creature created in the divine image. Jewish as well as non-Jewish unbelievers remain with a two-term relationship; but in the mind of a Jewish believer, the nonbelieving Jew fulfills a fragment of the divine covenant with Israel even while failing to recognize it.

Christian as well as Jewish believers stand in a three-term relation. The difference is that whereas Christian ethical life is lived in the context of a grace which has already redeemed the world, Jewish ethical life is premessianic, and finds grace primordially *in* the commandments, a grace which makes possible a human share in the preparation of the messianic kingdom. Only future dialogue can disclose whether this difference is as sharp as here stated. But even now a Jew knows that he can, however rarely, anticipate messianic redemption; and he sees many a Christian behaving as though the world were still unredeemed.

(4) To bind Judaism to any *one* political standpoint would be sheer parochialism. To make it hospitable to *all* political viewpoints would be to fall prey to a political quietism Jewishly tolerable only as a tactical device designed to avoid fruitless persecution. The God of Israel commands into a

human situation which has an inescapable political dimension.

At least some political viewpoints are clearly ruled out. No good Jew can support on principle (as distinguished from mere tactics) racial discrimination; for he knows that his God created only one man in the beginning, lest anyone regard his ancestors as superior to those of others. Nor can he be a Communist when Communism is based on the principle of total human self-redemption, a principle which implies atheism and is used to justify human totalitarianism. Least of all can he be a Fascist, since Fascism combines atheistic political totalitarianism with racism.

But such is the burden of man's premessianic condition that whereas Judaism rules out some political viewpoints, it does not entail an absolute and unalterable commitment to any positive viewpoint. The ideas of universal freedom, equality, justice, and peace are authentic secular expressions of divine commandments pointing to an ultimate messianic dimension. But by themselves they are not concrete enough to amount to a political viewpoint; and what *is* concrete enough can rarely be directly or unambiguously identified as the will of God. The basic dilemma is that the Jew must decide what to do toward the messianic end while living in the here-and-now of a premessianic present. That such decisions are rarely either simple or unambiguous is as clear in this age as in any—when few Jews dedicated to the messianic idea of total peace can advocate immediate and total disarmament. It is all the more profoundly exhilarating that moments of grace occur in history in which all ambiguity vanishes. Such a moment is occurring in present-day America, when the time is ripe for the total recognition of the humanity of the American Negro. Yet even here the ways in which this recognition is to be accomplished are not simple or unambiguous.

(5) The "God is dead" slogan covers a variety of different and even incompatible assertions: (a) that the "God-hypothesis" is no longer needed when science alone can explain the universe; (b) that *in point of fact* few contemporary men have a meaningful belief in God; (c) that whether or not they have such a belief, they *ought* not to

have it, inasmuch as it reflects immaturity, and modern man has "come of age."

(a) The first assertion restates the hoary positivistic view that religion is primitive science. But the biblical God is no hypothesis in need of empirical verification and capable of empirical refutation. Nor does He serve the prescientific function of explaining facts.

(b) The second assertion is true but not new to inhabitants of the secular city—only to those freshly arrived from the farm. By itself, it at most means that the long association between Christianity and majority opinion is ended: that henceforth Christian faith must choose between minority status and surrender to secularism. For the believing Jew, this choice never existed.

(c) The third assertion is religiously serious. Does *radical* human freedom necessitate the death of God? In view of centuries of religiously imposed unfreedom, this is no mean question. And yet, can a Jew believe that this of all ages— the age of Auschwitz, rarely mentioned by the Christian "God is dead" theologians and never, it seems, really faced— is the age of man "come of age"? Still more seriously, must God be dead in order that man may be free? Most astounding in all the present Christian turmoil is the lack of witness to a divine love which, rather than diminishing or destroying human freedom, on the contrary establishes and augments it. No doubt the present rebellion is the nemesis of past religious decadence. Yet, instead of rebelling against decadence, one may seek renewal. The Jew finds such renewal when his life bears witness that "when the Torah came into the world, freedom came into the world."

There is yet a fourth meaning to the "God is dead" slogan, most serious of all: that modern man is *incapable* of hearing the word of God *even if he listens*. Only to apply the slogan here is to prejudge what is in fact the central problem of religious faith in the modern world. According to Jewish tradition, God, often distant, "hides His face." Modern secularist man regards this distance as *necessary* distance, if not nonexistence; and he *a priori* regards moments of divine presence—if *per impossibile* they should occur—as human self-delusion. Modern man seems incapable of accepting himself as related to a divinity beyond him.

But does this seeming incapacity signify that God is dead? Or that the great religious demand made of this age is a radical *t'shuvah*—a *turning* and listening to the God who can speak even though He is silent? And is not, in that case, the Jew of the generation of Auschwitz required to do what, since Abraham, Jeremiah, and Job, Jews have always done in times of darkness—contend with the silent God, and bear witness to Him by this very contention?

Marvin Fox

Teacher of philosophy at Ohio State University.

❡ (1) It is essential to distinguish between the metaphysical aspects of revelation and the practical implications of revelation. With respect to both I believe in the traditional doctrine of *Torah min ha-shamayim*, the teaching that the Torah is divine. I also follow the tradition which allows great latitude in our theological understanding of the nature of revelation while insisting on rigorous adherence to fixed norms of behavior.

No one can reasonably claim to understand how God reveals Himself to man. The very idea of revelation leads us to paradoxes which defy rational explanation. We cannot make fully intelligible in the language of human experience how the eternal enters into the temporal world of man, or how the incorporeal is apprehended by corporeal beings. Yet we affirm in faith what we cannot explicate, for our very humanity is at stake. I believe, because I cannot afford not to believe. I believe, as a Jew, in the divinity of Torah, because without God's Torah I have lost the ground for making my own life intelligible and purposeful.

To believe because life demands it is not peculiar to religious men. It is something that reasonable men do as a matter of course in other areas. For example, most men in Western society believe that there is some necessary relationship between reason and reality, though no decisive evidence can be offered for this conviction. They hold to it

because if the world does not conform to human reason
then it is unintelligible, and we find that an unbearable
state of affairs. Rather than face the pain of an unintelligible
world we affirm, as an act of faith, that it must be rationally
ordered. We insist that whatever reason finds necessary must
be the case in reality and whatever reason finds impossible
can never be the case in reality. And we do so rightly, for
with anything less our lives would become a hopeless chaos.
The same holds true of the Jew who believes in the Torah
as divine, even while acknowledging that he has and can
have no decisive evidence. He believes because the order,
structure, direction, and meaning of his life are at stake,
because the alternative is personal and moral chaos. He
believes because all that he finds precious hangs in the balance—the quality, substance, and texture of his own
existence. His belief is not formulated as a set of dogmatic
propositions. It is, rather, *emunah*, trust in God and in the
tradition of the community of Israel. In that trust the believing Jew finds the ground of his own existence and opens
himself to unique and exalted possibilities. In that trust he
discovers that the truly human is a reflection of the divine,
a discovery which has the power to transform and sanctify
man and his world.

In affirming such a belief in revelation, I make no specific
claim about the way in which revelation took place, except
the traditional one that the biblical prophets are its only valid
channel. Moses holds a unique place among these prophets
and through him the Torah was transmitted to the community of Israel. Because prophecy transcends my own experience I cannot read the biblical descriptions of the prophetic
vision in simple literal terms. Jewish tradition offers ample
precedent for understanding the Torah in symbolic or
metaphorical terms. The text, of course, must be studied
perceptively and with meticulous care, but this is not to say
that it is to be read in literal or fundamentalist fashion. One
need only recall that *midrash* is a very early mode of understanding Torah in a nonliteral way, or that the first part of
Maimonides's *Guide* is a caution against blind literalism.
Even so recent an authority as the Nezib (Rabbi Naphtali
Zvi Yehuda Berlin of Volozhin) stresses that Torah must

be read and understood as poetry (cf. his Introduction to his commentary on the Pentateuch).

In effect, this suggests a wide range of ways in which we might formulate our admittedly inadequate ideas of revelation. Presumably, a highly sophisticated philosopher or theologian will view the matter differently from an unlearned man of simple faith. What all affirm, if they stand in the normative tradition, is that God has addressed us through His prophets. I share fully this classical Jewish belief.

In noting the latitude and diversity of theological understanding, it was not my intention to suggest that there are no limits or boundaries. As a believing Jew, I conceive of revelation as including *Torah she-be'al peh*, the oral tradition. Here we find the valid Jewish guides to understanding the theological as well as the legal teachings of the Torah. The range of possible approaches to revelation is rooted in and defined by this oral Torah.

While allowing diversity of theological insight, I also follow the tradition in holding that all the commandments of the Torah are binding upon every Jew. To know what these commandments are we must again appeal to the oral tradition which continues to unfold through all the generations of Jewish history. The judgments and decisions of recognized and qualified Torah scholars have the binding force of law, for they are the very substance of Torah. Hence, I accept not only the 613 commandments of the written Torah, but equally the explication of those commandments through the oral Torah. In fact, we cannot know clearly what is intended by the commandments of the Torah except through the teaching of the oral tradition. Here, in contrast to the abstractions of theology, we have a clear and concrete pattern of practice. Of course, there are disputed questions concerning practice also, but for these there is a clear technique for decision. It is this unified pattern of religious behavior which binds us as Jews. Through the fulfillment of God's commandments we serve Him, express our love for Him, and achieve the ultimate purpose of Jewish existence—the sanctification of our lives.

The distinction which is suggested (in the first question) between ritual and ethical commandments is untenable for a believing Jew. The tradition, of course, recognizes that some commandments regulate intrahuman relations while others regulate man's relation to God, but the Torah gives us no ground for accepting the one and rejecting the other. The ethical commandments bind us because they are laws of the Torah. Precisely the same is true of the ritual command-ments.

Those who think that moral principles are self-validating would do well to study the history of ethical theory. Contemporary moral philosophers are still struggling—with notably little success—to find independent foundations for their ethical principles. For a believing Jew the only foundation is the binding force of Torah which sets forth these ethical norms. But it is precisely the same Torah that prescribes the ritual rules as well. Moral and ritual commandments are inextricably intertwined in the Torah, as a glance at the context of the golden rule will quickly reveal. From the standpoint of Torah the rules governing our food, our clothing, our labor, our Sabbaths and festivals are as essential as the clearly moral rules. For if the latter are the foundations of a decent and humane social order, the former are the Jewish way of preparing one to live in such a society. The Torah has commanded us to bring holiness into our daily lives, to come to see the wonders of the commonplace, to revere all creation as God's handiwork. Through the ritual commandments we grow in our capacity to abide by the ethical commandments. He who eats reverently and dresses reverently may be expected to be reverent before the most precious of all things on earth—human personality.

Two final comments must be made. First, I have expressed in the preceding paragraph an ideal which is not always fully realized. Nevertheless, it is a valid Jewish ideal, and when we fall short of it we fall short of the teachings of Torah. Second, this brief explanation of the ritual commandments is not intended as a reason for observing them. Should the explanation be wrong the commandments bind us nevertheless, for they are commandments of the Torah. I only wanted to indicate one perspective from which the unity of the ethical and ritual elements can be perceived. For a believing Jew all the commandments have equal force, though he is free to understand their purposes and interrelation in a variety of ways.

(2) Just as I do not claim to understand revelation I do not claim to understand fully how the Jews were chosen by God, for this is itself an element of revelation. However, I believe in the chosenness of the Jewish people, both because the Torah affirms it and because our history justifies it. For the Jews to have been chosen suggests nothing whatsoever about their superiority. Nowhere in the Torah is the doctrine of the chosen people based on claims of special merit or natural superiority. On the contrary, the people of Israel are depicted in all of their human weakness. Consider the first generation after the Exodus from Egypt. They worship the golden calf immediately after the revelation at Sinai. They are exposed as a nation of whining complainers constantly dissatisfied with life in the desert. They are so lacking in faith that a whole generation must perish before they are fit to enter their promised land. Surely these are not claims to national or racial superiority. What was true of the first generation was, unhappily, all too often true of later generations, and for their sinfulness they earned the rebukes and the chastisement of the prophets. This supposedly superior people blames itself for its exile and the devastation of its land and records this blame in its own official literature.

As to the claim that this doctrine is the model for modern racialist theories, one can only dismiss it as a malicious distortion. The evidence is so well-known and so commonplace that one hesitates to cite it. There is a long list of outstanding Jewish sages—men whose names are honored and whose teachings are revered—who were not of Jewish birth but became converts to the Jewish faith. Others of great eminence are held to be descended from converts. Above all, the biblical record speaks for itself. King David, ancestor of the Messiah, is a direct descendant of Ruth, a Moabite woman converted to the Jewish faith. It is hard to imagine any more vigorous rejection of racialism.

What, then, is intended in the doctrine that the Jews are a people chosen by God? They were chosen, for reasons we cannot fully fathom, to bring mankind the message of God's existence and His teachings. "Ye are my witnesses saith the Lord." It is the task of the Jews to serve as teachers and models for mankind. Their duty is to bear witness to the truth of God both by their explicit teaching and by the quality of their lives. If this is a privilege it is also a burden. It confers no special rights, only special responsibilities. We were chosen to receive the Torah, commanded to live in accordance with its precepts, and thereby to bring divine truth into the world.

It is only honest to recognize that Jews have sometimes been guilty of arrogance and self-satisfaction. They have at times imagined that they were chosen because of their innate superiority. Such distasteful attitudes deserve only contempt and condemnation, though they are an understandable reaction to the oppression which Jews have so often suffered. Patriotism is easily distorted into ultranationalism or chauvinism, but this should not lead reasonable men to reject honest patriotism as evil. Nor should we feel forced to reject the classical image of the Jews as chosen to witness to God, merely because it can be distorted into racialism or smugness and pride.

(3) The notion of "several true religions" is ambiguous and requires clarification. If "truth" is intended here to refer to a set of true propositions, then clearly various religions which affirm contradictory or contrary propositions cannot all be true. If there are several true religions, in this sense, then they must all be asserting the same thing. But it is clearly not the case that, for example, Judaism and Christianity assert the same things. Judaism affirms the absolute unity of God and denies that the Messiah has come. Christianity affirms that God is triune and insists that the Messiah has already come. Viewed as statements about the world these cannot be simultaneously true, and in this sense every believer must affirm that his religion is the only true religion. His alternative is to claim that two contradictory statements are equally true, a move which no rational man can make.

However, the essence of Jewish faith, as I understand it, is not contained in the formulas of a dogmatic creed, but in a special way of orienting oneself to the world and to human destiny. The community of Israel has its own unique language of faith, its own symbols, its own mode of religious consciousness. These are not propositions in a theological system and they are not arguable. They derive from the historic experience of the Jewish people, especially from their confrontation with God. Viewed in this way, the truth of faith is an internal truth, a truth which we feel, to which we respond, and by which we are directed. No other pattern of piety can take its place; no other is open to the Jew as Jew. In making this exclusive claim I fully recognize that precisely the same things can be said of Christianity or of any other religious communion. For this very reason I respect the integrity and dignity of every sincere community of faith. I recognize that its symbols express for it the felt truth of an inner religious life substantially different from my own. At this level I make no judgments of independent truth or falsehood. As a faithful Jew I have access only to the way of serving God which comes to me through my own tradition. I leave open a similar possibility for other men within their own traditions.

Nevertheless, it is certainly the case that the special religious experience which is Jewish rests on certain explicit principles of faith. Judaism is not possible without belief in the existence of God, in His absolute unity, in His revelation (to name only a few). These I hold to be true beliefs, even though not demonstrable. Any beliefs contradictory of these or of other fundamentals of Jewish faith I must, therefore, hold to be false. Simple logic forces me to this conclusion.

Judaism continues to have a distinctive contribution to make to human civilization, but not primarily at the level of theology. Most of our basic theological claims have become part of Western culture through the spread of Christianity. Monotheism is hardly a unique Jewish teaching today. Nor can we claim any special possession of unique ethical principles. Here again traditional Jewish teaching has become part of the larger society in which we live. Decent men in all civilized countries accept the main outlines of Jewish moral teaching.

What is distinctive is the Jewish conception of how this teaching is to be put into practice, namely the *halakha*, the comprehensive norms of Jewish law which leave no area of human behavior unregulated. The world, indeed the Christian world, has yet to learn this lesson. In one of its major deviations from Judaism, Christianity has sought to overcome the law. Though the ancient controversy was usually expressed in terms of the conflict between the letter and the spirit of the law, the real issue is law versus no law. This point has been made eminently clear by some of the best Christian scholarship of our time.

Christianity supposes that love must be substituted for law, that love alone is the appropriate guide to all human behavior. In the moment of moral decision a man must be guided by love alone. To behave under the prescriptions of the law is, from this point of view, to behave mechanically or heteronomously. The highest achievement is thought to be the transcendence of the law by love. This position, formulated in the tradition of classical Christianity, is reaffirmed today particularly by those Christian thinkers who view ethics as situational. In a brief summary the Bishop of Woolwich expresses the matter thus: "Chastity is the expression of charity—of caring enough. And this is the criterion for every form of behavior, inside marriage or out of it, in sexual ethics or in any other field. For *nothing else* makes a thing right or wrong." Note that he speaks here about "every form of behavior" and affirms that only caring, i.e., *caritas*, is what makes any act moral or immoral.

As a Jew, I stand firmly inside a tradition that is more concerned with the act than with the attitude. Only with fixed norms of behavior can we guarantee the essential decencies of the human community. In the name of the abstract ideal of love, unimaginable cruelty has often been perpetrated. Jews have all too frequently been the victims of such perverted love. It is our conviction that unless love is guided by the law it can easily become demonic. Moreover, we know that human need cannot wait to be served only by the inspired moment of love. Instead our tradition requires a man to do his duty no matter what his inner state. This may not result in magnificent poetic outbursts, but it does guarantee essential human decency. It may seem less edifying than the appeal to love alone, but it does save us from the delusion that all is permissible so long as it is done from love. To take just one concrete case—contemporary Jewish ways of eliciting charity still reflect the old tradition that we are obligated to give in order to help those in need. Our fund-raising is sometimes crude and abrasive. We demand, we cajole, we embarrass people into giving. We hope that the gift is given with love, with deep and humane concern for those who depend on us. But if not, the gift still feeds the hungry, clothes the naked, and brings healing to the sick. For the law requires that we give, and those who are in need cannot wait until the spirit moves us. This is a fundamental principle of all Jewish practice—that the deed must be done when and as the law prescribes. Nothing less is acceptable. I believe that we have nothing more valuable to teach the world today, no lesson more characteristic of Jewish faith or more desperately needed by humanity.

(4) I interpret the question concerning the political implications of Judaism to refer to the contemporary secular state. Judaism, in these circumstances, does not entail any particular form of social or political organization. It is compatible with any social or political system, so long as it is one which preserves human dignity and is based on principles of justice. A faithful Jew cannot support any form of racial discrimination, because it is unjust and inhuman. This is not primarily a political judgment, but a moral or religious judgment.

No Jew can give his supreme loyalty to the state. His highest loyalty is to God and his highest duty is that defined in the Torah. Any state which claims absolute supremacy is a natural enemy of the believing Jew. For such a state idolizes itself and demands for itself the place which Jews must reserve for God. Insofar as Communist and Fascist states are guilty of the statist idolatry, no good Jew can be a Communist or a Fascist. When one adds to this the destruction of human dignity, the perverse forms of discrimination, and the cynical injustice of contemporary Communist and Fascist powers, it is evident that they categorically contradict essential elements of Judaism. Whenever a seemingly democratic state arrogates to itself absolute power it also merits the opposition of faithful Jews.

(5) The "God is dead" issue is open to several possible interpretations. The most radical is that it means simply that

there is no God and there never was. In this form it is straightforward atheism which Judaism obviously rejects. Another version is that God is currently dead, i.e., that He is no longer accessible to us. The Torah tells us that there will be times when God hides Himself from man, and this may indeed be such a time. However, the Christian theologians draw a conclusion from this which Judaism cannot accept. They conclude that because God has withdrawn from us, He has become irrelevant and that we must therefore live our lives without Him. Judaism teaches that when God hides from us we must make every effort to tear away the veils that separate us from Him. He is always relevant. It is we who have become obtuse and insensitive, thereby making ourselves irrelevant. Our task is not to try to live without God, but rather so to transform ourselves that we are again worthy and able to stand in His presence.

A third meaning of "God is dead" is simply that the symbol, "God," has lost its power over us and no longer points to the divine reality. This seems to me a sober and honest appraisal of our actual situation, a situation which contemporary Jews share with Christians as an effect of our secular culture. I applaud the honesty of those who recognize how little "God" means to contemporary society, who see how often we invoke God's name as a formalized social propriety rather than a living reality. Our empty pieties may well destroy us, and Jews should share this concern with all genuinely religious men. Though I can offer no easy solutions, I welcome the concern of those who are agitated by the problem and recognize it as a vital issue for Judaism as well as Christianity.

There is no significant danger to Judaism in any aspect of modern thought per se. A faithful Jew can live as a fully participating member of contemporary society and culture, so long as he is free to view that culture with a critical eye. Above all he must recognize the limits as well as the splendid achievements of the natural sciences and philosophy. Contemporary philosophy tends to avoid ultimate questions, but this does not free us of the need to answer these questions responsibly. Contemporary science, in its less guarded moments, is prone to treat all questions as if they were legitimate parts of its own subject matter. Here lies the one great danger to Judaism, the threat which is posed by an unrestrained and uncritical naturalism.

The most destructive aspect of this exaggerated naturalism is its denial of any qualitative distinction between man and the other animals. In the Jewish tradition, indeed in the whole Western religious tradition, man is viewed as unique, among all other creatures. This is expressed in the biblical statement that man was created in the image of God. It is on this view of man that we base our belief in the dignity and worth of every human being. It is from this view of man that we derive our notion of moral duty and our conviction that our obligations to men are of a different order than those we have to other creatures. Without·this foundation we forfeit all that matters to us as men. I do not believe that we can preserve the preciousness of human personality and our reverence for humanity while conceiving man as nothing more than another animal. It is this brutalizing element in modern thought which I consider the greatest challenge to Jewish belief. For it undermines that which Judaism conceives as its highest goal—the sanctification of human life so that through *imitatio dei* our godlike qualities might become the human norm. We cannot yield this goal without destroying all that matters in Jewish faith.

Solomon B. Freehof

Rabbi of the Rodef Shalom Temple (Reform)
in Pittsburgh.

ℂ (1) The simplest doctrine underlying the 613 commandments is the Orthodox one that all of them are derivable from explicit or clearly implied statements in the Torah. Even the elaborated details governing their observance are part of the oral law which was also given to Moses on Mount Sinai. Every correct elaboration of the law arrived at by a competent scholar is only a rediscovery of what was already said on Mount Sinai. Therefore we have no right to classify the commandments in any order of supposed relative importance. They are all God-given mandates.

This doctrine is clear-cut and has long been influential;

but by now it has lost its credibility. Only a small proportion
of world Jewry still believes that every detail of observance
is God-given. Furthermore, the classic doctrine now tends
to embitter Jewish communal life, for it leads those who still
hold to it to the conclusion that the overwhelming majority
of Jews in the world lives in violation of God's clear mandate.
There can be no statistics on the extent of present-day neglect of the law, but one has only to think of the Jews he
knows: how many of them, even those who consider themselves Orthodox, now obey the Sabbath laws strictly, or the
laws of kosher food, or resort to Jewish rabbinical courts in
business dealings? When one reads the Orthodox rabbinical
magazines, one gets the feeling that Orthodox leadership, to
the extent that it is aware of widespread nonobservance,
lives in constant apprehension of the effect of this mass nonobservance upon the future of Jewish life. They feel
hemmed in. Their outcries about kosher food are generally
bitter denunciations or cries of futility. They seem to feel
that the Jewish people itself has become a source of dangerous infection to the Jewish law. One may say that they are
now defending the fortress of the law against the Jewish
people.

All groupings in modern Judaism must face the realities
of Jewish religious observance. It is a basic fact. One can
either declare the overwhelming majority of Jewry to be sinful and retreat into a fortress, or else consider the widespread nonobservance or selective observance of the 613
commandments as a historical reality to which Jewish thought
and theology must be adjusted.

The search for a new theological basis for the commandments took place in Reform. The Reform movement was
founded by laymen, not by rabbis. The rabbis were of the
second generation of its pioneers. The laymen, disturbed by
the growing nonobservance of the commandments, sought
no new theology. They thought that aesthetic beautification
of the service would solve the problem. The first Reform
rabbis knew that mere modernization and beautifying of the
service would not be effective. They therefore sought for a
doctrinal revision of Orthodox theory, in order to build a
Judaism in harmony with contemporary reality. Holdheim
declared that most of the ceremonial commandments were

national in purpose, while some of them expressed spiritual and ethical ideals. Since the Jews of the world were not a nation any longer, he said, all the national commandments were void. Geiger stressed the evolutionary nature of Judaism: certain ceremonies were now outworn and others might take their place. Frankel, the founder of the Conservative movement, stressed the results of history: all the commandments which were deeply rooted in the Jewish past must, he said, still be held as valid. The difficulty with all these theories is that none of them gives a clear-cut rule whereby to judge specifically which commandment is incumbent upon us and which is not.

So today the situation remains as it has been for a century and a half. The choice of commandments is left to the emotions and preferences of the individual; and this has brought chaos. There is now a wide spectrum of varying observance throughout the Conservative movement, the Reform movement, and in the congregations which call themselves Orthodox. Hence all the discussion today about the *authority* of the commandments. The Orthodox can do little more than rebuke or sigh. Reform and Conservative leaders hope to maintain the *idea* of *mitzvot* but cannot arrive at a standard of selection. So far no one has come up with any logical doctrine which can convincingly say, "This is essential and this not essential."

My own opinion is that the Jewish people is spontaneously evolving a system of practice, and it must be given more time to work it out. In another generation, perhaps, custom, which is always a vital force in Jewish observance, will tend to clarify itself. For the present, we must use the Jewish legal literature and the codes respectfully but not subserviently. They must be our guides but not our governors until such time as the Jews of the various countries arrive at what corresponds to their feelings as to the essentials of Jewish life. Hillel said (of course in a much more restricted sense): "Let the Children of Israel alone. If they are not prophets, at least they are the children of prophets" (B. Pesahim 66a).

(2) Are the Jews God's chosen people? The question troubled the prophet Amos and his opinion is ambivalent.

He said that just as God brought Israel out of Egypt, so God delivered other nations. Therefore all nations are under God's mandate and will be punished for their violations of ethical duty. In his denunciations he includes Israel in a list with Damascus, Gaza, Tyre, Edom, Amon, Moab. But other of his speeches contain special denunciations of Israel and Judah. Evidently he felt that God's selection of Israel implied some additional intimacy (3:2): "You only have I known among all the families of the earth. Therefore I will visit your transgressions upon you."

The doctrine of the chosen people was the doctrine of a special responsibility, not of a special glory. The prayer-book always couples the idea of "chosen" with "commandments." "With great love hast Thou loved us . . . and statutes hast Thou taught us." The idea is therefore different from the vauntings of such other peoples who deem themselves unique in order to justify dominance over others. Jewry has been the people to bring the concept of ethical monotheism into the world and has maintained the purity of its God-conception. The idea that there are therefore special obligations to decency and kindness and justice is the actual meaning of the chosen people and is still a real motivation even in the life of modern Jews. When we say, "A Jew ought not to do this sort of thing," we are not scorning anybody, but are taking upon ourselves a higher standard. There is nothing ignoble in our assumption of a duty and in the belief that we have extra responsibilities.

(3) The Christian and Mohammedan religions are understood to be under the Covenant of Noah. Judaism is under the further Covenant of Sinai, which adds special obligatory commandments. Those under the Covenant of Noah are obligated to obey seven commandments (against idolatry, cruelty to animals, murder, etc.)—in other words, to observe ethical monotheism. All who obey these seven Noahide commandments belong to the category of "the righteous of the nations who have their portion in the world to come."

Jewish legal literature is the most trustworthy source for the realistic day-to-day attitude of Judaism toward other religions. Belletristic or polemical literature might be suspect of having been written for the eyes of Gentiles, but the legal literature, especially the legal commentaries, are almost never seen except by Jewish scholars.

The importance of the question springs from the fact that anti-Semites have used this Jewish legal tradition in their attempt to prove that Jews and Judaism are hostile to Christians and Christianity and that we are indeed commanded by our law to cheat them and even to destroy them. The fact of the matter is that the ancient repressive laws in the Bible and Talmud were directed against the idolators. Jews were forbidden to do business with them or to help them in any way. Jewish law, however, quickly indicated that Mohammedans and Christians were not idolators at all and that these older laws therefore did not apply.

Thus, for example, Rabbenu Tam, the great French authority of the twelfth century, says that we may make all business contracts with Christians, even when the business requires (religious) oaths to be taken, with the Christians swearing by the saints. Such oaths ascribing additional divinity or semidivinity to others than God would be forbidden to Jews, but is not forbidden to "the sons of Noah." He says, "These days they all swear by their saints but they do not really ascribe divinity to them. This is not to be deemed idolatry, for they intend their oath to be in the name of Him who created heaven and earth" (Tosfot in B. Sanhedrin 63b, also Tosfot in Bekorot 2b). In spite of "saints," "Trinity," etc., Christianity is deemed monotheistic. This opinion is embodied in the codes (see Shulhan Arukh, Orah Hayyim 156, Isserles). Moses Rifkes, who fled for his life from Vilna before the Chmelnitzki army in the seventeenth century, and would be expected to be bitter, nevertheless says (Hoshen Mishpat 425:5): "The rabbis made these [repressive] laws against the idolators of their day; but these nations under whose protection we live believe in God's creation of the world and the Exodus from Egypt and in many essentials of religion, and all their intentions [i.e., of the oaths they take by the saints and the Trinity, etc.] refer to God the Creator of heaven and earth." A still later authority, Israel Lifshuetz of Danzig (eighteenth and nineteenth centuries), says in his commentary to Mishna Baba Kama (Chapter 4, Note 17, speaking of Christians): "Our brethren the Gentiles, who acknowledge the One God and revere His Law which they deem divine and call it 'Holy Writ,' observe as is required of them the seven command-ments of Noah."

All these citations are in small printed commentaries which hardly a Gentile would ever see. They represent not a public-relations point of view but the precise opinion of Jewish law that the Christian religion is a true religion; that Judaism and Christianity are both under divine covenant, the Christians under the Covenant of Noah and we under the more demanding Covenant of Sinai. Therefore Christianity is the true religion for Christians and Judaism is the true religion for Jews.

Would that Christianity had the same respect for Judaism as Jewish law has for Christianity! The Christian missionary mandate leads them to hope that Judaism will disappear into Christianity. We have no such hope and therefore no such mandate. The list of 613 commandments contains no commandment to proselytize.

(4) It would be easy to derive a simple Communism from the text of the Gospels, but it would be difficult to find Com-munism in Jewish literature. Nevertheless, there is no basis for any economic orientation—capitalism, Communism, etc.—in Judaism. All that Judaism is concerned with is social justice. Any economic arrangement which achieves it is praiseworthy. As for race, any individual of whatever race who presents himself or herself for conversion may be accepted, if deemed worthy as an individual.

(5) The "God is dead" question agitating the so-called "radical Christians" is of comparatively small relevance for Judaism. First of all, it is not quite clear what they mean in saying that "God is dead." The phrase seems to be more sensational than precise. Apparently what these "radical Christians" mean is that since to most laymen God has ceased to be a living reality, theologians must now contrive a religious approach which will not repel the godless public with any teaching of the living God. They seem, then, to be suggesting that the new religious propaganda will be more successful if the teaching is about Christ but not about God.

For a number of reasons this agitation has little meaning

for us. If a Christian ceases to believe in God, he ceases to be a Christian and may be completely lost to the church. If a Jew becomes an atheist, he is still in many ways Jewish and his children will be among those who found synagogues. Since we do not lose our fellow Jews quite so easily, we have less reason for panic. Secondly, the central motivation of the movement comes from Bultmann, whose chief purpose is to "demythologize" the New Testament—that is to say, to teach its doctrines without incarnation, resurrection, etc. But these "mythologies" or miracles are the essentials of Christian doctrine. There are miracles in the Old Testament too; but neither the plagues in Egypt nor the splitting of the Red Sea are essential or indispensable to Judaism. There is less panic, therefore, among us if people do not believe in the biblical miracles. Then again, the arguments of the "God is dead" people, as summed up by the Bishop of Woolwich in *Honest to God*, are directed against the primitive idea that God has a *geographical* location, that God is "up there" or "out there": this concept of God, he says, must go. But it *has* been long gone from Jewish tradition. The Talmud speaks of God in analogy to life in the body; as life fills the body and is omnipresent in it, so God fills the world, God is the soul of the world (B. Berakhot 10a). Or the Midrash calls God *Makom*, "place," and explains that God is not in the world, but rather that the world is in God (Bereshit R. 68:9). I do not believe that intelligent Christians are as primitively geographical in their God-conception as this new group makes them out to be. There is hardly any Jewish leader who would feel the need to use the "God is dead" arguments in persuading Jews back to religion.

As to which modern philosophic attitude is of greatest danger to Judaism, I cannot answer. Judaism has managed to adjust itself to many a philosophic doctrine. Perhaps because Judaism has so many different roots in Jewish history and individual experience, it can afford to sway a little in changing winds.

Norman E. Frimer

*Metropolitan Regional Director of the B'nai
B'rith Hillel Foundations in Brooklyn, New York.*

❡ (1) Revelation in a religious context is used in our day in basically two ways. The one usually makes reference to the product of man's own inner moral and spiritual outreach as his creative genius soars upward and thrusts inward to explore the mysteries of the unknown. The other, however, expresses not a cultural phenomenon, the child of a cognitive or intuitive leap, but rather a nonnatural and noncultural occurrence which Professor Joseph B. Soloveitchik designates as "the apocalyptic." In this category, the will of the Eternal One paradoxically breaks through into the very midst of history and in the particularity of his divine-human encounter bestows upon man the gift and bounty of His wisdom. In the succinct formulation of Samson Raphael Hirsch, the distinction lies between the "Revelation of God through man, or the Revelation from God to man."

This latter view is the religious given of classical Judaism to this very day. It, moreover, characterizes the obvious claim made in the Torah itself. This becomes astonishingly evident to the reader of sacred Scripture when he is struck by the Pentateuch's total consistency—in contrast, for example, to the Hagiographa—in maintaining an incredible silence regarding any agonizing religious experiences on the part of man in pursuit of God. His heroic "fools" are not at all portrayed as panting or "thirsting for the living God" and burning with any mystical desire to rend the curtain separating them from divinity. Quite the contrary! The Creator alone takes the initiative in contacting and addressing Adam and in directing the footsteps of Father Abraham. Even Moses displays no intense passion for an unmediated meeting with the Other. The God of history calls unto him from the burning bush which cannot be consumed and to this compelling call, Moses submissively responds *"hineni—* I am present."

This quality of divine and unsynergic initiative seems to

pervade all the biblical records of prophecy. It is hardly likely, therefore, that this repeated pattern and portrayal of original divine incursion and subsequent human response are fortuitous and but a device for literary effect.

Add to this an even more amazing fact. In almost every instance in the Pentateuch where the will of God directly confronts man, the event of revelation is not expressed merely as mysterious divine presentness without content or specificity. Invariably the Torah associates the godly call with commission and command. "*Va-y' tzav*—And the Lord God commanded Adam" is the first scriptural record of God's address to man. "*Lekh l'kha* —get thee out of thy land" is the abrupt and radical calling card which the Almighty presents to our first patriarch. The master prophet, too, hardly has a moment in which to absorb the awesome and irresistible fascination of supernature in the very midst of nature when the bidding of God's command breaks in upon him. Whether it be the words of "Thou shalt . . . Thou shalt not eat" (Gen. 2:16), "Build for yourself an ark" (Gen. 6:14), "And go thee unto Beth El and dwell there" (Gen. 35:1), or "Go . . . take my people out of Egypt" (Ex. 3:10), the divine address is apprehended not just as universal *Gebot, à la* Buber, but as particular *Gesetz*, in Rosenzweig's term—a specific commission to order life in accordance with His will.

A similar pattern confronts us as we examine the record of the Sinaitic stand. On this occasion, to be sure, not just select individuals are graced with the gift of prophecy. A whole community participates in a national divine-human meeting. In fact, the revelation at Sinai itself, entailing a second creation, gives birth to a new people of Israel and constitutes it at one and the same time as both faith and nation. No wonder then that this scandalous Sinaitic portrayal represents, in the words of Martin Buber, "The only such claim in the history of civilization." Yet the inspiration of this event has seared itself into the collective consciousness of an erstwhile slave-rabble, called to become "a kingdom of priests and a people of the Holy One," as irrevocably as the sign of the Abrahamitic covenant is sealed into the very flesh of every male Jewish child.

Once again, however, the Torah does not describe this

"invasion" of the Timeless into the timely, the Eternal into
the momentary, merely in the universal terms of "Presence
as power." Sinai explodes in the concreteness not alone of
I-Thou but, in the words of André Neher, of an "I-Thou
shalt, I-Thou shalt not." The Torah speaks not just of *b'rith*
(covenant) but of *sh'ne luhot ha-b'rith* (the two tablets of
the covenant). Similarly, God's bidding, "Ye shall be holy
for I, the Lord your God, am holy" (Lev. 19:2) remains
not a call to some ineffable spiritual ecstasy or mystical
union. It is boldly set forth in a detailed outline of daily living, seeking to interpenetrate every nook and cranny of
experience with holiness.

From such a vantage point, all the commandments are
binding upon the community and citizenry of Israel. Either
at birth or by *b'rith* each Jew enters into the covenantal
obligation of directing his own life—not all or nothing, but
step by step—and of building the whole and holy community—brick by brick—in accordance with His revealed will.
In this task of personal and social reconstruction, Judaism's
unique principle of divine-human partnership emerges with
boldness. As in the conquest of nature, so in the constant
reordering of society, man as prophet and sage, as scholar
and teacher, has in every single generation the bounden duty
of leadership to explore creatively and to implement practically the architectural blueprint of Torah. God has pointed
the way by the first layer of highway; man must continue
the project. So, with insight and reason, God's gift to men,
they earnestly and desperately probe the precedents of principles and practices, of institutions and events recorded in
both the written and cumulative oral tradition, seeking to
distill from the wisdom of the total past glimmering clues for
the crucial needs of their own day. Whether in relationship
to God or to man, the unique image of God, Torah has
remained Israel's distinctive and sacred *vade mecum* on its
pilgrimage to messianic redemption.

The fulfillment of these commandments, however, is
clearly predicated on the ground rules set by the divine
legislator. When the operational conditions for their performance are absent, they are by specification suspended. So,
to illustrate, many of the Pentateuchal laws of purity are no
longer applicable since the Temple and its service are pre-

conditions for their observance. On the other hand, with the miraculous return of our people to the holy land, a good number of the *"mitzvot* which depend upon the soil" have once again been renewed. For no matter what the historical conditions or the times, the *mitzvot, in potentia,* can never be abrogated. The word of the Eternal One is everlasting truth.

For the very same reason, a hierarchical division of the commandments into the ritual and the ethical is not at all valid. Such an analysis may be pedagogically sound and critically indispensable for purposes of human appreciation. Man is a rational and challenging being and his reason hungers for the nurture of clarity and understanding. Inevitably, therefore, every age has sought, and will continue legitimately to seek, its own intellectual key to the very heart of His will. (The caveat of past experience should not be ignored, however. The reasoned insights of the fathers too often became the blind and unexamined dogmas of the children, *viz.,* the absolutized rationalizations of *kashruth* as cleanliness or survivalism and of the Sabbath as progressive laws to protect labor and mental health.) In addition, the religio-psychological problem of the "do-able," so widespread in our times, which Franz Rosenzweig, the contemporary par excellence, so thoroughly experienced and explicated, may persuade and even impel individuals as well as groups to prefer, as relevant or important, one part of Judaism over another, one *mitzvah* over another.

In substance, however, such fine and final distinctions are alien and contrived. In fragmenting the Torah, they rob it of its comprehensiveness and they give rise to an inauthentic order of means and ends, essentials and expendables, which in turn lead to consequences that are anarchic. That is why the Torah blueprint itself points to no such divine priorities. Neither do the prophets, popular opinion notwithstanding. Professor Harry M. Orlinsky stresses this in a recent article, where he writes: "It is true that scholars have tended to make a distinction between cult and social justice, between sacrifice and good deeds, in fine, between the priest and the prophet. This distinction is utterly unbiblical." Judaism does not deal merely with a sector of life called the religious. It confronts life itself, all of it, and through *mitzvot* attempts to define and fashion its totality of experiences. This human wholeness, which is existentially indivisible and greater than the sum total of its parts, the Torah seeks to undergird and encourage. Consequently, it says to man: "*Tamim tih'ye im ha-Shem Elohekha*—you shall be whole with the Lord, your God" (Deut. 18:14). Both Israel the collectivity and the individual Jew can achieve and retain wholeness through the added dimension of holiness channeled through the *mitzvot*.

When this inner view of life is lifted to an even higher perspective, Torah becomes far more than just an efficacious system of *technikoi*, a kind of religious methology or life style. Judaism then represents an ever-unfolding relationship between Israel and the Almighty in which each *halakha* literally denotes the way, the divine direction, and each *mitzvah* ("commandment" now begins to sound harsh and gauche) constitutes both the word and essence of a love which can be shared by the most humble but believing Jew with his loving and beloved God. To delineate and evaluate, then, the *mitzvot* purely in terms of their ceremonial, ethical, aesthetical, doctrinal, psychological, disciplinary, or even spiritual functions is to extinguish the flame, to be blind to their wholeness and holiness and to convert a living relationship into an inert datum of knowledge.

In this regard, even the inexplicable statute (the *hok*) prohibiting the wearing of clothing made of linen and wool, though seemingly devoid of any ethical or spiritual intent, is far from purposeless or blind performance. To the faithful, its observance is sustained by the conviction expressed by Maimonides in his *Guide* (11:26): "All of us, the common people as well as the scholars, believe that there is a reason for every precept, although there are commandments the reason for which is unknown to us, and in which the ways of God's wisdom are incomprehensible." Until the time that man does gain this comprehension, however, the sacred act constitutes an unstinting gift-offering of devotion to the Holy One, as he loyally and voluntarily struggles to bring his whole life and the whole universe under the sovereignty of the Creator.

This kind of biblical thinking has, it is true, become somewhat strange to contemporary man. He has been educated to insist with almost dogmatic fervor that all knowing must be conceptual and objectified. Yet for the Jew of classical commitment who strives to view life *sub specie divinitatis,* every act lifted to the dimension of the *mitzvah* becomes a rare and unrepeatable opportunity—not necessarily an achievement—for *kabbalat p'nei he-Shekhinah,* a meeting with the Divine Effluence. In the winged words of Professor Abraham Joshua Heschel, the sacred act is the very abode of the immanent God and in its fulfillment the Jew, every single Jew, can encounter his Maker. "The way to God," you see, "is the way of God."

(2) Jewish tradition stubbornly refuses, therefore, to seek justification for Israel's existence and vocation outside God's own mysterious choice. It contains no explicit reference to a distinctiveness related to any unique contribution made or to be made to the welfare of mankind. Actually such claims grate upon human sensibilities and as a result of continuous cross-pollenization of ideas and ideals they soon become archaic and shallow. The Almighty, insists Scripture, chose Israel and gave it His Torah out of love. Like any decision of love, this election was not necessarily based on analytical findings, nor must His decision square with some presupposed priorities of human biases and assumptions. "Not because ye were more in number than any other people did the Lord set His Love upon you, or choose you . . . but because the Lord loved you" (Deut. 7:7). In his anticipation of a challenge from the new, post-Exodus generation which did not itself stand at Sinai, Moses took great pains to make this circular kind of reasoning crystal-clear. Divine love requires no rationalization. It is its own excuse for being and it is also Israel's warrant for being. It does, however, impose upon this people a distinctive task of becoming and remaining worthy of that great love. Each successive generation is inescapably called to commit itself anew to the Sinaitic covenant of *"na'aseh venishma*—we will act and be obedient," and thereby to build itself as a community into a dynamic and living witness that God is living and ever-present, that life has meaning and direction, that man is free and not determined, that beyond the accidents of color, class, or national origin he has been endowed by his Creator with

an inalienable right and obligation to shape his own destiny.

Modern apologetical claims to a special national genius for religion or a superior gift of intellect or morality remain just that. Whatever their grounding in fact—or lack of it— they have little authentic grounding in Scripture. In reality, they represent an earnest but ersatz attempt to retain and maintain the claims for distinctiveness of the people of Israel on purely cultural and philosophical grounds. Judging from the contemporary scene, their efforts are not meeting with great success.

Of equal futility is the effort expended in apologetical arguments against the obvious distortions and corruptions of this basic article of Jewish faith. Those distortions are not the product of illiteracy or misunderstanding. The scholarly enemies of our people have not been unacquainted with our sources nor entirely ignorant of our ultimate aspirations, summed up so movingly by Maimonides in the penultimate paragraph of his magnum opus, the *Strong Hand* (11:4). "Our sages and prophets," he writes, "yearned for the days of the Messiah not to rule over the world, not to tyrannize over the Gentiles, not to be exalted by the nations . . . but to be free for the pursuit of Torah and wisdom, to be rid of all oppressors, and to strive to merit eternal life." What might validly be asked of these passionate defenders of equality and freedom is why they did not direct the arrows of their onslaught against Christianity which with equal zeal has made an identical claim for its devotees. From the early days of Paul (see Rom. 2:7-11) to our own days of *aggiornamento,* Church dogma has not retreated one iota from its consistent and insistent claim that by true faith the Christian has become the rightful heir to the role and status of God's elect. This position is made unequivocally clear in the Vatican Council's Declaration on the Relationship of the Church to non-Christians, which repeatedly reflects the conviction that "the Church is the new people of God."

"What will the Gentiles say?" is therefore not alone a craven but a fruitless excuse for denying the very foundation stone of Israel's covenantal relationship and existence. It might just as well be suggested that Americans give up their fundamental faith in the democratic process because of the willful distortion and misuse to which this word and doctrine have been subjected by the totalitarian and authoritarian proponents of a central or people's democracy. Religious men must be sustained by an unshakable faith that ultimately truth will be vindicated.

(3) A similar perspective is recommended toward the various claims about "the true religion." Modern men might well pay heed to the sage counsel of the prophet Micah, who even in respect to the heathen nations stated, "Let all the peoples walk each one in the name of its god" (Mic. 4:5). Whatever claims are made regarding Judaism as a faith are intended only for the Jewish people and any others who would voluntarily join its ranks. As for the respective truth and merit of other competing claims, let history cast the final verdict. But until that day, "We will walk in the name of the Lord our God for ever and ever."

All this represents classical Jewish belief. What about the actual situation of faith in the current American Jewish community?

Enough sociological data are available to convince us that we are in the midst of a serious religious crisis. Except for the scattered oases of commitment, Judaism is by and large not a vital faith which addresses the daily lives of our people, guiding and even commanding their patterns of personal and social conduct. Judaism seems more like an ancestral inheritance, sacred and hallowed, to be sure, but like any heirloom of the past, capable of eliciting reverence and obeisance only on certain occasions. It does not shape, fill, or move our whole style of life.

The causes of this over-all condition stem from no one single source. For some, God—and therefore Judaism—remains quite shadowy and unreal because as children of our age they have been trained to capture and encase truth and reality in the syllogistic proof of demonstrated reason or the experimental evidence of the scientific laboratory. Unfortunately, the confinement of such a universe of discourse leaves no room for Him. The God of Abraham, Isaac, and Jacob stubbornly refuses to be imprisoned in a word or formula. He loves freedom too much for this. Moreover, He has given Himself many names. Each of them represents an invitation to man to lift the hem of mystery just a little and to catch from a different prismatic perspective only a flashing and passing glimpse of His infinite and blinding glory. Consequently, from the idolatry and prison of his own thinking man himself will have to be his own liberator.

For others, God has "died" in torture and agonizingly not because of any intellectual challenges. It is not the mind that aches but the heart which is in cosmic revolt, so to speak, and calls the whole heavenly kingdom to trial for the betrayal of its elect in its hour of martyrdom. Lord, if Thou art our Lord, why hast Thou deserted us, is their convulsive shriek. These physical survivors of the Nazi holocaust as well as the many contemporary psychological victims of this experience find in Elie Wiesel's words their litany and their Kaddish: "This day . . . I was the accuser, God the accused. My eyes were open and I was alone—terribly alone in a world without God and without man." The smoke mixed with ashes from Maidanek and Buchenwald, Auschwitz and Treblinka, hangs for them like a pall over the universe. The lights of the *Shekhina* cannot break through, nor its warming rays penetrate, and a glacial freeze creeps over man. They find no consolation in tradition's assurance that He, too, in the hour of Israel's trial, weeps and laments. For His weeping is in the abode of His hiding, and no human ear can hear it. But the tears of their own little ones, the "holy flock" of His chosen ones, they beheld helplessly and in terror. They saw the world handed over to demons and piously they awaited an apocalypse. Yet only silence rewarded their expectations, a divine silence which, like a funeral dirge, accompanied the cremation of their beloved ones. Where was His promised mercy, let alone His claimed justice? For such as these, the earth itself must first be cleansed of guilt and shame before God can ascend to His throne in heaven.

The most serious challenge to Jewish convictions comes not from the death of God but the death of man. Faith is an answer to an agonizing search, a response to an excruciating will to find ultimate meaning and purpose. Modern man, however, seeks no such purpose and limits his search to the palpable and the possessable of each day. The magic of gadgetry has robbed us of our sense of childlike awe and wonder. The plethora of objects and stimulation has sated and dulled our inner responsiveness to the sanctity and mystery in life. Judaism as faith and religious experience therefore speaks to ears which are unlistening and hearts which are not attuned. The forms are gone through and the motions performed, but there is no glow and little flame.

There is one more grouping which deserves mention. This is the radical minority who are very much alive and responsive to the moral and social dilemmas of the day but who do not relate their idealism and activism to the religious tradition into which they have been born. In fact, many regard religious faith as irrelevant to their immediate or ultimate concerns, though admittedly they have no new sources for values which they can substitute for the old. Nevertheless, they are turning their backs on "organized religion" because in their eyes it is identified with the very "establishment" against which they are in revolt.

For all these postmodern men, new formulations, new theological schema, new or novel ideologies will not restore their extinguished or stoked faith. Like most people, they have had their fill of words and systems. Intellectuals, especially, recall vividly their sense of profound disillusionment with the promised utopias and the fraudulence of pseudomessianic visions. In the absence of some transforming experience like great tragedy or great bliss, God will come alive for them when "institutions of God" and "men of God" provide by their own lives—not just professions—models of proof that He is alive, when by their active involvement in the pain and plight of their concrete sharing in the struggles for human dignity and peace, they demonstrate that all men are genuinely their concern as brothers. The world has always had need of intellect and genius but the need of this generation is more desperately for men of saintliness and active faith. In the words of the founder of Hasidism, society needs not men who "say" Torah, but are it. This kind of Zaddik —and not in any cultic sense—has, in Jewish lore, been designated as the "foundation of the universe." The dynamic presence and example of such human beings can provide a resource for both Jewish and human revivification. For if faith, as the adage goes, "cannot be taught but caught," it will be caught only from contagious personalities.

The immediate and long-range task of the self-selected saving remnant—who stand both outside and inside the formal institutions—is to serve as powerful beachheads of living faith. Around each of them must be gathered communities of fellowship whose lives must communicate the conviction contained in the words carved over the door of the home of Carl Jung: *"Vocatus atque non vŏcatus, Deus aderit"*— "Evoked or not evoked, God is present." Or, to use the more traditional words of the daily liturgy: "The Lord hath reigned, the Lord doth reign, the Lord will reign forever and ever."

David Greenberg

Rabbi of the Scarsdale (New York) synagogue
(Reform).

℃ (1) When I say that Torah is divine revelation I mean that moral values are rooted in reason, in the mind of God. The Midrash says God looked into the Torah and created the world. Molotov said Fascism was a matter of taste. The difference between a pimp and a saint, between Eichmann and Leo Baeck, is not a matter of opinion to be decided by a majority vote of the citizens of Germany. At Nuremberg the world turned away from moral relativism—the notion that right and wrong are what those in power say they are—to a more traditional doctrine. Confronted by the ultimate horror of Auschwitz, Western civilization was shocked into sanity. If this is not so, then the trial at Nuremberg was sheer vindictiveness, the imposition of the will of the victors upon the vanquished. There are standards of righteousness by which states can be judged. Morality is not arbitrary caprice. This fundamental conviction unites believing Jews. It is more significant than our disagreements over ritual trivia.

Some of the 613 commandments apply to specific classes of people; others apply only in the land of Israel; still others applied only in the days of the Temple.

Man is to give his unconditional obedience to God and not to a book, not even the Torah. Though God is by definition infallible, man is not. Even in the Torah, God's light is refracted through man, an imperfect medium conditioned by time, circumstance, and mortal imperfection. It is possible even for Moses to misunderstand God.

I cannot believe that God sanctions slavery or capital punishment for murder, adultery, and desecration of the Sabbath. I agree with the rabbis who, in effect, nullified these laws through interpretation. I cannot believe that the bastard and his descendants must be prohibited forever from entering the congregation of Israel and the suggestion by some authorities in Israel that the Bnai Israel of India must be eternally relegated to the status of untouchables in the homeland to which they lovingly returned.

You can accuse me of being a relativist and a voluntarist because I believe that man ought to obey those laws which God addressed to him, to his heart and his mind and soul.

I am not so presumptuous as to assume that ritual laws which seem to me to be devoid of ethical or spiritual content such as the laws of ritual purity cannot be experienced by others, whose conditioning is different, as a refining discipline and a source of spiritual exaltation.

(2) If any Jew tells you he is not chosen, you had better believe him.

The claim to chosenness is a high claim, it is arrogance and blasphemy unless you intend to prove it by your life. But unless we take our stand on high ground we will not stand at all. It is a statement of moral aspiration, a kind of *noblesse oblige*. God's choice was not a unilateral act; it implies Israel's willingness to live in accordance with the moral law.

Robert Gordis points out that the concept of chosenness is invariably associated in the liturgy with the giving and receiving of the Torah.

Amos confounds the issue when he cries, "Are ye not as the children of the Ethiopians unto Me." He clarifies it when he says, "You alone have I chosen from among all peoples, therefore I shall visit your iniquity upon you." This assumption of ethical obligation is a far cry from the racism of the Nazis which claims automatic superiority for the master race and the right to enslave and murder the rest of mankind. It certainly does not deny the divinity of all men created in the image of God.

Chosenness can have another connotation. The peoples of the earth are the great protagonists upon the world stage and each nation in God's providence is called to fulfill some purpose. To be a Hebrew, to be a Greek, to be a Roman, is to be one of those who as a matter of historical fact was chosen to fulfill a role of more than ordinary significance. There were many tribes who walked the same desert as the seed of Abraham. They were descended from similar stock, spoke related languages, breathed the same air, shared the same sun; but one was chosen by God to be catapulted across the horizon of history to write its flaming message indelibly upon the hearts of men.

(3) The outlook of the world would be dim indeed if Jews had a monopoly on morality. There are universal moral laws accessible to reason and common to men of all faiths. They are symbolized in our tradition by the seven Noahide commandments given to all his descendants, as against the 613 directed to the children of Israel.

Judaism is distinguished from the classical expressions of Buddhism, Christianity, and Islam in its exaltation of intellect, in its stress upon the importance of this world and the sanctification rather than the rejection of nature, in its drive toward justice, in its faith in man, in its hope for the future of this world.

In its recognition of the passionate power of evil, Judaism has the advantage over secular humanism, which sometimes imagines that ideas will triumph by their own unaided logic. The believing Jew can summon a power and passion equal to that of the powers of darkness. He is saved from cynicism and delivered from despair. He is confident that the Messiah, even though he tarry, will come.

Of course, contradictory metaphysical statements cannot all be true. In this sense there cannot be several true religions. There can be and should be a pluralism of religious forms and rites, myths and symbols, to help the individual pass through the crises of life and dramatize the values of the group in terms of its history and hopes. "The attempt to speak without speaking any particular language is not more hopeless than the attempt to have a religion that shall be no religion in particular," says Santayana. In a religious culture as in language, each group selects a segment from the great arc on which are ranged the human possibilities provided by the life cycle and man's struggle with his environment. Even when the orchestra of humanity sounds a universal note, its overtones are altered by the material of the individual instruments.

Isaiah's vision of the end-time when nations will not learn war any more does not involve the disappearance of the nations nor the homogenization or wanton destruction of their disparate cultures.

(4) In its long history, Judaism has coexisted with every conceivable form of political and economic organization. It is anachronistic to imagine that Judas Maccabeus anticipated Thomas Jefferson, or Moses, or the welfare state. For that matter the Bible has been quoted in defense of witch burning and slavery.

Yet, if I have any understanding of the tradition which teaches that all men are created in the image of God, I must take my stand with the weak and oppressed, as I believe Moses and the prophets would if they were alive today. I cannot make my peace with any racist or totalitarian government.

(5) Atheism is not new; neither is the assertion that God does not function in the life of professed believers. What is novel is the fact that the current controversy takes place among clergymen. What is significant is the language in which it is expressed—"God is dead." God by definition cannot die and it is theological nonsense to speak of the death of the eternal Father while affirming His son.

Forgive my flippancy. Here Freud is more illuminating than Saint Thomas or Tillich. What conclusions would he draw about our society from the fact that first the Catholics put the mother, Mary, in heaven and then the Protestants killed the father? Recently a sick Jewish boy shot the rabbi.

It is not the challenges to Jewish thought which threaten the dissolution of Jewish life. Ignorance and indifference spawned by sociological causes are the true enemies. A chasm separates the atheist, who has some dignity, from the ignoramus and the opportunist.

No one since Kant has seriously attempted to prove or disprove God. We have the right to believe without doing violence to our God-given reason. The problem is not logical but psychological. Men are powerless to believe as they are powerless to love because they find it hard to become men.

Arthur Hertzberg

Rabbi of Temple Emanu-El (Conservative) in Englewood, New Jersey, and teacher of Jewish history in the graduate faculties at Columbia University.

⟪ The essence of Judaism is the affirmation that the Jews are the chosen people; all else is commentary.

Whether the Jews are indeed the chosen people is a matter for faith. It cannot be demonstrated by argument. In the Bible, and ever since, history has been invoked to "prove" this claim—that Jewish experience, in all its grandeur and in all the depths of its suffering, can be explained only on the presumption that it is the record of the hand of God writing, mysteriously, in human events. It is, of course, possible to argue against this thesis. It can be said that the exodus from Egypt was an insignificant incident, involving a paltry band of slaves, who then wrote myths about it, and that Auschwitz was but another instance of man's well-known capacity for murdering other men. It is possible to deny that any particular element in the history of the Jews is really unique, and to maintain that the whole of it, despite its obvious singularity, is only a tissue of accidents. But this is not the way the Jewish faith views the history of the Jews.

But why the Jews? In the eyes of faith, Jewish chosenness means that the Jews do not know why God chose them (Deut. 7:6–13); they claim no special privilege, except perhaps the somber one of suffering uniquely, of being judged by God, by the harshest standards (Amos 3: 1–2; 9: 7–10). What chosenness does mean to the faithful is that what has happened and continues to happen to Jews is at the very center of the meaning of human existence.

This assertion of chosenness is, of course, scandalous. It has been under attack from the very beginning of the encounter between the Jews and the West. The roots of modern racism are indeed to be found in this confrontation; those roots, however, are not in Judaism but in the Greek tradition. It is the enemies of the Jews who have used racist arguments against them.

For the Greeks and the Romans, the Jews were the most troublesome of all the peoples they encountered. The Jews persisted in believing that even high, philosophical paganism was wrong and blasphemous. They were preeminent in refusing to accept the Hellenistic notion that "barbarians"— i.e., non-Greeks—could enter culture only if they adopted the Greek outlook. Greek and Roman anti-Semites responded by attacking the apartness of the Jews as misanthropy and by repeatedly charging that these people were bad by nature. This notion recurred in the more anti-Semitic extravagances of the New Testament and of medieval Christian theology. The Jews rejected Jesus, so the argument has gone, because they were evil, by nature. The immediate forerunner of contemporary racism is in the attack mounted on the Marranos after the sixteenth century in the name of "purity of blood" —the notion that converts of Jewish ancestry could not escape the "taint" of their origins.

Jews have never understood the doctrine of the election of Israel as having anything to do with inherent biological superiority. They have always known that it is a religious category, not a racial one. What is new in the modern age is that Jews themselves have now joined the attack. Modernity brought with it the construction of an entirely new set of desires by Jews, and "chosenness," with all that it implies, has stood in the way of the new purposes.

The great commandment of the classic Jewish tradition was that the Jews should be "a people dwelling apart," that the community of the faithful should live in some detachment from the world around them. The dominant enterprise of the Jews in the last two centuries has been to achieve their complete emancipation. They have been laboring to establish the proposition that both what they are and what they believe belong in the same realm as the other faiths and communities of Western man. Obviously, the belief in "chosenness" and the practice of apartness stand in the way; it has seemed necessary that all obstacles to "integration" should be removed.

Modern Jews have been at great pains to prove that they are really "just like everybody else." Indeed, there has even been an element of homeopathic magic in their eagerness to play down their own doctrine of "chosenness." It is as though they were saying: Let us stop talking about our being radically different on religious grounds, and our enemies will be moved to stop attacking us as a radically dangerous race.

This has not worked. It has not worked as a counter to Jew-hatred, because no matter what Jews may say or do, they continue to be a visibly unique element in the world. The man of faith sees the divine choice ("and you shall be unto Me a singular people") finding, and even pursuing, those who would deny it. They must affirm it, inevitably, through their lives. The only people some modern Jews have ever convinced that Jews are "like everybody else" is themselves. Both their friends and their enemies outside the Jewish community have known that this is not so. Balaam has always seen what the descendants of Moses would pretend does not exist.

The modern attempt to deny "chosenness" has failed just as clearly to answer the crucial question that it raises internally, within Jewry: If Judaism represents a slightly different variant of the conventional Western outlook, why should the peculiar diaspora which is its bearer remain in being? The conventional rhetoric, of religious and cultural pluralism, is really no answer. If the observance of Passover is indeed the affirmation of a commitment to the freeing of all the oppressed, then perhaps the money spent on *matzoh* this year and the energies put into innumerable Seder observances should have been spent in Harlem or in Hong Kong. If the rituals of Judaism are devised by man to symbolize his values, why can he not freely change or abandon these symbols? If man's values are of his own devising, why can he not change those values and abandon the community that represented earlier stages of his moral outlook? If the meaning of Judaism is that it commands its believers to labor for social progress, why must the believer prefer for himself the Jewish community in America today to the community of the dispossessed in Watts?

There can be only one answer to this order of question. The Jewish faith is of lasting importance, and it is an ultimate sin to abandon it, *only* if it be conceived as divinely ordained; else what men have made they can unmake and the communities into which they were born are mere accidents. From this perspective, there is no distinction between the moral laws of Judaism and the ritual commandments. Contemporary Jewish religious apologetics cannot really barricade itself behind a distinction between a divinely ordained moral law and man-made ritual. The notion that God did indeed command Samuel to hack Agag to pieces before him in Gilgal is far more repugnant than the belief that He really cares whether I wear a suit consisting of both linen and flax. The theological difficulty is the same in both cases. We are, therefore, quite properly asked to explain by what principle one can affirm revelation and yet deny some of the commandments and much of the outlook of the sacred texts in which that revelation is presumed to be recorded.

The plain truth is that there is no clear dogmatic answer, and all the attempts that have been made in the last two centuries to provide one are more dangerous than leaving the question open. This is not unprecedented in Jewish theological thinking. Job was troubled by the question of God's justice. His friends suggested elaborate "answers" by which they justified the ways of God, but the author of the book was more impressed by the notion that the justice of God is a mystery, which men can understand in part, but only in part. Rabbi Akiba was troubled by the question of man's responsibility in the face of God's omnipotence, and Akiba's famous resolution ("all is foreseen but free will is granted") amounted to saying that man must live with this paradox, and that the content of much of his religious life is to wrestle with the mystery both in life and theory. Both Job and Akiba found that all the possible answers, including the one of denying God for the sake of logic and making an end of the problem, were shallower and more wounding than living with the question.

The crucial problem that confronts Jewish theology in our age can best be stated in a paradox comparable to the one with which Rabbi Akiba defined his dilemma. We must say: God exists and He has revealed Himself to man through the sacred texts of the Jewish tradition, and yet the individual must be free to make his choices as to what he will affirm as value and what rituals he will obey as representing, for him, authentic commandment.

The commitment of the man of faith to the tradition is under persisting challenge. The contemporary historical disciplines are more of a problem to him than modern science. Our growing knowledge of the physical universe can only call into question literalist versions of the cosmology of the Bible, or its miracles, but the essential religious assertion that there is a God who made the world is perhaps less out of fashion among men of science today than it was two generations ago. The "warfare of science and religion" has not been ended by an armistice and peace treaty, but the whole subject no longer seems important to either side. What continues to be troubling is the fundamental relativism about all the actions and all the faiths of man which is the prevailing temper of intellectual life. No one dares to discuss values in our day on the basis of the older premise that, quite apart from any utilitarian considerations, some values are better than others and some spiritual outlooks are of higher estate than any available alternates.

But is Judaism indeed a higher value, or a higher complex of values, than any possible contemporary alternate? The very form in which the question has been posed implies a relativistic scale, which presumes that all outlooks must be judged in the mode of comparative cultural and religious anthropology. The defense of an idea is to prove that it is more acceptable than some other idea, as democracy is more acceptable, at least to democrats, than Fascism. Judaism cannot possibly be explained or defended within such a context. Stated abstractly, as a set of moral concerns about human dignity and freedom, social progress and peace, there is nothing to distinguish Jewish ideas from conventional Western ones, or even from the moral content of some, if not all, of the high religions. (I would except the nonbiblical ones, because their fundamental notion of man's immediate life as incidental leads to quite different moral conclusions from the biblical ones.)

This does not, however, end the question of the unique significance of Judaism. It is too easy to say that the Jews remain, or ought to remain, an elite on the battle line for the realization of these values. This is a humanist concept, which is subject to the criticism that some other group might be arising to become the true contemporary elite. Such leadership cadres have arisen within society as a whole in the past and they will, of course, continue to do so. The Jewish faith and community cannot be asked at every specific moment in time to prove in argument, even to itself, that it is a more significant leadership than the one in fashion at the moment. What Jewish experience does prove is that the Jews have consistently played an astonishing role in the world. This does not mean that Judaism has had its purposes or self-definition clear in every age. Some centuries have been periods of waiting and even of confusion, in which the best the Jews could do was simply to maintain the community and the living tie with their past heritage. I think that this is such an age, of waiting, of looking for answers rather than of being able to give them.

In the moral realm Judaism does have, even in this age in which its distinctive accents are muted, one continuing great idea to suggest: its faith in the Messiah. For the last two thousand years there has been a continuing polarity within Judaism between the persisting main body of the faithful and recurring challenges arising among them in the name of an immediate messianism. Viewed from the perspective of continuing Jewish experience, there is a straight line from Jesus to Shabbethai Zevi to Karl Marx and Leon Trotsky. In all of these various permutations, men have arisen out of the soil of Judaism to announce the messianic age as near at hand and immediately achievable, and toward that end they or their disciples have offered up the existence of the Jewish community. Making an end of it has been regarded as a necessary preamble to some dawning "end of days." To inter Judaism, with thanks, as a superseded stage on the way to a greater new world has been regarded by all kinds of radical messianists not as treason but as a heroic moral act. But the Messiah has not yet come. The world is as yet unredeemed and all the various visions of a realized eschatology, both religious and secular, have obviously been premature. Faithful Jews have taken the risk in every generation of rejecting the notion that the end of days is really now announced. Their faithfulness has preserved Judaism in its proper attitude of waiting—and of being the soil out of which the Messiah will yet come, in a form we cannot imagine. Judaism will continue to breed those who would reject it for seemingly broader visions. The ʾman of faith must believe that such messianists, too, play some role in the divine plan, but the faithful must remain just that—faithful.

We cannot derive, and it is even dangerous to attempt to derive, from classic Judaism a specific and precise political and social outlook, except in the broadest terms. Believing Jews are forbidden to hate or to oppress other men; they can therefore not be totalitarians in politics. Nothing is clearer than that they must oppose the antireligious element of Communism, but there is absolutely no reason to say that only the capitalist economic order is acceptable from the perspective of Judaism. What Judaism can do for the individual Jew is to permeate him with the total feel of the tradition and then leave him to make his own personal choices in the realm of men's immediate actions. Many Jews remember, as I do, a grandmother who said often about some matters, out of the very depths of her being, that "a Jew doesn't do this." As political and social doctrine this may seem imprecise, but one who is not alien to the inherited Jewish experience finds this standard both precise and most exquisitely moral.

It should be clear by now, from the drift of my argument, that I regard any question about Judaism as the "one true religion" as irrelevant in the form in which it is put. Classical Judaism believes that the many faiths of man all play a role in the divine scheme. What Judaism does contend is that its divinely appointed role is uniquely its own, and that that appointment is both its task and its destiny.

In this age of waiting there is really one task for Jews, as a continuing community of believers. It is to eschew theological or ideological definitions of Judaism, which are particularly impossible in a period of general intellectual confusion and uncertainty, and to turn to the two things Jews can do: to reforge the link of personal knowledge and experience of the inherited Jewish learning and to maintain the Jewish community in being, as a distinctive entity. We shall not necessarily succeed with all Jews, and we shall perhaps fail even more today than we have in the past, but we must persevere in the effort.

It is not only Jews who know that the Messiah has not

yet come; the world knows it too. Is this not the meaning, ultimately, of the theological crisis of Christianity, which is inherent in the new death-of-God theology? Advanced Christians are confronting the unredeemed world. As they sit amidst the rubble of all the shattered hopes, including their own theological ones, advanced Christians are hoping to redeem the world by a new devotion to Jesus. This is a very "Jewish" stance, for we Jews have been in the business of living through and beyond tangible and intangible exiles and disasters from the very beginning of our experience. We know that all is never lost—but, for that matter, that all is never won, either. In the age of the concentration camps and of the re-creation of a Jewish commonwealth in Israel we have known both the greatest despair and historic comfort.

To be a Jew means to believe, and to wait.

Richard J. Israel

Director of the B'nai B'rith Hillel Foundation and chaplain to Jewish students at Yale University.

❡ The starting point of my credo is the absurd fact of my existence as a Jew. Personal religious experience leads me only to general religious concern, not to Judaism. Reason and history only tell me why I should not exist. I take my unlikely presence in the world as a Jew at this time not to be merely a biological or a sociological fact, but a theological one. The positivist cannot explain me without standing on his head. Given the character and quality of the Jewish experience, it is impossible for me to conceptualize it without attaching to it a teleology.

There are two *midrashim* which describe the giving of the Torah. One tells of the people of Israel standing at the foot of Mount Sinai while God informs them that if they do not take the Torah He will turn over the mountain upon them and it will be their burial place. A second tells of God, in effect, peddling the Torah from people to people until Israel finally accepts it freely and enthusiastically.

The first *midrash* describes my willy-nilly chosenness, the fact that my parents were Jews and didn't ask me if I wanted

to be born that way, any more than did their parents and
their parents' parents, all the way back to Sinai. How I respond to the fact of my Jewishness seems to be described by
the second *midrash*, for here, with respect to response, I am
not chosen, I choose. I either choose willingly to accept the
Torah or to run the risks and escape from the covenant. I
inherited a house. Whether or not I choose to live in it is
my own decision.

The question as to whether my sense of being chosen is
related to doctrines of national and racial superiority strikes
me as silly. The covenant has nothing to do with the virtue
of Israel. Quite the opposite. It can be suggested that Israel
was chosen at least partly for its insignificance (see Deut.
7:7). If Israel has no importance of its own, that which God
achieves through such a people is a greater tribute to His
own power. Many peoples, both before and since the appearance of the Jews in history, have held to doctrines of
chosenness and doctrines of superiority, generally as a way of
justifying their own power. Jewish chosenness emerged from
a situation of impotence. Whistling in the dark perhaps? In
any event, the notion that we should be held responsible for
any doctrines arising from misinterpretation and misuse of
the Jewish doctrine of chosenness is foolish. I take chosenness to mean that the Jew has yet a role to play in God's
plan for the resolution of history. I see no great intellectual
scandal in assuming that God wants to work out history
through particular peoples as opposed to all of humanity
together. One makes as much or as little sense as the other.
In either case, the reasons would be those best known to
Him and need not be intelligible to me.

The event at Sinai places me here today. I believe that
the Torah is a record of the response to that event whose
precise nature is not clear to me from the texts. It is clear
that it had an irrevocable impact upon a people for several
thousands of years. I, as a member of that people, am affected by, and thus ultimately am a participant in, the
event. The acceptance of the commandments was the response of the people of that time. Insofar as I wish to participate in and personally recover the event, I find that I
must participate in the commandments. Insofar as there is a
lack of clarity about the events, there is a lack of clarity

about the commandments. The 613 commandments are a
test number, an entrance requirement to the club of the
"authentic." They are a way of asking whether one accepts
normative Orthodoxy. I can only understand them as a theoretical dogma. As a theoretical system I can accept them. I
can hold that the totality of the law is binding upon me as
well as upon all other Jews, but I am not willing to claim
clear divine authority for any given one of them. There is
serious disagreement even among the great codifiers like Maimonides and Nachmanides as to which the 613 commandments are. I can accept the idea of the Law and its general
structure. I am not certain about the authority of its particu-
lars. There is a revelation, but its full content is not always
obvious. There are commandments, but I must struggle to
discover them.

The traditional *mitzvot* affect me variously, and I am not
free to ignore consideration of any of them. I should like to
describe a number of my responses.

Some, whether in the ethical or ritual realm, are rare opportunities, to be passed by only at my own deep personal
loss. Rabbi Mendel of Kotzk once said, "I don't want you to
sin, not because it is wrong, but because there isn't enough
time." I cannot feel that the important issue in nonobservance
of the Sabbath is sin, but it certainly is a missed opportunity
which can never be recovered. A *Shabbat* that I miss can
never happen to me again. I have lost it.

I do not feel the same about all *mitzvot*. Some are deeply
enriching, some are a big bother, and still others are silent.
But my negative response to a *mitzvah* does not necessarily
provide me with an immediate release. I know that the easi-
est way for me would be to bring everything in my tradition
up-to-date, to rearrange and reinterpret until the entire corpus is in comfortable accord with the very latest in modern
thinking. But if history teaches me anything, it teaches that
today's fads are not necessarily tomorrow's faith. God may
be dead this week, living in mushrooms the next, and the
following week be merely a figure of speech for Another,
who is really God. My own religious temperament requires
a certain amount of rootedness. I am prepared to live in
contact with the *mitzvot* so that they may teach me, while I
suspend judgment about their metaphysical validity.

The obligatory daily reading of the *Shema* constitutes such a case. Its second paragraph really puts me off, speaking as it does about immediate reward and punishment on this earth, through changes in atmospheric conditions. I flatter myself in thinking that I am as able as anyone else to find a first-rate interpretation, to explain that I really haven't understood the text properly. What it really means is . . . But nonsense! I have understood what it really means and I don't like it. There is a point beyond which the neat reworking of mythological content is just a way of concealing our discomfort with the expressed ideas. I should prefer to leave the text just as it is, understanding it the way I think it means itself to be understood. It tells me that God acts in this world in a very direct way. This is an idea which has spoken to religious thinkers for generations. It doesn't to me. Nevertheless, I do not want to cut myself off from the possibility of being judged by the tradition. If I drop bothersome aspects of the tradition, I will never again have the opportunity to be challenged by its difficult ideas, nor will I give the generations that come after me the opportunity to recover a meaning which I have lost. I am involved in a holding operation.

The observance of *kashruth* is an example of an annoying series of *mitzvot* which I am glad not to have dropped because of some of the rather important surprises it has offered. Because it is a public observance, I have to justify it rather frequently, to my friends and certainly to myself. I find that whether I like it or not, *kashruth* brings me into contact with a series of rather important questions: What is my responsibility to the calf that I eat, or to the potato? Is the earth and the fullness thereof mine to do with as I will? What does it mean that a table should be an altar? Is eating, indeed, a devotional act? Does God really care whether I wait two or six hours before drinking milk after a meat meal? If *kashruth* makes me ask enough questions, often enough, I discover that its very provocative quality is one of its chief virtues for my religious life.

The prohibition against clothing made of linen and wool is an example of a *mitzvah* which has suggested to me no inherent meaning whatsoever. I don't like it, especially since it doesn't even offer me the liberal's convenient way out:

". . . after all, it is only a late rabbinic injunction." There it is, big, bold, and clear in the Torah. It is not the *mitzvah* I like best in the world. It just sits there poking fun at me. But it does rather mercilessly tell me not to be such a know-it-all, that the law cannot be translated into simple humanistic terms.

I do not mean that I find it possible to take the other end of the rope and successfully observe or confront all the *mitzvot* which my tradition hands me. Some *mitzvot* are more do-able than others. Some are more confrontable than others. But I do not find it sufficient to settle for that which I personally happen to find meaningful at this particular moment. I feel under constant pressure to push myself forward to explore as much new material as I can, to try to observe one more *mitzvah* than I did yesterday.

It may be that the *mitzvah* system is unique to Judaism. For me, however, that is an uninteresting historical fact. What really distinguishes me from other people is an internal response; my acting in order to fulfill the terms of the covenant. I have my contract with the Lord. I assume nothing about the contracts of others, however. Invidious distinctions drawn between traditions don't get very far.

For example, it strikes me that we have gotten ourselves into something of a bind by renouncing Torah's divine significance and then trying to prove that Judaism is humanistically superior to Christianity. We have managed to achieve this sleight-of-hand by carefully selecting our citations and our Christian theologians, thereby conjuring up an image of an ascetic, quietistic, irrational Christianity. Over and against this, we have picked our own scriptural verses and theologians so that they will be sensible, down-to-earth, practical people, concerned with the redemption of this world, in time, exclusively through our own efforts, with just an occasional bit of inspiration from the Lord. In so doing, we have quite thoroughly ignored the opposite themes in each of our traditions. Now that contemporary Christians are running circles around us working in this world, when Christian theologians celebrate a "world come of age" which looks suspiciously like a "Torah given into the hands of man," we find that we have lost our sales pitch. We must then scramble to try to justify ourselves not in terms of our inherent humanistic superiority to Christianity, but on the even flimsier grounds that we got there first.

Judaism cannot make a strong case for a set of unique political values. Jewish political attitudes have been conditioned considerably more by the political situations of the Jews than by their religious outlook. I should think that a Jew could legitimately support any political system which would guarantee the dignity of its citizens, not using them as tools of the state. Though contemporary historic experiences would make it difficult for me to conceive of situations in which a good Jew could support Communism or Fascism philosophically, I think it would be hard to show that by their natures they or democracy are necessarily either friendly or hostile to Judaism. Justice has been the concern of Judaism, not any particular forms of political life.

Insofar as the traditional sources make any claims for the ideal state, they would probably favor a constitutional monarchy, the nature of its constitution determined not by what the people wanted, but by what authoritative scholars of the Torah interpreted as law. This, however, is an eschatological hope. Such a government need not be sought by any Jew until the end of days. Until then, a Jew would have the obligation to encourage those forms of government which were most likely to promote the justice and humaneness of the Noahide Laws for non-Jews and would permit Jews the freedom to observe their own traditions in a reasonably peaceful and tranquil situation. Prudential choices would be required, not judgments about the inherent virtue of any political system.

Racial segregation is an altogether different matter. Although I do not always rest easily with some of the ways in which the Law works out its attitudes to non-Jews, I can think of no way within the normative tradition by which distinctions between people could be made on the basis of race. Only if a few biblical passages are cited out of context can they be construed to mean that a good Jew, or anyone else, could justifiably believe in racial segregation.

The announcement of God's death by current Protestant theologians is certainly likely to evoke little more from the Jewish community than, "So what else is new?" After all, He has been in retirement for some time. The Jewish funeral was a much more private affair. We buried Him quietly and in the middle of the night. In recent years, the awareness of a living God has simply slipped away from most Jewish circles without a fuss. We regularly read in contemporary Jewish texts of the talmudic dispute between Rabbi Joshua and Rabbi Eliezer in which the latter produces miracles as the proof that God agrees with him. We have generally sided with Rabbi Joshua, who, rejected such proofs, holding that "We pay no attention to a heavenly voice." The heterodox use of the *midrash* on Jeremiah 16:11 which makes God say, "Would that they had forsaken Me and kept My commandments," has come to be taken as a basic doctrine. The rest of the passage which explains that the power of the Torah would bring the people back to God has been forgotten. What goes on in the Jewish community might have been God's business once, but it isn't any more.

With this kind of neglect of the religious dimension of Jewish life in America, I would not hold that any particular aspect of modern thought is a major challenge to Jewish belief. Judaism is a self-contained coherent system which hangs together as well as any other. But one philosophy almost never refutes another. It ignores it. The present dilemma of Judaism seems irrelevant to modern Jews, not even worthy of serious consideration.

As one who is, I think, not untypical of these times, I find that it requires a considerable act of will to take the Jewish categories seriously. It is much simpler to live cozily with the twentieth-century liberal, pragmatic, empiricist tradition into which I was born. But I was born into two worlds, and there is more to my life as a Jew than today's intellectual climate alone can sustain. The *mitzvot* at least offer me an opportunity to be in continuing contact with the categories of the Jewish tradition, that I may come to grips with them in their own terms.

Yaakov Jacobs

Editor of the Jewish Observer *(Orthodox).*

⟪ "Let us make man," G–d* declared on the eve of the first *Shabbat.* The use of the plural raises the question: To whom was G–d speaking? One of the Hasidic teachers tells us that G–d was addressing man himself: "Let us *together* make man."

Herein lies the essence of Jewish belief: Man is granted the raw material of existence and, in the talmudic phrase, he becomes a partner in his won creation. The instrument with which he fashions his own nature is the Torah revealed to us on Sinai. Observing each of the 613 *mitzvot* thrusts man forward in his striving for *shlemut,* wholeness and oneness with G–d. The word *"shlemut,"* which has a common root with the word *"shalom,"* also shares in the elusive nature of peace: we cannot achieve one without the other.

The search for *shlemut* is at the core of the Jew's religious belief and experience. It is achieved by narrowing the gap which separates man from G–d, and by the growth of awareness of the needs and sensitivities of others and the willingness to share their burdens. It thereby becomes the measure of man's spiritual progress.

Tradition—the Decalogue itself—divides the *mitzvot* into two categories: *ben adam la-Makom,* governing man's relationship with G–d, and *ben adam la-chavero,* governing his relationship with his fellowman. Yet the two categories of *mitzvah* are identical in their objectives. Love of man and a willingness to share his burdens bring man closer to G–d; and love of G–d and obedience to His will open the heart to greater love of man. In this sense, *mitzvot* governing man's relationship with his fellows, the laws of *kashruth* and *Shabbat,* the prohibition against *shatnez* and other laws of the Torah which appear to have no social significance, are all instruments with which the Jew pushes himself up in his climb toward *shlemut.*

* Some Orthodox Jews extend to English the prohibition against the utterance in any context other than prayer of the various Hebrew words suggesting the name of God.—*Ed.*

T'filah, often translated as prayer, though this is only one aspect, is a basic tool in the struggle for *shlemut*. The word "*t'filah*" derives from the root "*palel*" and connotes the act of judging; the reflexive form in which it is commonly used indicates that at the heart of the experience of prayer is the act of judging oneself in confrontation with G–d. The search within contemporary Judaism for "creative prayer" is a futile search so long as prayer is thought of in a narrow sense. The efficacy of *t'filah* lies in the potential it offers for achieving *shlemut*, for growing in the act of self-judgment. It offers the opportunity for actually changing the identity of the *mitpalel*. Perhaps it is this concept which is embodied in the tradition of adding a name to one who is critically ill, in the hope that the experience of *t'filah*, the anguish and the nearness of death, will change the nature, the very identity, of the individual.

The search for *shlemut* is endless. When a Jew achieves a measure of *shlemut*, he is cast down by conceit, the mortal enemy of *shlemut*. But unlike Sisyphus, who forever climbs the same mountain, never growing, never progressing, the Jew renews his climb with greater energy; refreshed, rather than fatigued by the previous climb.

The search for *shelmut* is a highly personal endeavor, yet it demands interaction with society and the world. Reb Yisroel Salanter put it this way. There are *milei d'almo*, worldly needs, and there are *milei d'shmayo*, heavenly needs, but the *milei d'almo* of another are for me *milei d'shmayo*. More simply, if another human being is in need of bread, a mundane need for him, my responsibility to feed him is a spiritual challenge. Certainly, such awareness will influence the outlook of the Jew on the world around him; it will influence his political orientation, for he will gravitate toward those forces in the body politic which share his concern for the weak and the underprivileged. Since it is his obligation to be concerned for the welfare of a single man or woman in need, this concern must be no less relevant when a mass of men, women, and children is involved. The precise political base he will choose for himself must be determined by the political circumstances which prevail in his community or society. The individual Jew alone can determine how to translate his concern into political action, and what priorities he will set up in dispensing his energies and his abilities. In this regard he is little different from any of his fellow citizens with a strong commitment to justice and righteousness.

Nevertheless, no Jew who believes firmly in Torah and commits himself to observance of all the *mitzvot* can support racial segregation; he cannot accept any criteria for judging any man other than that man's intrinsic merit. In his own search for wholeness, he must come to appreciate *shlemut* wherever he finds it.

This total commitment to G–d and His Torah is asked only of the Jew. The Torah recognizes the validity of the search for G–d by other faiths and therefore the Jew feels no need to win others to his faith. The would-be convert is told that he seeks admission to a brotherhood which is oppressively restrictive for its adherents; that he will be exposed to hostility directed at him for his Jewishness; that he may even be called upon to forfeit his life because of his Jewishness. Only when he convincingly demonstrates that he is willing to enter the faith with full awareness of the consequences, is he permitted—and then joyfully—to become a Jew.

It is in this sense that we are a "chosen people," chosen for commitment to G–d and His *mitzvot*; chosen to live the godly life at risk to life and limb; chosen to demonstrate the presence of G–d's kingdom on earth and to plow incessantly forward to the days of the *Mashiach*, when all mankind will achieve *shlemut* and *shalom*.

Is every "religious" and "observant" Jew so motivated? The Chofetz Chaim was once asked to explain why scholars are frequently contentious, when it is written: "*Talmidei chachamim marbim shalom be'olam,*" that they generate peace in the world. "*Siz a probe,*" he replied (in Yiddish) —the formula is reversible; one who does not generate peace is not a *talmid chacham*.

A group that claims national or racial superiority is by definition a closed group; one cannot be inducted into superiority. The Jewish people is an open group, and anyone may become "chosen" if he chooses to take on the responsibilities of being a Jew. To suggest that this concept of being chosen has served as a model for racial and national superiority—if there is any validity at all to the theory—is to suggest that the one G–d has been the model for false gods.

"Everything in G–d's creation has a purpose," a rabbi once told his disciples. "In that case," asked one disciple, "what is the purpose of *apikorsus* [heresy]?" "*Apikorsus* is indeed purposeful," the rabbi replied, "for in respect to our own needs we must have complete faith in the Creator; but in responding to the needs of others, man must feel that he alone, and no other, can meet these needs."

The "God is dead" theology may also be said to serve a purpose. The Midrash writes that in the days prior to the coming of *Mashiach*, "*p'nei dor k'pnai kelev*, the face of the generation will be as the face of a dog." The Chofetz Chaim explains this enigmatic statement by reading the word *p'nei* in the sense of leadership: "When a dog walks with its master, it appears to be leading the way. When they come to a crossroad, the dog looks back to see which way his master is preparing to turn. He then runs up ahead, again appears to be the leader." It is this state of "leadership" which will exist in the difficult days before the *Geulah*, the redemption. The "new theology" is the *reductio ad absurdum* of a theology which looks to external forces and to popular opinion to determine its belief.

Modern man is said to be no longer able to speak of or to experience G–d. He cannot reconcile the existence of evil with the existence of G–d: evil refuses to go, and so G–d is asked to leave. Yet the inability to find the terms with which to speak of G–d is an age-old problem and lies at the core of religious experience. This frustration was expressed centuries ago in words which have been incorporated into the *Shabbat* morning liturgy:

I must tell of Your glory though I have not seen You,
I fumble with comparisons, I list your attributes, yet
I know You not.

Interestingly the modern physicist experiences a similar frustration. Isaac Asimov writes:

How could one determine where a particle [is]? The obvious answer is: Look at it. Well, let us imagine a microscope that could make an electron visible. We must shine a light or some appropriate kind of radiation on it to see it. But an electron is so small that a single photon of light striking it would move it and change its position. In the very act of measuring its position, we would have changed the position.

So the physicist too may declare of his particle: "I have named you and catalogued you, but I shall never see you." The Creator and the material of His Creation both refuse to reveal themselves to the eye, but their existence is no less evident.

H. Richard Niebuhr, in his work *The Social Sources of Denominationalism,* which has been labeled "one of the real classics of the sociology of religion" yet is rarely referred to in the literature on the subject, writes that a religion "which surrenders its leadership to the social forces of national and economic life, offers no hope to a divided world." He demonstrates the manner in which various Protestant denominations arose in reaction to changes in social and economic factors in the growth of the United States—the frontier churches, for example—where the denominational theological structure was an afterthought to bolster changes generated by nontheological forces. In one of the first reports of the "new theology" to appear in *The New York Times,* one of its adherents was quoted as saying that "several New Testament scholars had shown an interest in the movement and that efforts will be made to establish for the new theology a historical Scriptural base."

Christian theology has drawn its beliefs and religious practices from Torah, yet it has rejected Torah and heaped scorn on the Jew who symbolizes Torah. It introduced into theology the concept of a man-god, and now rebels at speaking of G–d in "human terms." Some have found a new fascination in the Jew, and "Old Testament studies" are now enjoying a flair in the seminaries and universities. It is difficult to pinpoint the precise origin of this interest in the Jew now manifest in scholarly and popular literature. Perhaps it began when the bomb dropped on Hiroshima and mankind was faced with fear, uncertainty, and homelessness, which is *galut,* and started looking around for someone with the know-how of living in exile.

I am a Jew because I stood at Sinai. My G–d lives because He "took me out of the land of Egypt," and being the G–d of all men, became my G–d in a very special way. I must attempt to live G–d's Torah because it the only way in which I can live as a Jew. Anything less than Torah—even the omission of a single letter—leads ultimately to the "New Theology" and the "death of G–d." Every man may, if he chooses, reject the experience of Sinai, just as every man may reject the G–d who lives in his heart—that is a right granted to us by G–d Himself. But in rejecting Sinai, the Jew must be aware of the far-reaching consequences of his rejection. G. K. Chesterton has perhaps said it best in the modern idiom.

> The moment you step into the world of facts you step into the world of limits. You can free things from alien or accidental laws, but not from the laws of their own nature. You may, if you like, free a tiger from his bars; but do not free him from his stripes. Do not free a camel of the burden of hi: hump: you may be freeing him from being a camel. Do not go about as a demagogue, encouraging triangles to break out of the prison of their three sides. If a triangle breaks out of its three sides, its life comes to a lamentable end.

Free a Jew of his "stripes" and you free him from being a Jew.

Immanuel Jakobovits

Formerly the Rabbi of the Fifth Avenue Synagogue
(Orthodox) in New York City. He is now
Chief Rabbi of Great Britain.

❡ (1) To me the belief in *Torah min ha-shamayim* (the divine revelation of the Torah), in its classical formulation by Maimonides, represents a definition of the essence of Judaism as inalienable as the postulate of monotheism. Until the rise of the reform movement in nineteenth-century Germany, this axiom of Judaism was never challenged or varied by any Jewish thinker or movement, whether traditional or sectarian.

Torah min ha-shamayim essentially means that the Pentateuch as we have it today is identical with the Torah revealed to Moses at Mount Sinai and that this expression of God's will is authentic, final, and eternally binding upon the Jewish people. Immaterial to this belief is the mode in which the Torah was communicated to Moses—whether by "dictation," "verbal inspiration," or some other mystic communion peculiar to prophecy.

But intrinsic to this doctrine, as painstakingly emphasized by Maimonides, is the equal sanctity of all parts of the Torah and of all its laws. To my mind, this is dictated by reason no less than by the explicit claims of the Torah and its classic exponents. Any substantive division between ethical and ritual laws is arbitrary and altogether foreign to the text and religious philosophy of the Scriptures. Both types of laws are featured quite indiscriminately in the Ten Commandments and throughout the Torah (see especially Lev. 19) as well as in the Prophets and the Talmud. In Judaism's penal legislation, too, ritual and ethics are treated alike; every offense against man at the same time constitutes a sin against God requiring ritual atonement, while any religious transgression is also a crime against society. All biblical laws equally derive their validity from their revelation by God. "Love thy neighbor as thyself" is a norm of virtue only because "I am the Lord [who commands it]" (Lev. 19:18), and the social statutes of the Torah have the same Sinaitic origin and *raison d'être* as the ritual precepts *par excellence* about the altar (Ex. 20:21;21:1 ff.), as several exegetes are careful to stress.

This is fundamental rather than purely fundamentalistic. If ethical laws were good, immutable, and divine *because* their virtue is manifest to reason, intuition, conscience, or any other human faculty, or if the validity of any law in the Torah were subject to human discrimination—accepting those as "divine" which appeal to our present-day notions and rejecting as "man-made" those we do not understand— the whole structure of Judaism as a revealed religion would collapse. We would create a god in man's own image; for man, not God, would determine what is "divine" law, using Him only as a rubber stamp to "authenticate" purely human judgments. Judaism stands or falls by the heteronomy of the law: "*He* hath told thee, O man, what is good" (Mic. 6:8), not the reverse.

Moreover, any system of ethics contingent upon the arbitrary and fickle whims of the human consensus (which varies from time to time and from one individual to another) would lack all virtue as well as true religiosity. Relying on man's reason, intuition, or utility as its source and compulsion, such a system would make the interests of man and his faculties the ultimate object of his service. In the significant words of Maimonides, good conduct determined by "the verdict of the intellect" rather than by revelation might be "wise" (expedient) but could never be "saintly" (meritorious) (*Hil. Melakhim,* 8:11).

(2) Yes, I do accept the chosen people concept as affirmed by Judaism in its holy writ, its prayers, and its millennial tradition. In fact, I believe every people—and indeed, in a more limited way, every individual—is "chosen" or destined for some distinct purpose in advancing the designs of Providence. Only, some fulfill their assignment and others do not.

Maybe the Greeks were chosen for their unique contributions to art and philosophy, the Romans for their pioneering services in law and government, the British for bringing parliamentary rule into the world, and the Americans for piloting democracy in a pluralistic society.

The Jews were chosen by God to be "peculiar unto Me" as the pioneers of religion and morality; that was and is their national purpose. From this choice flow certain privileges (above all, the perennial survival of Israel and its role in the messianic consummation of man's final destiny) and obligations (such as self-discipline through the *mitzvot* and frequently martyrdom). This concept, more than any other, has sustained the Jewish resolve to remain distinct in the face of endless persecution and in defiance of tempting (or violent) inducements to merge with the majority. And this concept has inspired the will to submit to a severely exigent code of laws (hence the mention of the "chosen people" promise, and not of any other reward, immediately prior to the revelation at Sinai [Ex. 19:5]).

I think few factors are more deleterious to Jewish life today than the widespread rejection of this "chosenness." The humblest Jew in the Middle Ages had a greater awareness of his and his people's indispensable part in realizing the prophetic vision of human perfection than most Jewish leaders have in our times. Without the incentive of serving a (religiously and morally) superior purpose, the Jewish commitment to that purpose—individually and nationally—was bound to give way to leading an "ordinary" existence like others, just as Americans, deprived of the belief in the superiority of "the American way of life," would lose the distinctiveness of their national genius and cease to shoulder their special burdens in the world. Only the promise of a "chosen" role can educe the ambition and energy needed for exacting tasks and ideals.

The Jewish "chosen people" idea has nothing to do with national or racial superiority as currently understood. The idea never justified, or led to, discrimination against strangers in Jewish law, expansionism or political domination in Jewish history, or conversionist aspirations in Jewish theology. It was invariably directed at exacting greater sacrifices from the Jew, not at imposing them on the non-Jew.

(3) As a professing Jew, I obviously consider Judaism the only true religion, just as I would expect the adherents of any other faith to defend a similar claim for their religion. I assert this claim on three compelling grounds:

Firstly, it is intrinsic to Judaism, as averred both by its teachings and by the unique covenantal bond between God and Israel. The recognition of other faiths as "equally true" is branded as apostasy in Jewish law (Sanhedrin 63a, based on Ex. 22:19). Judaism, to be true to itself, is bound to reject, for instance, the divinity of Jesus or the prophecy of Mohammed as false claims; otherwise its own claims, such as the supremacy of Moses's prophecy and the finality of the Mosaic law (the seventh and ninth of Maimonides's Thirteen Articles of Faith), could not be true.

Secondly, the claim is grounded in logic. Two mutually

exclusive and conflicting statements of fact can never both be true. The only logical alternative to Judaism's being the only true religion is not that another religion is equally true but that Judaism is equally (or more) untrue.

Thirdly, to me Judaism's claim is an ineluctable personal credo. I could not subscribe to the rigorous demands of Jewish practice and thought if I had the slightest reason to believe that other faiths, far more widely professed and easier to practice, might be equally true. In fact, I feel any such egalitarian view of religion is no religion at all; it lacks the passion and depth of conviction which must inspirit any truly religious faith if one is to love it "with all one's heart, and all one's soul, and all one's might" even to the point of dying for it, if necessary, as much as living for it, whatever the cost. A religion which demands nothing is worth nothing; and the least a religion is entitled to demand from its devotees is the kind of exclusive love spouses may expect from each other, parents from their children, and a country from its citizens. For me, in the telling phrase of the Zohar, "God, Israel and the Torah are (equally) one"—each is unique and incomparable.

Judaism will have something distinctive to contribute to the world (as well as primarily to the Jewish people!) until the end of days. I have already mentioned some singular features which distinguish Jewish ethics from secular ethics. In many respects the Jewish moral code is also distinct from its counterpart among other religions. It has its own norms and rulings on such subjects as abortion, birth control, divorce, and illegitimacy—to mention only a few examples from a single area of human relations.

But these ethical and moral distinctions—even if they could be shown to produce better human beings, nobler family life, etc.—represent only an insignificant part of the Jewish claim to survival as a separate faith-community. More significant would be the uniquely Jewish commitment to intensive and lifelong learning for its own sake (whereby a house of study is holier than a synagogue!), Judaism's emphasis on righteous deeds rather than faith, its concept of corporate responsibility, its invocation of duties—not rights—in man's moral constitution, and its passionate affirmation of life in this world. These and other distinctively Jewish con-

cepts, if implemented, would go far toward ridding contemporary society of some of its worst ills.

Of still greater importance is the spiritual force of an
entire people committed to the promotion of religion and
morality as its supreme national task. It is one thing for
religion to be the business of some professional clergymen,
but quite another for a whole people to be nationally dedicated to these ideals, in the way that others may aspire to
the Great Society or the welfare state or scientific excellence.
If all Jews everywhere would become conscious—as they
eventually will, I am convinced—of their charge, as children
of the Patriarchs and heirs to the Hebrew prophets, to be "a
kingdom of priests and a holy people," if, pointing at any
Jew in the street, office, or home, people would say, "Here is
an agent of God, governed every minute of the day by His
law, and therefore incorruptible and unable to do any evil
deliberately," no one would ask whether Jews still had something distinctive to contribute to the world.

Transcending all these contributions is the Jewish hope
of redemption as the ultimate fulfillment of the human
destiny on earth, the messianic dream centered in Zion
spiritually restored as "the light unto the nations." Beyond
achieving economic prosperity, national security, international goodwill, eradicating crime and disease, and making
the sciences and arts flourish, Judaism raises man's sights to
higher goals. Longing for the day when men will "not hunger
for bread nor thirst for water, but for hearing the words of
the Lord," when "the knowledge of the Lord will fill the
earth as the waters cover the sea," it seeks the Good Society,
led by rulers who will "not judge after the sight of their
eyes" (by self-interest or personal conscience), but by the
universal code of God's moral law. Judaism looks to the
fatherhood of God universally acclaimed as the means to
realize the brotherhood of man. For without a common father
there can be no brothers.

Judaism, by nourishing these hopes, provides the rationale
of human history and the thrust toward its consummation.
Like the Hebrew language, it knows no present tense; it
values the here-and-now only insofar as it vindicates the
past and serves the future. In relating the reality of history
to the blueprint of its vision, it supplies the criteria by which

to judge whether civilization advances or retrogresses in its tortuous evolution.

In more pragmatic terms, Judaism envisions the time when governments will invest no less money and brainpower for achieving moral and spiritual excellence than for the conquest of nature; when there will be crash programs to produce, not merely more scientists, but more solid marriages, wiser statesmen, and nobler citizens; when people will seek entertainment from feats of moral valor and intellectual triumph, not from scenes of crime and marital faithlessness; when the leisure gained by automation will be used for the pursuit of learning, not for idleness or mischief; and when individuals and nations alike will rejoice in the happiness of their neighbors as in their own. Without this vision life loses direction, history lacks meaning, and the struggle for loftier aims than personal happiness and social welfare is stifled in the rout of hope.

(4) Like the attributes of God, the political sympathies of Judaism are easier to define in negative terms than as positive affirmations. While, with a social legislation of its own, it would tend to favor or oppose some political ideologies more than others, its support of a particular political viewpoint is more tenuous and qualified than its incompatibility—by virtue of its broadly liberal outlook and its emphasis on the dignity of man—with such extremist doctrines as racism, Communism, or Fascism. Yet I could not state with any precision how far a "good Jew" would be expected to expose himself and his community to economic pressure, persecution, or martyrdom in fighting such doctrines where they are dominant. That would depend on many circumstantial factors.

(5) I cannot see the relevance of the "God is dead" theology to Judaism, except insofar as the absolution of Jews from the "deicide" charge called for the invention of some new "god-killer."

To my mind, by far the most serious challenge to Jewish thought today lies in secularism, whether of the Communist brand in the East or the materialistic type in the West, whether expressed as crass nationalism or as philosophical humanism. To turn man and his universe into a hedonistic, soulless, senseless, and purposeless product of chance rather than choice, accountable to no one and serving only himself, and with nothing but bland question marks to explain his origin and his destiny, is a form of idolatry more pernicious than the worship of graven images.

This is not to deny the need for a reappraisal of Jewish teachings in the light of modern thought, just as Judaism reacted to similar challenges in the past. The confrontation with the ritualistic paganism of antiquity witnessed the rise of prophecy, which stressed the then neglected ethical elements of the Torah. The impact of the Greco-Roman age was met by the Talmud, the presentation of Judaism in preeminently legal terms. The encounter with Arabic philosophy during the Spanish period produced the classics of Jewish philosophy, or the formulation of Judaism in philosophical terms. Conditions in eighteenth-century Poland led to the rise of Hasidism, while the rational humanism of nineteenth-century Germany found its Jewish reaction in the Orthodoxy of Samson Raphael Hirsch and other thinkers. All these developments and movements were equally authentic expressions of Judaism, beginning and ending—as the prophetic books do (Josh. 1:7 and Mal. 3:22)—with an unqualified endorsement of "the Torah of Moses, My servant," though particularly stressing or evolving different facets of it in response to the challenges of the times.

No doubt the impact of the revolutionary changes in the thinking and living of our age will likewise spawn new orientations of Jewish thought. The scientific explosion and the resultant new insights into the nature of man and the universe, the advances of technology and automation, the development of interreligious relations, the human-rights movements, the growing concern over social inequities, and notably the restoration of Jewish statehood all present challenges which are bound to generate new creative religious forces within Judaism. But, like all historic processes, this must take time to grow organically. When it is remembered that almost five centuries had to elapse following the exodus from Egypt until conditions were ripe for building the first Temple in Jerusalem, and that the composition of the Talmud took even several centuries longer, we may be wise not to confound our expectations with the impatience so characteristic of our times.

I have attempted to answer the editor's incisive questions without sophistication, ambivalence, or equivocation, and close to within the confines of space allotted to me. But one can no more present the complexities of Jewish thought in a few thousand words than Hillel could do justice to his impatient questioner, who wanted to learn the essence of Judaism while standing on one foot, by simply telling him, "What is hateful to yourself do not do unto your neighbor" without adding, as Hillel did, "Now, go and study!" With Jewish education today usually ending, instead of starting in earnest, with bar-mitzvah age, most Jews have an exceedingly rudimentary and juvenile understanding of Judaism, hardly sufficient to resolve or withstand even the simplest challenges. How could they confront other problems in modern life, if their education in science, literature, history, philosophy, etc., ceased at the age of thirteen? In order really to appreciate the response of Judaism to the stirrings of our times, years of intensive and mature studies in the vast sources of Jewish thought are required, not to mention the even more indispensable experience of Jewish living. "Now, go and study!"

Mordecai M. Kaplan

Founder of the Reconstructionist movement.

❡ In answering the questions submitted to the rabbis of different denominations, each rabbi is bound to reply from the standpoint of his own particular version of Judaism. Mine is the Reconstructionist version of Judaism, with which *Commentary* readers are likely to be less familiar than they are with the ideologies and programs of the four Jewish denominations: Orthodox, Conservative, Reform, and secularist. I shall therefore try to acquaint them with it.

According to the Reconstructionist version, Judaism is more than a religion. It is an *evolving religious civilization.*

(a) *As a civilization,* Judaism is the ongoing life of the Jewish people, with its ancient homeland, its history, its language, its culture, and its code of laws.

(b) *As a religious civilization,* Judaism expresses the purpose and meaning of Jewish existence in terms of the belief in one God.

(c) *As an evolving religious civilization,* Judaism has reinterpreted the original formulation of its religion, which belongs to the monotheistic, this-worldly, mythological universe of discourse, into: 1) a monotheistic, otherworldly mythology (rabbinism); and, 2) a monotheistic, otherworldly metaphysics (Philo and Maimonides).

If Judaism is to survive creatively, and not as a mere fossil, it has to make room, alongside the existing denominations, for those who cannot subscribe to any of its past theologies, by allowing them to formulate a theology of their own, which would give a humanist, instead of a supernaturalist, interpretation to the history and life-style of the Jewish people. Such an interpretation, proceeding from the known to the less known, is based on a religiohumanist version of salvation, or human destiny.

The traditional version of salvation, or human destiny, is based on the dogma of divine reward and punishment, either in this world or in the hereafter. The humanist version of salvation is the maturity of the individual and the creative survival of society. According to the secularist version of humanism both purposes can be achieved by means of social ethics. According to religious humanism, both purposes can be achieved by social ethics, provided such ethics are motivated by an awareness of that, in the cosmos, of which man himself is a part, and without which the only basis for ethics could be the individual (prudential ethics), but not society. Man, besides being an individual, is also an integral part of the cosmos. God is that aspect of the cosmos which has to validate the standards of social ethics. Thus, according to secular humanism, "man is the measure"; according to *religious* humanism, that which makes the cosmos possible is the measure of man.

Judaism is presently evolving a reinterpretation in terms of monotheistic, this-worldly functionalism.

To clarify the forthcoming stage of Judaism, it is necessary to have in mind the following modern technological universe of discourse, which is based on functionalism:

Existence is potential power or functioning. In the human mind, potential power takes three forms: fact, action, and value. Reason distinguishes between appearance and reality; intelligence, between illusory and authentic means to worthwhile ends; wisdom, between an illusory and an authentic scale of values, as a means to the art of living and self-fulfillment.

To the ancient Greek thinkers, intellect as such (the synthesis of reason, intelligence, and wisdom) was of supreme value. Hence God, who represents the supreme value in the scale of values (the "unmoved mover"), was Active Intellect. To the Hebrew prophets, headed by Moses, righteousness was of supreme value. Hence "the way of God" (Gen. 18:19) was righteousness and justice. To Greek philosophy, society existed for the sake of the intellectual elite To Judaism, the individual exists for society and through society.

As a consequence of historical experience, man's intelligence has come to regard democracy as the most authentic method of human creative survival, since both the maturity of the individual and international peace call for a conception of human life in which the individual and society have to be conceived as means to and ends for each other. Consequently, the next stage in Judaism has to incorporate democracy into its set of values.

The natural agencies, or sources of values, which constitute *wisdom* (as defined above), are: the family, the clan, the tribe, the intermarried community, and the nation. The purposive agencies or sources of values are: the state, the ecclesia or church, and the various purposive or ideological organizations, whether economic, political, social, cultural, or religious. *Natural agencies, on the whole, exercise greater value-forming power than purposive ones.* In the long run, Russian nationalism is bound to exercise greater influence on the Russians than Russian Communism. That is why Jewish peoplehood is indispensable to Jewish religion.

There are three types of ethics as a branch of wisdom: (a) prudential ethics, the purpose of which is the preservation and good of the individual; (b) political ethics, the preservation and good of society; (c) cosmic ethics, the preservation and good of mankind. Each type is determined by the scope we assign to the function of reciprocal responsibility (righteousness and justice). Prudential ethics is narrowest in scope, and cosmic ethics, widest in scope, being coextensive with all of mankind.

The purpose and meaning of Jewish existence must henceforth be the maturation of the Jewish individual (i.e. the maximum functioning of his creative potentialities) and the creative survival of the human race. The creative survival of the human species is no longer possible, unless nations limit their respective sovereignties, submit their domestic and foreign policies to the standards of cosmic ethics, and outlaw war. That imposes upon the individual the responsibility of choosing political, economic, and cultural leaders who are morally responsible.

If Judaism is to contribute to the moralization of the nations of the world, it can do so only in the capacity of an evolving religious civilization. That is the main thesis of Reconstructionism.

And now the replies: (1) Instead of assuming the Torah "to be divine revelation," I assume it to be the expression of ancient Israel's attempt to base its life on a declaration of dependence upon God, and on a constitution which embodies the laws according to which God expected ancient Israel to live. The declaration is spelled out in the narrative part of the Torah, and the constitution is spelled out in the law code of the Torah.

Due to the evolutionary character of Judaism, its declaration and its constitution have undergone considerable change. It is meaningless, therefore, to speak of the 613 commandments as "equally binding."

The decision as to which of those commandments are binding depends on the particular stance one adopts and the general perspective one entertains. My perspective is Reconstructionist. The principle of selection is the extent to which commandment contributes to: (a) self-identification with the Jewish people and its civilization; and (b) the attainment of the twofold goal of individual and collective maturity. To me the prohibition against clothing made of linen and wool is as archaic as the law against taking interest on a loan.

(2) The belief that the Jews are the chosen people of God belongs to the original formulation of Jewish religion during the monotheistic this-worldly mythological stage of the Jewish civilization. Like the reinterpretation of the original idea of God in Jewish religion, the reinterpretation of the original idea of the Jewish people has come to be indispensable to the purpose and meaning of continued Jewish existence. The tenable implication of the ancient doctrine of the chosen people is the assumption that the Jews, as a people, are committed to the high vocation of being "a light unto the nations." The only way they can live up to their commitment is to translate into a program of daily living the cosmic ethic of reciprocal responsibility that takes into its scope the whole of mankind.

The best way, according to Reconstructionism, to answer the charge that the chosen-people doctrine has been "the model" for theories of national and racial superiority is to eliminate that doctrine from the Jewish liturgy, as Reconstructionism has done. It thereby proves that the nation or race that adopts the theory of national or race superiority has at last arrived where the Jews were three thousand years ago.

(3) The Jewish religion is the most authentic religion in the world, for the following reasons:

It is *indigenous*, in that it is the natural expression of the concrete historical career of the Jewish people, in the same way as good and wholesome character is the expression of a person's reactions to the vicissitudes and experiences of his individual life. An *adopted* religion like Christianity is all too likely to be based upon some metaphysical or supernaturalist dogmas. When those dogmas become irrelevant, the church loses its *raison d'être*.

In contrast, the value-forming power of a people or nation does not cease when any of its dogmas become irrelevant. They can be given new meaning which enables the people to resume its function of providing its members with wisdom in the art of living. Being indigenous, Jewish religion can afford to evolve, without jeopardizing its continuity, when a new universe of discourse replaces the one in which its values happen to be articulated. That is the case because its *continuum* is a living people, with a social heritage, or civilization, which it transmits from generation to generation. As the people evolves, its religion matures together with its civilization.

In the sphere of religio-ethical values, adopted religions generally subscribe to Reinhold Niebuhr's thesis, which is elaborated in this book *Moral Man and Immoral Society*, as a naturally inescapable fact. Jewish religion, however, though traditionally assuming "original sin" as a fact, maintains that repentance and the study of Torah nullify it. By the same token, it assumes that the essence of morality is moral responsibility. *If individuals would learn to choose political, economic, and spiritual leaders who are endowed with a sense of moral responsibility, society would become moral.*

(4) The main point made in answering the third question with regard to the unique contribution of Judaism to world civilization is that its religion, to survive creatively, has to show the way to the moralization, not only of the individual, but also of society. Moreover, the moralization of society is synonymous with choosing leaders who have a sense of reciprocal moral responsibility. It therefore follows logically that a Jew who favors any political or economic movement like the Communist, Fascist, or segregationist would be acting unethically, if he were to support it, and all the more if he were to affiliate with it.

(5) Experience has shown that anything that has relevance to Christian theology is bound to have relevance to Jewish existence. That is what Heine meant when he quipped: *"Wie es sich christelt, so judelt es sich"* (What Christians make of their Christianity, Jews make of their Judaism). By the same token that Christians are influenced by Buber, Jews are influenced by Tillich. Sociology, with its law of social imitation, is far more effectual than theology with its law of *imitatio Dei*.

Rabbis who are likely to imitate the Christian death-of-God theologians should be made to realize the *irrelevance* of the question which has of late been agitating those Christian theologians. Christianity as an adopted religion is based upon dogmas about God which are syncretisms of Jewish revelation mythology with Greek metaphysical mythology. The rejection of a dogma is the rejection of what the dogma affirms. A dogma as such does not lend itself to reinterpretation. Someone who wishes to see an end to all theologies said: "What the world needs most is an expert dogma catcher." In rejecting the Christian dogmas concerning God, the Christian theologians virtually deny the existence of God. Hence the term "death of God."

That is by no means the case with the Jewish idea of God, which is a formulation concerning the existence of God based on the cultural perspective of the age in which Jews happen to live. Thus Maimonides' idea of God is radically different from the biblical idea of God as expressed by the prophets. They unquestionably conceived God in humanlike terms, whereas Maimonides accepted Aristotle's idea of God as "unmoved mover" and Active Intellect! Only an indigenous religion can afford to reinterpret its idea of God. Far from being a rejection of the belief in the existence of God, the reinterpretation is, indeed, a confirmation of the belief in His existence.

In Jewish religion, *the continuum*, amid all the changes in its idea of God, is the Jewish people, with its aspiration to what God is to effectuate in the world—the advent of the messianic era, when all the nations will destroy their armaments, and unite in submission to His law of justice and righteousness.

Norman Lamm

*Rabbi at the Jewish Center (Orthodox) in
New York City.*

❡ I have always felt that Shammai's policy was wiser than Hillel's in their respective reactions to the Gentile who challenged them to teach him the whole Torah while standing on one foot. It is probably better not to try at all than to risk all the ambiguities that must necessarily attend a condensation of one's religious outlook to a couple of thousand words. Nevertheless, out of deference to the preference of the Jewish tradition for Hillel, I am willing to take my chances and come armed with naught but naïve trust in the reader's fairness, no matter what his convictions.

(1) I believe the Torah is divine revelation in two ways: in that it is God-given and in that it is godly. By "God-given," I mean that He willed that man abide by His commandments and that that will was communicated in discrete words and letters. Man apprehends in many ways: by intuition, inspiration, experience, deduction—and by direct instruction. The divine will, if it is to be made known, is sufficiently important for it to be revealed in as direct, unequivocal, and unambiguous a manner as possible, so that it will be understood by the largest number of the people to whom this will is addressed. Language, though so faulty an instrument, is still the best means of communication to most human beings.

Hence, I accept unapologetically the idea of the verbal revelation of the Torah. I do not take seriously the caricature of this idea which reduces Moses to a secretary taking dictation. Any competing notion of revelation, such as the various "inspiration" theories, can similarly be made to sound absurd by anthropomorphic parallels. Exactly how this communication took place no one can say; it is no less mysterious than the nature of the One who spoke. The divine-human encounter is not a meeting of equals, and the *kerygma* that ensues from this event must therefore be articulated in human terms without reflecting on the mode and form of the divine *logos*. *How* God spoke is a mystery; how *Moses* received this message is an irrelevancy. *That* God spoke is of the utmost significance, and *what* He said must therefore be intelligible to humans in a human context, even if one insists upon an endlessly profound mystical overplus of meaning in the text. To deny that God can make His will clearly known is to impose upon Him a limitation of dumbness that would insult the least of His human creatures.

Literary criticism of the Bible is a problem, but not a crucial one. Judaism has successfully met greater challenges in the past. Higher Criticism is far indeed from an exact science. The startling lack of agreement among scholars on any one critical view; the radical changes in general orienta-

tion in more recent years; the many revisions that archae-
ology has forced upon literary critics; and the unfortunate
neglect even by Bible scholars of much first-rate scholarship
in modern Hebrew supporting the traditional claim of
Mosaic authorship—all these reduce the question of Higher
Criticism from the massive proportions it has often assumed
to a relatively minor and manageable problem that is chiefly
a nuisance but not a threat to the enlightened believer.

Torah is not only God-given; it is also godly. The divine
word is not only uttered by God, it is also an aspect of God
Himself. All of the Torah—its ideas, its laws, its narratives,
its aspirations for the human community—lives and breathes
godliness. Hillel Zeitlin described the Hasidic interpretation
of revelation (actually it was even more true of their oppo-
nents, the Misnagdim, and ultimately derived from a common Kabbalistic source) as not only *Torah min ha-shamayim*
(Torah *from* Heaven) but *Torah she'hi shamayim* (Torah
that *is* Heaven). It is in Torah that God is most immediately
immanent and accessible, and the study of Torah is therefore not only a religious commandment per se, but the most
exquisite and the most characteristically Jewish form of
religious experience and communion. For the same reason,
Torah is not only legislation, *halakha*, but in its broadest
meaning, *Torah*—teaching, a term that includes the full
spectrum of spiritual edification: theological and ethical,
mystical and rhapsodic.

Given the above, it is clear that I regard all of the Torah
as binding on the Jew. To submit the *mitzvot* to any
extraneous test—whether rational or ethical or nationalistic—
is to reject the supremacy of God, and hence in effect to
deny Him as God. The classification of the *mitzvot* into
rational and revelational, or ethical and ritual, has descrip-
tive-methodological but not substantive religious significance.
Saadia Gaon, who a thousand years ago proposed the
dichotomy between rational and nonrational commandments
as the cornerstone of his philosophy of law, maintained that
even the apparently pure revelational laws were fundamentally rational, although man might not, now or ever, be able
to grasp their inner rationality. At the same time, far
greater and more genuine spirituality inheres in the acceptance of those laws that apparently lack ethical, rational, or

doctrinal content. It is only these performances, according to R. Hai Gaon, that are prefaced by the blessing, "Blessed art Thou . . . who has sanctified us with His commandments and commanded us to . . ." Holiness, the supreme religious category, contains an essential nonrational core; and this state of the "numinous" can be attained only when man bows his head and submits the totality of his existence to the will of God by performing His *mitzvah* for no reason other than that this is the will of the Creator. R. Nachman of Bratzlav recommended to his followers that they observe the "ethical" laws as though they were "ritual" commandments. In this manner, the ethical performance is transformed from a pale humanistic act into a profound spiritual gesture. I do not, therefore, by any means accord to ceremonial laws any lesser status than the others. On the contrary, while confident that these *mitzvot shimiyot* are more than divine whim in that they are ultimately of benefit to man and society, I prefer to accept even the *sikhliyot,* the rational and ethical, as "ritual" in an effort to attain holiness, the ultimate desideratum of religious life.

(2) It should be unnecessary to have to clarify to sophisticated readers, at this late date, that the Jewish doctrine of the election of Israel is not one of racial or ethnic superiority. The chosenness of Israel relates exclusively to its spiritual vocation embodied in the Torah; the doctrine, indeed, was announced at Sinai. Wherever it is mentioned in our liturgy—such as the blessing immediately preceding the *Shema,* or the benediction over the Torah-reading—it is always related to Torah or *mitzvot.* This spiritual vocation consists of two complementary functions, described as *goy kadosh,* that of a holy nation, and *mamlekhet kohanim,* that of a kingdom of priests. The first term denotes the development of communal separateness or differentness in order to achieve a collective self-transcendence. The *halakha* is the method par excellence for the attainment of this goal. The second term implies the obligation of this brotherhood of the spiritual elite toward the rest of mankind; priesthood is defined by the prophets as fundamentally a teaching vocation. The election of Israel "because all the earth is Mine"

was understood by Seforno (to Ex. 19:5) to mean, "because I love all the peoples of My world, I have elected you to teach all mankind to call upon the Name of the Lord and serve Him in unison."

These two functions, the tension between which is inherent in the concept of chosenness, are not antonyms, mutually exclusive, but supplementary ideas. In a study of how this doctrine was treated in Tannaitic times, a contemporary scholar has discovered that the greater the emphasis by an individual sage on chosenness and its inescapable particularism, the greater the breadth of his universalism. This separateness of Israel, its "holiness" function, may both result in and be fostered by a sense of alienation. But to assert, as some have done, that it is *exhausted* by the experience of alienation is to misread the whole meaning of election by eliminating its clear *telos,* that of holiness. There is no virtue in alienation, or particularism, or an inclination for dissent, for their own sake. They may be characteristic, respectively, of modern man's psychological condition, or the aspirations of Jewish secular nationalism, or the liberal credo; but they are not Judaism. And, ultimately, they cannot nourish the soul or provide an answer for the spiritual yearnings of men.

Can the idea of chosenness give birth to the wild *Herrenvolk* theories that have proved so catastrophic in our times? Of course it can, and possibly has (although it never has with Jews). But such noxious notions are not legitimate children of the biblical doctrine of election; they are monsters, genetic mutations. Any idea contains the risk of distortion; and the nobler the idea, the greater the danger and the uglier the perversion. The concept of government can be reduced to tyranny; must we, therefore, all be anarchists in order to avoid such dangers? Religion can become superstition; democracy, mobocracy; liberty, libertinism; respect, subservience; love, lechery. Shall we abandon the former because they can and often do degenerate into the latter?

The same holds true for the chosenness of Israel. It is a teaching of service and a service of teaching. It is concerned with the attainment of spirituality. Its particularistic aspect, while essential and indispensable, is propaedeutic; its universalist element remains the ultimate *telos*. Israel may be a reluctant teacher, and the world an unwilling pupil. But the methodology of divine pedagogics is rarely directly didactic. The teaching occurs on many levels and is expressed in many ways: by word, by sublime example, and most notably by the very mystery of Jewish history. That Israel is the chosen agent for this education of mankind does not reflect either on the superiority or inferiority of this people— although intimations of both may be found in Jewish literature. The nearest that any major Jewish thinker has come to a biological interpretation of this spiritual elitism is the highly ethnocentric "historiosophy" of Judah Halevi. But only a deliberate misreading of the *Kuzari,* the work in which this idea is proposed, can mistake it for a precursor of modern racialism. The whole of the argument is addressed by the rabbi in the book to the pagan king of the Khazars in an endeavor to convince him of the truth of Judaism. At the end of the book, the king converts to Judaism—surely an astonishing conclusion to a tract supposedly elaborating an exclusive doctrine of Jewish racialism!

(3) The nature of Israel's priesthood, its teaching to all of mankind, can be divided into two: the social-ethical and the spiritual-metaphysical (the two, of course, are ultimately interrelated). The *halakha* articulated the first in the form of the "Seven Noahide Laws" which, in effect, mean civilized behavior. (Nachmanides considers these as seven categories of law, rather than as individual commandments.) These are essentially negative: the rejection of immorality and brutality and lawlessness. The only "religious" one of the seven laws is also negative: the proscription of idolatry. To this the prophetic tradition adds a second element—the spiritual-metaphysical content of priesthood, positively formulated: the recognition and service of God. This is the vision of a day when "the Lord will be King over all the earth," and the redemptive future when "the knowledge of the Lord" will fill the earth as the waters cover the seas. This acceptance of God, of course, comprehends the good life. Maimonides distinguished between the first and the second of these two elements—the humanitarian-humanistic and the profoundly theistic ethos—by referring to the practitioners

of the first as *wise* Gentiles, and to the second by the more honorific term, *pious* Gentiles.

That a number of these ideas are shared by the major religions, some as a result of Jewish influence and some independently, cannot and ought not be denied. But this by no means relieves Israel of the obligation to pursue its vocation without relaxation. Surely this post-Auschwitz era needs education in civilized conduct as much as did the Canaanites of antiquity; and contemporary man—whose avant-garde theologians have killed what he had of God and directed his religious concerns solely to the worship of a man—needs, no less than the fetishistic primitive, the constant reminder that "the Lord [and not an apotheosized human] is God" and that the Lord is One. And perhaps the most significant teaching, the uniqueness of Judaism, is the coalescence of these very elements—the spiritual and the practical, the theological and the ethical, *aggada* and *halakha*. Judaism has always resisted the effort to foist on it—as metaphysical truth rather than as merely analytical device—the bifurcation of body and soul, of letter and spirit, of ritual and social, of cultos and ethos. The restriction of religion to worship and cult was accepted quite naturally by the ancient pagans, and the confinement of the spirit to cult in modern times, despite all gallant attempts at developing a "social gospel," is one of the sad triumphs of secularism. We have cornered God, locked Him up in little sanctuaries, and now complain that we cannot find Him in "the real world." Judaism's unique contribution to modern man may well lie in its insistence that God is very much alive, that He is *not* absent from society (even "secular" society) for those who invite Him in, and that the best way to achieve this goal is to release Him from His incarceration in our barren and dessicated temples. In a word: *halakha!* Through a sanctifying of all of life, meaning and purpose return to man, God is once again accessible, and human spirit can be affirmed in the very midst of life in all its existential tensions and the wealth of its variegated phenomena. It is through *halakha* that a new relationship is established between the sacred and the secular (Rabbi Kuk referred to them as the holy and the not-yet-holy), and that man can reorient himself toward nature in a manner that affirms joyously the development of technology.

(4) I do not believe that Judaism commits us to any specific social, political, or ideological system, but I do believe that it may negate certain viewpoints. Fascism and Communism, for instance, insofar as they offend human dignity and strip men of certain human rights, are obviously in violation of the principles of Judaism. Just as Judaism allows, within certain limits, a latitude for various philosophical tenets, and does not bind us to any one comprehensive metaphysical outlook, so there exists an area of freedom for different social and political philosophies. Much work remains to be done in elucidating the limiting principles beyond which a political theory is considered offensive to Judaism. It should also be emphasized that not all contemporary political issues can be resolved by immediate reference to Jewish sources. The attempts to align Judaism as a religion with either side of the Vietnamese question is a case in point. The naïveté in proposing simplistic solutions to enormously complex international issues, and the almost incredible *chutzpah* in labeling one's prejudices as official "Judaism," point to the danger in making religion *too* relevant. Judaism certainly has something to say about every significant issue in life, but this judgment can be meaningful only if it is applied to a problem that has been properly defined. Neither world political and social matters nor individual halakhic questions can be decided when they are enshrouded in an impenetrable vagueness. Appeals to sentiment and good intentions cannot substitute for the intellectual exertion that is the task of man in clearly formulating the problem for which guidance is sought in divine revelation. The giants of *halakha* have always emphasized that enlightenment cannot be acquired cheaply. Judaism may be neglected if it is too remote from the issues that agitate contemporary men; it will surely be held in contempt if it presumes to offer snap judgments in the form of pronunciamentos by self-proclaimed spokesmen on every issue that journalists and politicians consider of abiding importance.

(5) Space does not permit me to dwell upon what I believe is an authentic Jewish reaction to the current "God is dead" controversy. I have commented on that in a recent article in *Jewish Life*. Briefly, I do not believe that the entire

issue has any real relevance for Judaism, except insofar as it emphasizes the element of *hester panim,* the "hiding of the face" of God, by which is meant the absence of men's personal religious experience of the presence or nearness of the Creator. Christian theologians, however, have gone beyond this to a far more radical position. Insofar as I can understand them at all, they have banished the Jewish or genuinely theistic elements of their faith in favor of the Christian myth which is its specifically pagan character. Fundamentally, therefore, the issue has no special importance for Jews.

I feel quite differently about the exciting talk of the relation of religion to the secular world, as propounded by Cox and others. Here I think that Judaism has a great deal to say, if we are willing to liberate ourselves from the defensive, apologetic positions that we have taken vis-à-vis Jewish secularists in the last hundred years. I suspect that research into the philosophy of *halakha,* the thinking of the founders of Hasidism, and the writings of Rabbi Kuk will offer a great deal of enlightenment on this problem.

The real challenge to Jewish belief in our day will come, I believe, from the cyberneticians who have been developing a metaphysics of cybernetics in which they attempt to use theories of communication and control to establish criteria for a materialistic conception of meaning and purpose. If the source of human purpose is in the neuronic feedback circuits of our nervous system, then we have snuffed out freedom and established a new and imposing materialism.

But challenging though it may well be, I do not fear it. The computer is an extension of the human brain even as the scissors is an extension of the hand and the automobile of the foot. Just as we need our limbs to operate our instruments, so will we need our minds to ask the right questions of our omniscient answer machines. I have faith that mindlessness will not prevail, and that human dignity—the divine image—will not be proven obsolete. And after all, it is that historic and personal Jewish faith, that *ani maamin,* that has prevailed and kept us alive to this day.

Aharon Lichtenstein

Professor of Talmud at Yeshiva University
(Orthodox) in New York.

❦ (1) The Torah, both the written text and the oral law, constitutes divine revelation in three distinct senses. It was revealed *by* God, it reveals something *about* Him, and it reveals Him. First, the Torah comprises a specific narrative or normative *datum,* an objective "given" invested with definite form and content, which was addressed by God to Israel as a whole or to its leader and representative, Moses. This datum consists of two elements:

(a) The *revelatum,* to use the Thomistic term, whose truths inherently lie beyond the range of human reason and which therefore had to be revealed if they were to be known at all; and

(b) the *revelabile,* whose truths—be they historical facts or the norms of morality or natural religion—could have been discovered by man in any event, and whose transcendental status therefore derives from the relatively extrinsic fact of their having been divinely expressed. The present character of both as revelation, however, is crucial. After the fact, both constitute God's living message to Israel.

Secondly, the Torah reveals something about God, and this in two ways: it presents direct statements about divine attributes; and, inasmuch as it is not merely a document delivered (*salve reverentia*) by God but composed by Him, it constitutes in its normative essence an expression of His will. As such, it affords us an indirect insight into what is otherwise wholly inscrutable. He who is hidden in His numinous "otherness"—*El mistater b'shafrir chevyon, ha-sechel ha-ne-elam mikol ra'ayon*—or transcendent in His luminous majesty—(Milton's "Dark with excessive bright thy skirts appear")—has chosen, *mutatis mutandis,* to condense His infinite will in the very act of its expression. Finite man is thus enabled, though ever so haltingly, to grasp it somewhat. Hence, as the *Tanya* emphasized, the tremendous importance of the study of Torah for traditional Judaism. It is the one means of embracing and absorbing, as it were, God's presence as manifested through His revealed will. It becomes, therefore, not only an intellectual exercise but a religious experience.

But the revealed character of Torah does not exhaust itself in propositions imparted by God or concerning Him. It is realized, thirdly, as a revelation of the divine presence proper. Revelation is not only an objective *datum* or the process of its transmission, important as these may be. It is the occasion, exalting and humbling both, for a dialectical encounter with the living God. Revelation is not only a fixed text but, in relation to man, an electrifying I-and-Thou experience. Moreover, this experience is not confined to the initial moment of divine giving and human taking of a specific message. It is repeated recurrently through genuine response to God's message which ushers us into His presence. The rapture and the awe, the joy and the tremor of Sinai were not of a moment. They are of all time, engaging the Jew who truly opens himself to the divine message and God's call. "Every day let them [the words of the Torah] be in your eyes as if newly given." The experience of revelation is repeated through response, be it study or action, to its content, and conversely, the awareness of its content is sharpened through an intensive sense of its experience.

To the committed Jew, this experience, at Sinai or at present, is not simply a momentarily rapturous encounter. It is enthralling in *both* senses of the word. It imposes binding obligation. The Torah, although it includes sizable narrative segments, is, in its quintessence, normative. Indeed, the rabbis felt constrained to explain why it had not begun with the first command addressed to Israel (Ex. 12) rather than with the story of creation. At its core, the Torah is a body of law. *Halakha*, its heart and soul. To respond to the Torah, at whatever level, is not just to undergo mystical or even prophetic trauma, but to heed a command. Or rather, to heed God as the giver of commands. To the pure ethicist, obligation may perhaps be rooted in an autonomous moral law. Religiously speaking, one is bound by the person-to-person encounter. Not just the law but the King, not only the *mitzvah* but the *m'tzaveh*. "Why [in reciting the

Shema] does the portion of *Shema* precede that of *v'haya im shamoa?* In order that he [who recites] should first accept the rule of the Kingdom of Heaven and then the rule of *mitzvot.*" This is the crux of the precedence in Exodus 24:7, of *na'aseh*, "we shall do," to *venishma*, "we shall hear," which the rabbis saw as being so basic to Israel's acceptance of the Torah.

From this perspective, it is obvious that all 613 commandments are equally binding. Not that they are all of equal importance. Some outweigh others, and in cases of conflict, the *halakha* provides criteria for choosing between them. All are similarly obligatory, however, for it is their source rather than their content which binds—and Him they share in common. Whether a particular commandment has "ethical or doctrinal content" is not the heart of the matter. The crucial point is that it *is* a commandment, that it elicits a response to the divine call. To put it more sharply, there always is "ethical or doctrinal content." In the age-old controversy—dating from Plato's *Euthyphro*—as to whether things please God because they are good or they are good because they please Him, traditional Judaism has certainly held with Socrates that the divine will is not arbitrary but rational. As regards commandments, however, even if we ignore the intrinsic content, perhaps hidden from us, of a specific *mitzvah,* its merely being such has moral and religious import. It widens the scope of religious awareness. It inculcates the habit of acting in response to the divine will in all areas of endeavor. It develops a sense of the divine presence. It integrates all of human life into a normative and purposive existence. It enables the Jew to attain not only dignity but sanctity.

(2) This normative existence is the key to Israel's election as God's chosen people. Generally speaking, our election may be viewed as the result of the interaction of divine grace and human merit, of supernal love and yearning aspiration. Specifically, however, the vehicle through which this election has come into being has always been the covenant. And a covenant—be it with the patriarchs, in Egypt, at Sinai, upon entering the promised land, or, in a slightly different sense, with every individual Jew throughout the genera-

tions—has invariably entailed a key element: the acceptance of divine norms. Not Luther's feminine waiting for the seed of grace but active submission to a divinely ordered discipline—that has been the core of the process. Moreover, the normative element is not only the genetic and historical source of our election. It defines, in large measure, the heart of the concept proper. In what does our chosenness consist? It consists in being singled out as a unique instrument for the fulfillment of God's purpose in history. This, in turn, entails commitment to unique responsibilities and special obligations—a "Jewish man's burden," if you will. It involves a closer relation to God; responding more fully and more frequently to a divine command. There is, to be sure, an obverse—the dispensation of special grace and the bestowal of particular favor. Furthermore, our covenantal relation being dynamic rather than static, it has led us to develop through the years a distinctive national character. The essence of our election, however, remains our unique commitment and its attendant responsibilities; these may, no doubt, produce special consequences. For better: "Rabbi Chananya son of Akashya used to say, the Holy One, blessed be He, wished to render Israel more worthy. Therefore, he provided them with much Torah and commandments." Or for worse: "You only have I known of all the families of the earth; therefore I shall visit upon you all your iniquities." These are ancillary, however; the basic ground of our election is normative existence and obligation.

The concept of Israel's chosen status is therefore substantively different from the theories of racial and national superiority formulated by Gobineau, Treitschke, and their confreres. Chosenness, as we understand it, resides in our covenantal relation with God rather than in any inherent superiority. It is, of course, quite conceivable that the doctrine of Israel's national election has indeed served as the model for these theories. I am not historian enough to judge. It should be clear, however, that there is no real analogy. We do not boast of our prowess. We lay no claim to aboriginal merit. Rather, we humbly thank God for assigning us a unique destiny, and we strive to fulfill the responsibilities of the covenant which He proffered and we accepted. To the relativist, this will no doubt still sound naïve. But the believing Jew can assume no less.

(3) This concept of normative existence, of a life governed by divinely ordained law and organized as an all-embracing religious discipline, constitutes Judaism's most distinctive contemporary hallmark. *Halakha* is its *principium individuationis.* The ideal of personal dedication to God's purposes in the broadest sense is by no means uniquely Jewish. However, our means of attaining it—and therefore the specific content of the ideal proper—clearly is. Life dominated in every area and for every individual by constant reference and response to divine commandments is qualitatively different from an existence generally committed to religious goals. The Jew's whole life is permeated by an awareness of his relation to God. In every sphere of endeavor—be it social or economic, physical or intellectual—conscious choice and religious response are operative. The *halakha,* through its numerous laws concerning various areas, directs the Jew in the sanctification of himself and his environment. It suffuses his life with spiritual significance, and integrates his activity into a divinely ordered whole. It gives the Jew a sense of purpose—and of God's purpose.

While the halakhic ideal of normative existence represents the distinctive hallmark of Judaism, it has both particularistic and universal implications. In its specific form, the Torah's total discipline was addressed to the Jew and to the Jew alone. It constitutes the crux of our covenant with God and we neither expect nor encourage the world as a whole to adopt it. Within a purely monotheistic framework, we regard the Gentile world as fully entitled, indeed mandated, to develop its own true and valid religious approaches—to institute modes of worship, to formulate religious philosophies, to seek out, and, if it so wishes, to invest with a public character vehicles of bringing man closer to God. Hence, our view of the relation between the Jewish and the Gentile worlds with respect to the over-all Torah discipline differs radically from that which obtains with respect to monotheism. Monotheism is an idea which we may have developed but which is nonetheless universally binding. It was not only something which the world could observe *in* us but which we insisted it should learn *from* us. The halakhic discipline, on the other hand, is specifically Jewish and bears no normative relation to the Gentile. And yet it too has universal implications. While the details of halakhic living and its formal regimen do not relate to the non-Jew, the ideals and values embedded within the *halakha* addressed themselves to mankind as a whole. The degree and the obligatory means of attaining these ideals, as well as the normative and covenantal framework within which they exist, are Israel's and Israel's alone. However, the central underlying purposes—of integrating the secular and the holy, of suffusing all human activity with a pervasive sense of religious meaning and direction—these belong to everyone and to no one. Imprinting them upon the universal consciousness of all men would constitute Judaism's greatest contribution to the modern world.

The pervasive character of Torah discipline permeates the ethical sphere as well as the "religious." Indeed, the inner logic of the halakhic ideal clearly dictates that social and personal ethics (the ethical includes much more than interpersonal *ben adam lachavero*) are an integral aspect of religion proper. The impact of this ideal upon ethical thought and behavior is, in part, simply the general impact of religion upon morality. It provides a conception of the nature of man as a moral agent; it posits an absolute rationale for moral action; and it defines a set of desiderata toward which such action ought to be directed. It thus transmutes morality from a drifting pursuit of relative goods—in the naturalistic universe of the secularist, even were an autonomous morality conceivable, it would have no absolute goals to seek—into a dedicated quest for the intrinsic Good. The ethical thrust of *halakha* goes beyond this, however. It extends to positing specific ideals and designating modes and standards of their fulfillment. While genuine morality can never be fully legislated in detail—virtue, justice, or wisdom ultimately depend upon inner commitment—the Torah's guidelines, besides setting a minimum standard, provide a direction for, and add a religious dimension to, moral action.

Hence, the Torah ethic—together with numerous other factors, of course—distinguishes the committed Jew from both a secular humanist on the one hand and a Christian or

Moslem on the other. He differs from the one with respect to the elemental questions of the nature and destiny of man. And while he would essentially agree with the other as regards the basically religious character of human existence, he would challenge him with respect to specific goals. Nor are these minor questions of technical implementation. Our opposition to the dualism pervading much Christian thought is hardly a petty trifle.

(4) As with the ethical sphere, so with the political. Judaism could hardly countenance political systems or philosophies which regard man as nothing but *homo economicus*; which deny the essential worth of the individual; which renounce the concept of distributive justice; which arbitrarily discriminate against one group in favor of another; or which disregard the concept of collective responsibility for the welfare of each and every person. In this sense, Judaism definitely entails a particular political viewpoint. A spiritual conception of man and society and dedication to a just social order are a *sine qua non* of any political outlook which a Jew could legitimately adopt. As to the optimum means of attaining these ideals, however, Judaism—despite the fact that the *halakha* does provide specific direction on certain points—could allow for considerable latitude. Indeed, it is the acolyte of a political ideology who finds himself with little practical leeway; his specifically political "system" often binds him with dogmatic pronouncements of a party line geared to this very area. The religious devotee, whose ideology is essentially spiritual rather than political, may have far greater pragmatic latitude. Never, of course, an unlimited spectrum; but still a fairly wide range.

(5) Such, in summary substance, is the bedrock upon which the Torah *Weltanschauung*, as both belief and experience, rests. It is a position which has always been under attack—in modern times, more so than previously. What aspects of contemporary thought challenge it most severely? There are, unfortunately, numerous candidates for this dubious distinction, but a few may be singled out for special mention. They—I refer to intellectual rather than social pressures—fall roughly into two classes: those which under-

mine religion generally and those which challenge Judaism—
and, to an extent, all revealed religion—specifically. Foremost among the first are: materialism, Marxist or other;
pseudoscientism, especially as manifested in the social
sciences; deterministic psychology, especially behaviorism;
and, in the sphere of both ethics and religion, utilitarianism.
Within the second group, the major challenge is presented
by liberalism (I use the term in Cardinal Newman's sense,
i.e., rampant intellectualistic individualism) and, though to
a lesser degree than at the turn of the century, by biblical
criticism. Probably the greatest over-all challenge is posed,
however, by two elements which straddle both categories:
positivism, logical or otherwise; and historicism, not so much
because of its critique of specific traditions as because of
the relativism which almost inexorably attends it.

Not to be included in this list, however, is the so-called
death-of-God issue currently being bandied about in Christian circles. To the extent that this notion is more than so
much doublethink and disguised atheism, it constitutes a
reaction against sentimental anthropomorphism—the
"Grandfather in Heaven," to use C. S. Lewis's phrase, of
popular liberal theology. Despite its appeals to realism and
morality, however, it represents a reaction which has gone
haywire. Essentially, its advocates hold a transitional position. It is only a matter of time before they fragment
into two groups—secular moralists, and devotees of what will
turn out to be a conception of God after all, if a somewhat
unconventional one. I do not quite see how one can hold
this position seriously and remain a believing Christian,
but that no believing Jew could hold it is beyond question.
And not only because Jewish dogma contravenes it. It is not
just that the believing Jew *may* not hold it. He *cannot.*
"The lion hath roared, who will not fear? The Lord God
hath spoken, who can but prophesy?" To the Jew who is
called upon to respond to Him constantly, can God be anything but a living presence?

David Lieber

*President of the University of Judaism
(Conservative) in Los Angeles, California.*

❡ I consider myself to be a "modernist" for whom reason
and experience are the touchstones of knowledge, and not
the authority of a text or tradition, hallowed though it may
be by centuries of saints and scholars. At the same time, I
cannot accept the methods either of the behavioral scientists
or of the philosophical analysts as adequate to an understanding of the condition of man. Nor do I believe that they
can provide a way out of the egocentric predicament in
which man presently finds himself. Moreover, I am impressed
by the moral and spiritual insights which have resulted from
authentic religious experiences, as well as by their power
to move men and mountains, and reshape entire civilizations.
Finally, while I freely recognize that ours is not an age
which takes religious categories seriously, there is, in my
estimation, an increasingly felt need for a "shared object of
devotion" which the traditional God-faith provided, and a
desire for some kind of community of faith which will buttress the individual in his search for meaning and significance
in the friendless world in which he finds himself.

Historically, Judaism provided both this community of
faith as well as the structure within which it could grow and
function. It withstood political crises and sweeping social
changes alike, even as it met the intellectual challenges of
increasingly sophisticated systems of thought. In part, this
was due to the comparatively slow rate of change, and its
uneven character. Even more, it was due to the extraordinary religious civilization which was classical Judaism, biblical and rabbinic—a civilization at once receptive to new
ideas and new values, and true to the fixed points of the
Mosaic religion. The latter included the doctrine of the
election of Israel; the covenant between God and Israel;
the revealed system of law and morality which constituted
the terms of that covenant; and Israel's special role in human
history until the ultimate establishment of the Kingship of
God on earth.

To me, these still remain the anchor-point of the Jewish religion—though I must hasten to add that I do not accept the traditional interpretation of them. More pointedly, my conception of God is such that it does not permit me to speak of Him in any anthropomorphic terms whatsoever, including those which appear to have been taken quite literally by many of the Jewish religious authorities of the past. In fact, my position is that even to speak of the existence of God is to reify Him, since existence requires localization in time and space, both of which He transcends.

Fundamentally, then, God, the source of all existence, is unknown and forever unknowable. At the same time, He does seem to reveal Himself in human experience in unexpected moments and in a variety of circumstances. In any case, He functions as the symbol of all human aspirations for self-transcendence, as the ideal limit of man's notion of supreme value. He is "the 'beyond' in our midst," and faith in Him is an awareness of the ideal possibilities of human life, and of man's ability to fashion his life in the light of them. To speak of the "death of God," if it is not merely to deny a traditional conception of Him, is to destroy the most adequate symbol thus far available for the realm of the spirit which transcends man, challenging him to realize his human potentialities and strengthening him in his efforts. It also eliminates the possibility of worship, which is, in effect, a spiritual exercise, opening man to influences which go beyond the narrow confines of his own immediate interests and needs, and enabling him to catch a glimpse of himself from another perspective—*sub specie aeternitatis*, so to speak.

In fitting Judaism into this scheme, I believe we have to begin with the recognition that the basic unit is not the individual, but the group into which he is born. It is in his childhood years that the child develops not only his motor skills, but his fundamental value system, his basic attitudes, and his general outlook on life. It is the group which provides him with the emotional support he requires, and which helps develop within him a sense of responsibility for his actions. It cares for his biological and psychosocial needs, and at the same time awakens him to the spiritual dimension of his existence.

It is essential, then, that the group be a wholesome one, if the children who are raised in its midst are to become sensitive, responsive human beings. Hence, the need for social and personal norms, for rites and practices, which will sensitize the human being to his fellow man, as well as to the larger world about him, and which will provide him with a sense of awe and reverence in the presence of the cosmic forces which sustain him. Hence also the need for the kind of education which will at once help him to identify himself with his group and its purposes, and accept its discipline for himself and his family.

Here is where both the notion of "the election of Israel" and the "covenant" have played a major role in Jewish history, and still have an important role to play. Both of them, incidentally, are key concepts in biblical religion. They signify Israel's consciousness of its special place in human history, as the first people bound together not primarily by ethnic or cultural ties, but by their readiness to accept a special obligation imposed upon them by God and history to be a "covenant people," and thus a source of blessing not only to themselves and their neighbors, but to all the nations of the earth.

That there was a danger that this doctrine would be misunderstood even by the Israelites themselves, as it is misunderstood in our own time, is quite clear from the sources. Still, history has taught us that even the most obvious notions will be misunderstood, and it makes little sense to change them for the sake of those who suffer from "invincible ignorance" and simply will not see. Moreover, it is precisely the possible chauvinistic misinterpretations of these doctrines that called forth some of the most inspired comments of the Deuteronomist, as well as of the prophets, and left us no doubt as to their meaning.

For me personally they signify both Israel's special role in human history—as the "People of the Book," and as the martyr people par excellence in the original Greek sense of the term—and its continued desire to survive as a "sacred community" whose members will testify by their deeds to the power of the spirit and to the blessedness of the lives that have been touched by it. The election of Israel, then, is both a descriptive and normative term, referring not only to a fact of history, but to my own judgment of that fact. The covenant of Israel, on the other hand, refers to the conscious resolve to accept the election and to fashion the life of the people in accordance with it.

Like all ancient covenants, the covenant of Israel entailed specific obligations. In the Torah, they are enumerated not only in the Decalogue, but in the various codes of law which follow. As is well known, the Torah is not limited to the Pentateuch, but was expanded in the oral law, beginning with the time of Ezra, and continuing—theoretically, at least—on to our own day. For traditional Judaism, of course, all these laws —ritual, moral, civil, and criminal alike—were revealed by God and were all considered to have equal authority. Still, it is clear that, beginning with the prophets, the moral law was given precedence over the ritual one, and it is a distortion of traditional Judaism to argue, as some do, for example, that the laws of the Sabbath were as important as those governing the saving of human life. This is simply not true, as anyone who is familiar with some of the better-known rabbinic exegeses can testify, nor is it true that traditional Judaism is a parochial, legalistic system which choked off the spirit of the religion of the prophets and their universal message.

For myself, I accept the notion of a religious law as being a corollary of, and flowing from, the notion of the covenant. A community must have rules and regulations to function; its individual members must be guided by norms, standards, and laws. Furthermore, since I do recognize the desirability of maintaining continuity with the past, as well as a measure of unity with Jews the world over, I am prepared to guide myself by those rules and regulations which have been accepted through the ages, provided they do not conflict with my ethical or aesthetic sensibilities. Beyond that, I am anxious to reexamine the whole corpus of Jewish law to point up, wherever possible, its relevance to contemporary social and personal issues—such as war and peace, the rights of minorities and of majorities—and to expand it so that it may speak to those questions for which the tradition offers no guidance to date.

I do this in full consciousness of the fact that I do not believe the law and its details to be of divine origin, but rather Israel's response to what it considered to be the divine call. On the whole, I think that this response was unexceptionable and that it has elevated and ennobled Jewish life throughout the ages. To the extent, however, that the development of the law became an end in itself, and the fundamental principles upon which it was based were forgotten, it did become necessary from time to time for courageous religious leaders and teachers to set themselves against the trend. They had to blaze new paths so that the fundamental respect of the people for the law would not be destroyed, and Judaism might remain relevant to the Jews' highest aspirations and meet the needs generated by new ages and new surroundings.

Ours, it seems to me, is just such an age. Regrettably, respect for Jewish law is at a very low ebb in our time. In part, this is due to the disintegration of the organized Jewish community, and to the permissiveness which characterizes a democratic civilization. In large measure, however, it is due to the unwillingness or inability of the halakhic authorities to come to grips with the real problems of Jewish living. What is required is first an updated Code of Jewish Practices to guide those who wish to live within the framework of the *halakha,* and ultimately a revision of the *halakha* itself in the areas both of ritual practice and of personal and social norms.

We cannot do without ritual practices, not alone because they help maintain the unity of the Jewish group, but because it is through them that we express our desire to belong to the Covenant Community and by their aid that we internalize its values and attitudes. Furthermore, to the extent that ritual practices and holiday observances are worship in action, they help us keep open the channels between ourselves and the God in whose presence we seek to live.

At the same time, the *halakha* cannot restrict itself to rituals and religious observances. There can be no community without rules and regulations governing such matters as membership, marriage, birth, education, interpersonal relations, etc. Nor can any religious tradition worth its salt—and certainly not one which is based on the Bible—refrain from offering guidance to the individual and making demands on him in the area of moral decision and social concern. Nor again—since in a democracy social action can scarcely be divorced from political issues—can the *halakha* avoid dealing with such questions as the ethics of government, welfare legislation, relations with totalitarian states of all stripes, etc.

What is required, then, is the recognition by Jewish leadership, lay and professional alike, that the greatest contribution the Jewish community can make to its members, as well as to the world at large, is to reconstitute itself as a Covenant Community, which will take seriously the biblical injunction that it is to be "a kingdom of priests and a holy nation." This is not to imply any claim of Jewish moral or religious superiority. Rather, it is to insist that each group must aspire to the same type of distinction and fashion its culture and civilization so as to enable it to realize its highest spiritual potential as well. What will separate the groups will be their distinctive "languages"—their historic institutions and practices. What will unite them will be far more important—their common desire to help their individual members make the most out of their lives as moral personalities, and their desire to help one another in raising their levels of aspiration and achievement.

That we are still far from this desired goal, the daily headlines can attest. Alas, we are as far from it in Jewish life as the rest of the world is generally. The distinctive contribution of the Jew, then, can be to show the way in our time, just as his ancestors did many centuries and millennia ago. For this we are uniquely suited, not only because of our experience in the past, and the rich heritage it has bequeathed to us, but because of our sad experience in the most recent decades. More than anyone, we know the crying need of our time for a spiritual and moral awakening. More than anyone, we are aware of the beast which lurks just below the veneer of civilization and the need to tame and restrain it. Hence our problem is a dual one: to persuade ourselves that we can best serve mankind at large by making the Jewish people a more effective and meaningful unit; and to come to the realization that the survival of the Jewish people, nay of all of mankind, depends on our finding a way out of the naïve hedonism which characterizes our *Weltan-*

schauung, to a positive affirmation of the spiritual potentialities of man as he sees himself an earthbound creature, but one whose gaze nevertheless is directed to heaven.

Hershel J. Matt

Rabbi of Temple Neve Shalom (Conservative)
in Metuchen, New Jersey.

❆ (1) At the center of my religious affirmation is "Torah from Sinai," the conviction that the Torah contains the word of God revealed to Israel in the wilderness. This word, however, though issuing from God, was addressed to men, received by men, transmitted by men, recorded by men, copied and recopied by men—and thus to some degree was subject to the limitations of men: their inadequacies, inaccuracies, misunderstandings. Our Torah-text, therefore, though containing the word of God, cannot be assumed entirely to be the word of God. Man's continuing and never-ending task is to identify (with God's help) which among the Torah's words are God's own words and therefore absolutely binding.

The absolutely minimal statement of God's word in the Torah is "I, YHVH, am your God, who brought you forth from the land of Egypt, from the house of bondage"—and theoretically this would be a sufficient statement: it identifies the God; it affirms the I-Thou relationship between God and man; it implies both God's love and power to redeem and to command, and man's privilege and obligation to obey and to respond. Since this minimal statement, however, may be too meager, the basic and all-inclusive affirmation-and-command of the *Shema* should be added: "Hear, Israel, YHVH is our God, YHVH alone; and you shall love YHVH your God with all your heart, with all your soul, and with all your might." (Alternative formulations, of course, could be cited from the Torah. But the *Shema* is most familiar and, because of its absolute "with all," perhaps the most adequate as well.)

The command to "love your fellow man as yourself" is, like all the commandments, included in the command to love

God, and theoretically need not explicitly be stated in the minimal formulation of God's command. Lest the cynical nonbeliever or the self-righteous believer fail to see the obvious implication, however, it is advisable to make explicit statement of this second great command.

Concerning all the remaining commands of the 613, they are to be considered binding insofar as they are seen, upon humble and careful study, to be alternate formulations or specific instances of the two chief commands. (For this reason it would be proper to say that there is one additional basic command: "Go and study.")

The commandments involving my relations to my fellow man are all to be tested against the inclusive "love your fellow man as yourself"—remembering, of course, that "love" refers here not to romantic feeling, but to the practice of justice in the highest degree; the manifestation of care and concern in the highest measure; full regard for the true welfare of my fellow man as one who is infinitely precious—having, no less than I, been created in the image of God. Whenever any of the other commandments concerning fellow man are seen, upon careful study, to constitute an unnecessary denial or restriction of love, they are no longer to be considered as God's command, absolutely binding. In boldly asserting the right of such private judgment, I ought, of course, to give much attention and weight to the wisdom, experience, and piety of the talmudic and post-talmudic sages (including those of the present age as well), but since I am the "you" who is being commanded, mine is the ultimate human responsibility to decide what it is that I am being commanded.

Similarly, the "ritual commands" are meant to be instances of the command to "love YHVH your God"—and are to be considered binding only insofar as they are seen to be reflections of, vehicles for, or aids to the love of God. Again, much weight should be given to traditional explication and interpretation, but the privilege and obligation to examine and decide are a personal privilege and obligation. Despite the risks of subjectivity, there is no acceptable alternative; indeed, there is ultimately no alternative at all.

And yet, a crucial additional consideration is involved. To some extent, even the "ethical" commands, and to a vast extent the "ritual" commands, are addressed to me by virtue of my membership in the covenant people, Israel. I was commanded, but I was commanded as one of the children of Israel, along with all other children of Israel; we were commanded together, collectively and not only individually; my hearing and responding to God's commands involves and implicates all Israel as well. A crucial dimension of my life—indeed, the whole normal context of my "ritual" life (including Sabbath, holy days, many aspects of sex and diet and clothing, etc.) —is thus the shared way of the people Israel, summoned at Sinai to be a unique and separate "kingdom of priests and holy nation." Whether the particular ritual acts, objects, and occasions were God-originated or God-designated or God-approved, they came to be accepted as God's prescribed way for Israel to respond to Him. To increase or to reduce excessively the Torah-ordained pattern of Jewish practice, as understood by the sages of Israel and accepted by the people Israel, is to endanger the solidarity, identity, and survival of His Holy people, to dilute my own participation in its holy function, and to constrict the dimensions of my very own being. But once again, this corporate acceptance of the Torah's commands as God's commands, crucial as it is, cannot be the ultimate consideration. It is as one of Israel, to be sure, that I am commanded, but it is I who must acknowledge the command.

When I fail to see myself commanded to observe such-and-such of the 613 commandments, there are several options available: I can observe the commandment nevertheless, choosing to accept the discipline of Israel's traditional way, even though lacking the conviction that it is God's command (as long, that is, as I do not consider it a violation of God's command!); or I can cease from observing it ("no longer"); or I can hold back from observing it ("not yet"). All three of these options I find myself taking at various times; no one of them is improper—as long as I take it in reverence rather than from indifference, in humility rather than in self-righteousness.

Note, however, that I do not, need not, and dare not say that I will accept only those commandments whose observance I find pleasant or convenient; or whose origins I find identifiable or acceptable; or even whose specific purpose I find understandable. For the very notion of being commanded by God involves the acknowledgment, at least in principle, that God can command that which is contrary to my preference, for reasons that are beyond my understanding. Indeed, I must even grant that, since His thoughts are not my thoughts, it is likely that with regard to at least some of His commandments, such will be the case. I am grateful that God, having created me in His image, has enabled me to understand some of His purpose; having given me the Torah, He has enabled me to understand considerably more; having promised to send the Messiah, He has assured me that someday I will understand far more. Often I crave to understand that "far more" here and now; in moments of deepest faith, however, I am able to cease insisting that I understand exactly *why* I am commanded; it is enough for me to know *that* I am commanded and *what* I am commanded. The only "why" I must know now is that whatever I am commanded is for the true welfare of all men (including me), for the glory of Israel, and for the sake of God's Holy Name.

(2) I believe that YHVH, Lord of the universe, has singled out Israel from the nations of the world, establishing a covenant with Israel by which it has been summomed to be "a kingdom of priests, a holy nation . . . My first-born son . . . first fruits of His produce . . . My servants . . . My witnesses . . . a light unto the nations."

Is any superiority involved in this singling-out?

In attempting to answer, one must beware of two perils: the peril of chauvinistic self-righteousness and the peril of apologetic equalitarianism.

On the one hand, if any superiority is involved, it does not lie in Israel's greater original merit as grounds for the choosing ("not because of your righteousness"); nor in Israel's lesser obligation as a consequence of the choosing ("*therefore* I will visit upon you all your iniquities"); nor in Israel's consistent faithfulness in response to the choosing ("you have been rebellious against the Lord from the day I knew you"); nor in Israel's greater ease and comfort—at least in this world-and-age—as a result of the choosing ("for Thy sake are we slain all day long").

On the other hand, it would be foolhardy and unworthy to deny that Israel's chosenness is meant to constitute supreme honor and blessing—certainly a superiority of sorts. But the choosing was of God's doing: at His initiative, by His will, through His love, in His time and way, for His purposes—and only partially open to our understanding.

At least these aspects of the choosing we have been given to understand: The *reason* for God's choosing "an Israel" was that man, though created in God's image and thus able to know His will and free to do it, had shown himself far too disobedient and unfaithful; what was now required was a greater measure and more intimate degree of God's guidance, instruction, discipline—involving more concentrated attention, as it were, upon a smaller segment of mankind. The *purpose* of God's choosing Israel was the enrichment and blessing of all nations. The *goal* of God's choosing Israel was the eventual disappearance of that Israel—in the messianic day, when "the earth would be filled with the knowledge of the Lord."

(3) Since the God who redeemed Israel from Egypt and established the covenant with Israel at Sinai is affirmed to be the only true God, He is thus the God of all men, and His word in the Torah is addressed to all men (except for those "ritual" commands that are addressed to Israel in its separation). In one sense, therefore, Judaism—insofar as it faithfully preserves and conveys this word of the one true God—can properly be termed the one true religion, and its ethic, grounded as it is in the word of the one true God, can properly be termed the one true ethic.

But in another sense Judaism should be termed not the one true religion and ethic but the one criterion of true religion and ethics. If non-Jews—in concert with or in contrast to their particular society; in any place or at any time; prior to the Torah, or subsequent to but uninfluenced by the Torah—are found in fact to have enunciated the same truth concerning God and man as that contained in the Torah (or some part or measure of that same truth), then their religion and ethics are to that extent also true. (That men should be found to have arrived at this same truth, at least to some degree, should of course not surprise or disturb us;

the Torah itself, after all, teaches that *adam*, man-as-such, every man, is created in God's image, and is thereby endowed with the capacity to hear and respond to God's word concerning man's relation to Him and to his fellow man.)

Christianity, however, stemming as it does from Judaism, occupies a very special place among the other religions of mankind (Islam, too, to some extent). The central "vehicles of revelation" of Judaism and Christianity—the people-Israel-as-bearers-of-the-Torah in the one case, and Christ in the other—are radically different; the two communities are different; their roles are different. But the content of the two faiths, as regards man's proper relationship to God and his fellow man, is—despite differences in emphasis, tone, and mood—basically the same. Christianity can properly be viewed as a second and equally valid form of God's covenant with Israel—the missionary arm of Israel, serving to bring under the covenant those who, unlike the Jewish people, are not yet under it.

Every believing Jew takes for granted, of course, what few believing Christians can fully grasp: that the people, Israel, is in no sense supplanted by the Church, and that Israel's own role remains indispensable—to remain apart in holy separation, serving as God's witnesses and resisting the forms of paganism to which Christianity is prey; insisting upon the need for justice as the ground of love; constantly exposing the unredeemed character of the present world-and-age; holding up the vision of a truly redeemed world-and-age; and stressing both man's task and God's role in hastening the establishment of His Kingdom upon earth.

In that "final day," when God's purpose for mankind will have been fulfilled, the differences between Judaism and Christianity will no longer be necessary, and will therefore disappear—the one true religion having by then been accepted by all.

(4) As regards the compatibility of Judaism with any particular political, economic, or social system—and advocacy or support thereof—one absolute and several relatives are involved.

The absolute is the Torah's standard of perfect justice, which is love. Every political system, economic arrangement, and social pattern is to be measured against that standard and judged in terms of that ideal. We can thus expect—pending the coming of the Messiah—that every system will be found to be only relatively good, and thus also relatively evil.

But a second relative factor must at once be introduced. Though all systems known to us are relatively evil, they are not equally evil: some involve a greater degree of injustice, or cruelty, or dehumanization, or enslavement than do others. A "good Jew," therefore, must at every moment discriminate among the available alternatives, supporting the least evil of them and working to reduce the degree of evil involved (in addition, of course, to praying for forgiveness for his own complicity even in the unavoidable evil).

It is thus easy to answer whether a "good Jew" can be a segregationist, or a Communist, or a Fascist. Of course he cannot—since to be any of these involves a denial in principle and a repression in practice of the basic equality and fundamental rights that belong to all men as created in God's image.

But though it is easy to say who is not a good Jew, it is indeed impossible to say who is. For, since almost all available alternatives at a given moment involve at least some degree of evil, there is no complete escape from some taint of evil—and complete noninvolvement is not an available option.

The term "good Jew" should therefore be dropped from our vocabulary; or, rather, it should be held aloft to describe the ideal Jews, but never should it be applied by man to an actual Jew. God alone can and will decide.

(5) From the point of view of Judaism, the "God is dead" argument is either relatively meaningless or deeply troublesome or absolutely crucial—depending upon the terms of the argument.

If the statement that "God is dead" is meant to convey the notion that "once God lived, but then He died," it is for Judaism a self-contradiction and thus meaningless. The Living God YHVH is eternally living; if He no longer lives, He never lived; if He is not God now, He never was.

If the statement means, however, that God is deathly still

and silent, that He does not appear any longer to act in history, that He does not intervene when men defy His will and torture His children—then the challenge is real and profound, and ancient as well. All that the believing Jew can do is to offer an answer to the proximate "why" by pointing to the awesome reality of man's freedom to do evil; and to the ultimate "why" by reaffirming his faith in God's original good purpose in creating man; his trust in the eventual fulfillment of that purpose on "the final day"; and his "acceptance" of God's "right," in the interim, to hide His face in anger or in anguish, with thoughts that are not ours.

But perhaps "God is dead" means that God is not—and never was—a living being but a force or energy, a system or process, a near-perfect mechanism; that He is not a "he" at all; that all the attributes of a living God were erroneously attributed, were but illusions. To which the believing Jew can of course offer neither rational nor experimental refutation, but only the humble yet confident testimony of his own personal encounter with the living God, of his own reenactment of Israel's encounter at Sinai. And if the believer hesitates to quote to the nonbeliever that "the Lord is near to all who call upon Him in truth"—lest he appear overly self-righteous—he has but to couple his quotation with a twofold confession: first, that often the religious establishment itself has been responsible for exiling God from His house, muffling and stifling His voice; and second, that all too frequently, in the attempted encounter of prayer, the believer himself meets only with dead silence.

Have we now perhaps reached the crux of the whole argument? God's silence may be due not to any defect in His voice but to a defect in our ear! In that case, the very first challenge—that God once lived but now is dead—which I dismissed earlier as meaningless, may be the most meaningful of all. We used to hear the voice of God—in pleading and command, in judgment and forgiveness—but now, because we have for too long turned away and shut our ear, that voice has become almost totally inaudible. How hopeless! But if we once were men, or even once knew men, who heard the living God and spoke to Him, perhaps there is yet a thread of hope: perhaps—for God is merciful—we, for whom He has become dead because we have become dead to Him, may yet be revived sufficiently to find His living presence once again.

I do not believe that any aspects of modern thought pose an ultimate challenge to Jewish belief, except perhaps to a fundamentalist version of Jewish belief.

Two tendencies of modern *thinkers*, however, pose a challenge by preventing a confrontation. One is the strange tendency of many profound minds and sensitive spirits, who in all other fields approach their subject with creative openness to the multiple dimensions and levels of truth and beauty and meaning, to approach Judaism rigidly, narrowly, literalistically, dogmatically, and one-dimensionally. The other tendency is to overlook existentially what they know intellectually: that the secularist position, no less than the religious, operates with certain assumptions of faith—so that not whether to believe, but what to believe, is the only option open to men.

Jacob Neusner

*Associate professor in the Department of Religion
at Dartmouth College.*

❡ I lay no claim to theological sophistication or profundity. I am a mere historian and a believing Jew, and most diffidently offer these reflections about the substance of that belief.

(1) By "Torah" I understand instruction, or truth about reality. Revelation may take many forms; in this age, prophecy is in the hands of fools and children. Whatever truth we apprehend, therefore, emerges from our minds alone. But our minds have been shaped by God in His image. Truth reaches us through revelation in one mode or another, and represents the result of the mind's instruction, or insight into the world. All that we know we ultimately learn through God, who gave us minds and the capacity to think, and who forms the world that we may know it with our minds. Just what constitutes "Torah" once seemed more cer-

tain than it does today, but however tentative or fragile truth may now appear, it comprehends all the revelations we shall ever know or have. And by truth I mean a mature vision of reality.

I do not know what the "613 commandments" are, nor does anyone else. In referring to R. Simlai's lovely homily, we ought not to ignore the concluding remarks of R. Nahman b. Issac, "It is Habakkuk who came and based them all on one principle, 'But the righteous shall live by his faith'" (Habakkuk 2:4). I believe what the believing Jew must do is to strive toward perfect faith in God, therefore, and that this "commandment," if assumed, will illumine all the others.

I know of no ritual commandments lacking in ethical or doctrinal content, for however arcane a commandment may be, such as the one cited, it still provides the opportunity to sanctify a corner of the day-to-day world, humble or remote as that corner may seem.

(2) The Jews are chosen in Amos's sense, "You only have I known of all the families of the earth; therefore I will punish you for all your iniquities." Our chosenness is vindicated by our suffering. This has nothing to do with tribalism.

(3) We differ very little, if at all, in our view of what functionally constitutes a definition of ethical behavior, but we differ greatly, as is quite natural, about the proper motives and ideals, and the theology which ought to underlie that behavior. These differences are significant. We differ even more on the ways in which men can so purify their hearts that they may act ethically. All religions which teach that one God made the world, cares for what happens in it, and directs human affairs toward His providential goal are true religions. These are Islam, Christianity, and Judaism. Judaism is obviously distinguished from its daughter religions in numerous significant ways, but it needs to recognize that Christianity and Islam, and not Judaism, have been redemptive instruments for much of mankind. That is a fact of history. If, as I believe, it is God who directs the course of history and reveals His will, in part, through it, as through nature, then one cannot fail to recognize that men have

found more than one well from which to draw uncontaminated waters. It is, however, through the sacred events in Israel, both past and present, that life is best known. Auschwitz is ours, but others have had their Hiroshima, Stalingrad, Coventry, Berlin, and Dresden. Judgment proceeds from Israel to the nations. We suffer first, in the hope that others will gain insight from our chastisement, for upon us is the chastisement that can make man whole. We have been the sin-offering for humanity, and we have borne the sins of many. Indeed, our very condition vindicates in a terrible way our view that man is not yet redeemed. Unredemption begins with us. Our distinctive gift to mankind? Ourselves, our suffering, and our vindication in the end of days. These mankind shares.

(4) Judaism may provide political insight. It is to be discovered in part through a search for the political dimensions, or implications, of its theology, surely not through a hunt for texts proving whatever we have already decided we want to do. It is, secondly, to be found in the attitudes of the living community, which have a right to form, and not solely to be formed by, Jewish tradition, and whose historical collective experience, even in the most secular ways, bears witness to God's will. I do not think we have been sufficiently serious about either a study of Jewish tradition, or reflection upon Jewish realties today, to say just what political insight, if any, Judaism has now to offer. The accepted answers to whether a good Jew can identify himself with the positions cited are therefore too obvious to be really true.

(5) I do not fully understand what the "God is dead" theologians are saying. It seems to me they *may* be saying two things. First, the experience of the sacred, or God, is no longer widely available; second, that experience is no longer available *in the classical ways.* Both of these statements describe Jewish existence, and have for some time, though we may prefer to phrase them differently. I think it clear that God is hiding His face from our world. (I should not want to reduce the experience of *hastarat panim,* a hiding of the face, to its obvious sociological, cultural, historical com-

ponents, though these are very real and explain much.) We are no longer able to approach the gates of heaven, surely not to open them with the keys that used to work. God is surely "dead" for many Jews. In the Jewish community, even the flame of the *yahrzeit* candle long ago flickered out. In the synagogue, however, Jewry still keeps up the graveyard. I do not despair. We Jews have passed this way before. We have known ages in which God was very present for all Israel as today He is not. A handmaiden at the Red Sea saw what Ezekiel was not privileged to see. If we believe, as our tradition teaches us to, in the resurrection of the dead, then we need not doubt with Whom the miracle must begin.

The most serious challenge to Jewish belief is posed by the need to investigate what we mean by that belief, by the use of theological language, however we use it and whatever its specific vocabulary. If we say, God made the world, we are forced to contemplate the world and its emerging infinities. We must wonder what it is that we can be referring to when we speak of a "Creator" or an "act of creation." If we say, God gave the Torah, we need to consider what it is we are saying: the Creator of infinities handed on sacred stories, cared about what happened to an ox in its plowing, or to a worker's salary, or even to an organism in a test tube. Once we leave off repeating a stream of monotonous, unfelt words, and abandon our sentimental attachment to the given, we face the finite and unsatisfactory quality of our language and its metaphors, for that is all we have. The issue is not belief or unbelief. It is, for those who *say* they believe, how to contemplate the reality in which they believe. Those who say they do not believe need also to reflect upon their unbelief, unless they hold, as do some, that all we are, and all we shall ever be, is here and now. I envy the certainty and security of such a belief. Mine seems to me a more uncertain way, but it is one to which I feel called, and to explore which, as a "believing" Jew, I have been created.

Jakob J. Petuchowski

Professor of rabbinics and Jewish theology at Hebrew Union College (Reform) in Cincinnati.

❡ (1) It was, of course, a pagan who expected Hillel to teach the whole Torah while standing on one foot. A Jew would have known better. A Jew would have been overwhelmed by the seriousness of the topic, and would have refrained from asking for shortcuts. Not so the pagan. He had a polite outsider's interest. If you have something important to tell me, go ahead. But make it short and painless. Otherwise, my interest will not be sustained. Shammai had already thrown that pagan out. He had reacted to him the way he could legitimately have reacted to a Jew who would ask that kind of question. That is where Shammai made his mistake. Hillel, on the other hand, realized that he was dealing with a pagan who did not know any better. That is why Hillel agreed to give an answer of the requested length.

In agreeing to participate in this symposium, I rely on the authority of Hillel. No "Jewish" Jew would expect answers to five serious questions—questions which go to the very root of Jewish being—in twenty-five hundred words. But a polite outsider might. I take it, then, that I am answering the questions of polite outsiders, to whom Judaism is a matter of some intellectual curiosity—as long as the demands which it makes are not too heavy. Yet I am no Hillel. Hillel could give a one-sentence answer, and then follow it up by saying, "The rest is commentary. Go and study!" What Hillel said last I have to say first. The reader who is truly and sincerely interested in the answers to the five questions posed here should go and study. He cannot, and he must not, rely on a twenty-five-hundred-word summary by any rabbi or theologian. Within such limitations of space, there can be no reasoned discourse, no substantiation of personal affirmations. There can only be the merest hint of the respondent's convictions, but no satisfactory answers. If you really want to know, if the questions truly bother you, go and study! I once tried to compress my answer to the question "In what sense do you believe the Torah to be divine revelation?" into 132 pages. You can read it in my book, *Ever Since Sinai* (New York, Scribe, 1961). But even 132 pages did not really suffice. How much less the number of words allotted to me here!

Try to make sense of the following: I believe that the Torah is a document of revelation; but I am not a fundamentalist. I believe that the words we read in the Torah were written by men; yet I am not a nontheistic humanist. The men who wrote the Torah wrote it under the impact of a religious experience—an experience of God's concern for Israel, of God's incursion into history. And not only the men who wrote it. The experience was shared by the men who accepted it—or there would have been no such acceptance. Moreover, it is not merely a question of a written text. Torah, for the Jew, is the oral as well as the written Torah; and it is the function of the oral Torah to keep the moment of revelation alive, to apply the underlying principles of Torah to circumstances and conditions which could not have been described in the original written text. With Franz Rosenzweig, I would distinguish between "legislation" and "commandment" in the Torah. The "legislation" can be a mere matter of academic study for me. But it need not be. Approached in the right frame of mind, Torah "legislation" can yield *commandments* addressed to *me*. I am aware of the danger of religious anarchy inherent in such an approach, though I am not sure that it is really a "danger." I can respect the Jew whose pattern of religious observance differs from mine, if only his observance derives from a like desire to hear God's commandments. Yet there are also laws in the Torah which should be observed by all Jews—whether or not they feel personally "addressed" by them. For it is one of the functions of the Torah to be the "constitution" of the holy community. The preservation of that holy community is itself a positive value of supreme concern to the Torah and, as I believe, to God. It would seem to me, therefore, that an agreement on what the "constitution" of the holy community implies today is one of the most pressing tasks facing the Jewish religious leaders of all schools of thought.

Yet, neither the individual listening for the commandments addressed to him, nor the community deciding upon its constitution, has any right to approach the Torah with a priori notions about the inferiority of "ritual commandments lacking in ethical or doctrinal content." It is true, the prophets have taught us that ceremonies are blasphemy when those who observe them do not lead a moral and ethical life. But that does not yet mean that religion is exhausted by the ethical (and doctrinal) sphere. Such an identification of religion with ethics must inevitably lead (and has already led) to the discovery that one can be ethical without being formally "religious." (Yes, I know some very moral and ethical people who have no religious commitments!) If religion addresses itself to the whole personality, then it obviously will have to provide something for those levels of our being which lie below the layer of consciousness. And that may very well be one of the functions of the so-called "ritual" commandments. Not every "ritual" necessarily has to teach a "ethical" lesson in order to be a valuable component of religion—though even such "rituals," in their aggregate, could conceivably mold the type of personality receptive to moral imperatives. A "ritual" serving as an expression of the Jew's love for God, or as a reminder of a historical encounter, is as much entitled to our consideration as are the more pronounced "ethical" commandments. Of course, in the final analysis, it will depend upon the individual whether or not he feels addressed by the prohibition against mixing linen and wool. Chances are that, in determining what is meaningfully "do-able" among the various components of the Torah, the modern American Jew is not going to put that particular prohibition on top of his list—not because it is not "ethical," but because there is a host of other observances that more nearly express his religious needs.

(2) As far as I know, the ancient Greeks were not influenced by the Jewish doctrine of election when they distinguished between Greeks and barbarians. Yet I would not deny that the biblical doctrine of the chosen people might lend itself to perversion. What doctrine or idea does not so lend itself? Even the espousal of the cause of social justice has, in some quarters, been turned into an excuse for a tyrannical totalitarianism. When I accept or reject a doctrine, I do not

do so on the basis of its possible perversions, but purely on the basis of its intrinsic merit. Each time I observe a *mitzvah*, and praise God for having made us *kadosh* by means of His *mitzvot*, I affirm the doctrine of the chosen people. For the meaning of "Thou hast sanctified us" and the meaning of "Thou hast chosen us" are identical. And when I approach the Torah, I assert explicitly: "Thou hast chosen us . . . and given us Thy Torah." My possession of the Torah is really all the proof I need for the doctrine of the chosen people— all the proof I need, and also the meaning which "chosenness" has for me. But there are other indications as well. There is the miracle of Jewish survival which, but for my belief in the chosen-people doctrine, I would have to put down to a freak of history, or to some process of "fossilization." There is the sense of mission which has been transmitted to me together with the Torah, the idea that I belong to a people called upon to witness to God. The history of Jewish martyrdom would be completely senseless if I did not read it from the perspective of mission and chosenness. And as long as I myself feel the need to make my contribution to the world *as a Jew*, it will be my belief in the chosen people which motivates me to do so. So far removed, indeed, is my belief in the chosen people from any notion of chauvinism that I see the doctrine of the chosen people as completely at variance with any attempt to translate the meaning of Jewish existence into the terminology of modern nationalism and territorial sovereignty.

(3) According to Jewish teaching, God has had dealings with others besides Israel. The Father of all mankind has made Himself known to more than one single group of His children. There is, therefore, no reason for assuming that truth is limited to Judaism. What is limited to Judaism is the specific historical experience through which God has manifested Himself to Israel. God may have chosen other experiences in which to reveal Himself to Christians, Moslems, and Buddhists. Yet, being a Jew, I cannot help applying my Jewish yardstick to other religions; and, doing so, I find elements which I can reconcile with my own religious orientation, as well as elements which strike me as utterly foreign and incomprehensible. Incidentally, Judaism not only

"once had monotheism" to contribute to the world. It still does. My concept of the messianic future includes the prospect of a united mankind, proclaiming that "the Lord is One, and His Name is One." But it is not necessarily the ethical sphere as such which distinguishes the believing Jew from other believers and from nonbelievers. It is the ethical sphere within the context of a total commitment which is made up of the acceptance of two "yokes": "the yoke of the rulership of God," and "the yoke of the *mitzvot.*"

(4) Surely, the readers of *Commentary*, well schooled in the social sciences, do not seriously expect that Judaism—a historical growth of millennia—would entail any particular political viewpoint! Only in its biblical phase did Judaism map out a complete social system which, combining elements of monarchy, theocracy, and democracy, cannot be said to have been identical with any one of the current political philosophies. Whether even the social system of the Bible was ever completely put into operation is a historical question about which one might be skeptical. At any rate, we are no longer living in the biblical period. The task of the modern Jew, therefore, is to find out what the underlying motivations of biblical social legislation were, and then to apply them through such political channels as are available today. However, since no single modern political channel reflects the entire spectrum of the biblical ideal, it would be foolish to identify any such channel with the absolute demands of Judaism. Much nonsense has been said and written about this problem of late. Judging by some of these latter-day pronouncements, it would be virtually impossible for a political conservative to be a "good" Jew. Yet were we to eliminate all political conservatives from our roster of good Jews, we would not only deplete the ranks of good Jews unnecessarily; we would also be historically wrong.

As I understand them, the underlying principles of biblical social legislation are two: (1) God is the true "owner" of the world. Man does not own things in any absolute sense. His role is that of a steward, who has to make the best possible use of the property put at his disposal. In determining that use, man must bear in mind the second underlying principle, i.e., (2) the commandment that we love our fel-

low man because he is as we are, since he stands in the
same relation to God as we do ourselves (Leo Baeck's translation of Lev. 19:18). Communism would seem to deny the
first underlying principle, and Fascism the second. Nor would
it seem to be possible to reconcile the more virulent forms
of racism with the belief that we share a common humanity
with all men. Judaism is certainly against discriminatory
treatment of any section of the population, where such discrimination is inimical to the enjoyment of equal rights. But
Judaism also opposes *preferential* treatment, even if the
recipient of such preferential treatment be one of the "underprivileged." (See Ex. 23:6, 9, but also verse 3!)

Judaism's over-all objectives in the social and political
realm are easy enough to delineate. The prophets paint the
picture of "every man sitting under his vine and under his
fig tree, with none to make him afraid." The Torah, with its
institutions of the sabbatical and the jubilee years, aims at
an equitable distribution of property. The Talmud, with its
detailed legislation of the rights of both laborers and employ-
ers, wants to see work adequately rewarded, and investment suitably protected. Yet no single modern political philosophy is exclusively derived (or even claims to be so
derived) from the sources of Judaism. Every Jew will have
to study the tradition as well as the modern political alternatives, and then he will have to consult his own conscience
before he can, as a Jew, commit himself to one political
philosophy or another as the best road toward a *partial*
fulfillment of Judaism's aims. He will also have to realize
that the Messianic Age has not yet dawned and that all
human efforts are under the judgment of God. For any religious body today to invoke the authority of "Judaism" in
support of a given political platform, or a plank thereof, is
not only a historical impossibility. It is also a theological
monstrosity, if we remember that those very religious bodies
are a great deal more hesitant in proclaiming the "Word of
God" when it comes to those more specific commandments,
like the Sabbath, about which the traditional sources have
been far less equivocal.

(5) In some respects, the current "God is dead" debate is
strictly an internal Christian affair. This is all the more

evident once we see that, in spite of the death of the Father (or because of it?), the Son continues to reign. But there are also certain implications which are of great significance to Judaism. What the death-of-God theologians are trying to say is that yesterday's "God concepts" have become untenable today. "God concepts" are subject to revision and retirement. They always have been, though the terminology previously used may not have been quite so shocking. "God concepts" are man-made, and, of necessity, they have to reflect any major change in man's thinking. Some of them, no doubt, may be completely outgrown. This may well be the case with the "God concept" of nineteenth-century philosophy. Twentieth-century man no longer stalks the earth proudly as a particle of the Absolute. The god who thought man's thoughts, and who was expected to behave according to a pattern predictable by man, that god has died. But that god—cases of mistaken identification notwithstanding—had not been the biblical God to begin with. The biblical God is not a concept. He is not dependent on man's syllogisms for His existence. He is God, and, as such, He is free to make Himself known to man, or, as the Bible puts it, to "hide His face" from man. His thoughts are not man's thoughts, neither are His ways man's ways.

Our philosophical tradition has tried valiantly to domesticate this God of the Bible, to contain Him within the categories of human reason. For a long time, too, it looked as though philosophy had succeeded. And then came the shock of recognition: the God of the philosophers turned out to be a hypothesis which was no longer needed! It is this shock of recognition which, as I see it, has given rise to the talk about the "death of God." To that extent, then, the "death of God" is not only a Christian problem. It is very much a Jewish problem, too. The modern Jew, like the modern Christian, is dissatisfied with yesterday's "God concept." His choice is now one between atheism (of the avowed kind, or by circumlocution) and a return to the biblical God. Each alternative has its own problems. Atheism, because it leaves our spiritual craving unsatisfied, and because it forces us to invoke psychopathology in order to account for such intimations of the divine as theistic believers have claimed to have experienced. And the return to the biblical God, because the modern Jew cannot really keep his faith and his scientific orientation in watertight compartments. He needs, in other words, a philosophy and a scientific orientation which could go hand in hand with his faith in God.

Yet it is precisely at this point that modern thought presents its most serious challenge to Jewish belief. Science is no longer satisfied to remain a method. It becomes scientism, a totalitarian outlook. Psychology is no longer content in its role of investigating one aspect of the human personality. It becomes psychologism, confidently explaining all. The challenge, then, is not science as such, or psychology as such, or even philosophy as such. Rather does the challenge lie in the inability of the various disciplines to admit that there are dimensions beyond their ken, or, at any rate, beyond the capacity of their quantitative measurements. In such a climate, religious belief is severely challenged. It may, on occasion, even have to modify its own cognitive assertions. But, by the same token, so long as religious belief itself remains, it, too, presents a challenge to the totalitarian claims of various intellectual disciplines. The necessary and inevitable interaction may prove to be beneficial to all concerned.

W. Gunther Plaut

Senior rabbi at the Holy Blossom Temple (Reform) in Toronto.

℃ (1) In what sense do I believe the Torah to be divine revelation? In no sense and in every sense. The answer is meant to be neither paradoxical nor evasive; it is conditioned by my understanding of the two key expressions "the Torah" and "divine revelation."

Divine revelation is a self-disclosure of God. It requires God as well as man to give it reality, for all revelation is a form of communication. To reveal need not imply speaking-and-hearing—perhaps it never does; it always means the communication of selfness and essence. Divine revelation is God's-accessibility-and-man's-knowing.

To know the Other One is to grasp part of His reality.

It is a knowledge based on greater certainty than that accorded our sensual or logical apprehension. When we "know" a person or a thing or a situation in this sense, we commit not our skill but our selves to this knowledge. We grasp it and are grasped by it. "I know that my Redeemer liveth" expresses such certainty. And to the man who can say this, God has revealed Himself.

Orthodoxy believes that such revelation has, in Torah and Prophets, implied a verbal communication. I do not believe this. I do not believe that man's spiritual reach exceeds the knowledge of God's being and essence. This is what Rosenzweig meant when he said that at Sinai God revealed no words, no commandments, only *Anokhi,* "I am." The rest was, literally, commentary—human commentary, the attempt to translate the apprehension of God's being into the imperatives of human behavior. "God spoke" is a figure of speech, denoting, "This is what I know God wants of me." It is the consequence of revelation, not the revelation itself.

Every communication is conditioned by the way in which the communicants interpret the message. Divine revelation is a direct relationship between man and God; when it is communicated to others and reduced to speech or writing, it becomes interpretation. Torah and Prophets are records of Israel's interpretation of divine encounters.

The plural is used advisedly. Revelation is not a single act but a process, a succession of events culminating in the supreme experience of knowing, which in turn, in the very attempt to prolong the experience and to interpret it, yields to elation-and-agony, certainty-and-doubt. The consequences of revelation are both the healing and the hurt; the concomitant of divine knowing is divine doubt. The possession of things brings in its train the fear of losing; friendship and love carry the potential of painful separation; and thus, when man has heard the divine question, *Ayekka?,* "Where art thou?," he at once, having answered, *Hineni,* "Here I am," feels constrained to ask in turn, *"Where art Thou?"*

Revelation is, by its nature, neither confined to one time, nor to one man, nor, for all I know, to one people. Applied to the relationship of God and Israel, revelation was not limited to Sinai, even if Sinai represents, as I believe it does, not a single place but a series of events. Each generation

stands at Sinai; each generation has the opportunity of "seeing the thunder," as the process of knowing God is so tellingly
called in Exodus.

This understanding of revelation precludes my giving
assent to the proposition that the Torah (i.e., the five Books
of Moses) *is* divine revelation. It is the mirror of God's
presence, but not the presence itself. The mirror is flawed
because it is human; it is recapitulation of the essence but
not the essence itself. This is why I said in the beginning
that the Torah can in no sense be called divine revelation.

Yet not only *the* Torah, but Torah in the wider meaning
(denoting Israel's progressing, ongoing encounter with God)
represents what record we have of our people's spiritual
reach. All of Torah, down to our day, wrestles with confrontation and turning away, with what was and what is,
with reality and potential, with certainty and doubt. While
the Torah *is* in no way revelation, it does *manifest* it in
every way. It is record and failure to record, *mitzvah* understood and misunderstood, God known and God forgotten.

This is, of course, a liberal's approach. It implies the need
for human judgment, my judgment, with its potential and
its limitations. It carries the burden of choice; it speaks of
freedom which must forever guard against the temptation of
convenience. The 613 commandments are my starting point;
I observe what I, listening for the voice, can hear as being
addressed to me. What I hear today is not always what I
heard yesterday, and tomorrow may demand new *mitzvot*,
for I may be capable of new insights, a wider reach.

Time was when *Taryag*, the 613, represented a consensus,
the evolutionary agreement of how the record of revelation
was to be read and interpreted. The mainstream of Judaism ran clear and strong as long as this consensus existed.
Since it ceased, in the wake of Enlightenment and Emancipation, the waters of revelation have rarely broken through
the surface rock of indifference and doubt. Since then, we
have all become searchers for the living waters, each of us
in his own way, each with his own divining rod.

Today, a newly emerging consensus among the non-Orthodox is slowly taking form. It will be some time before it
becomes clearly discernible. When that time comes, the people as a whole who have hidden themselves from God may

once again, together with their traditional brethren who have guarded the old way, bear witness to the incursion of the divine into the realm of Israel. Until then, I listen to and take counsel with those who, liberals like myself, strain to be what they must be as Jews, and I seek their guidance. This joint and yet individual hearing, weak as it may be, is my only channel of understanding. There is none other, at least not for me.

(2) Having devoted an entire book to the subject of chosenness I will touch on only a few relevant aspects.

I affirm chosenness, albeit in a special sense. I know little about the *content* of chosenness, except that it cannot—any more than the content of any other relationship—be static. The burden at Sinai differed from that of the prophets; Israel in Babylon had a task different from that it faced in Auschwitz. The world is not what it was, despite Koheleth's assertion to the contrary. In facing our world we meet challenges indigenous to our age. It is the task of each generation to search for the meaning of its chosenness, the "perhaps" of its existence.

The use (and misuse) to which choice and chosenness have been put is of historic and political interest only. From a theological viewpoint it is irrelevant. In any case, *atta v'hartanu* has nothing to do with superiority, even if Jews and non-Jews have at times so construed it. And despite Toynbee's vocal asseveration, the sins of chauvinism and racism were not fathered by the Jew.

Chosenness does not imply limited access to God; there are many ways of serving Him. Nor is Israel by definition a limited people. It is so by dint of history and circumstance. Israel's unique way of serving God is open to all who would join in.

(3) Is Judaism the one true religion? A strong strain in our tradition answers this question in the affirmative, despite the oft-quoted meliorating dictum that "the righteous of all nations have a share in the world-to-come." Agreeing for a moment that Judaism can be classified properly as a "religion," and holding subsequent thereto that it is *a* true religion—i.e., a true way of serving God—I cannot believe that

it is the only way of serving Him. For the Jew it is; for him the covenant provides the framework of his divine and human relationships. For those outside of the *b'rith* there are many other opportunities.

What distinctive contribution can Judaism make to the world? Itself. The Jewish way of serving God is not the only way; it is, for humanity's sake, an *essential* way. The presence of the Jew and his tradition, his mood, his stance, his special accent on life—all these have a pivotal role in the society of men. The believing Jew sees himself as a child of the covenant and hence always *sub specie aeternitatis*. That he does so both as an individual and as a member of a people gives his striving a unique dimension. The believing Jew is always engaged in the salvation of the world rather than of his own soul; in doing so he pursues *mitzvot* rather than proclaiming a system of thought.

(4) All religion, it has been said, begins with mysticism and ends in politics. At this late date one need hardly affirm that Judaism is deeply concerned with the condition of the *polis*. Consequently, Judaism has something to say on all political matters which involve moral judgments.

The Jew, like everyone else, ought to make his decisions out of the moral imperatives that govern his life. I act on the basis of Judaism, as I understand it. For me, a particular political viewpoint is in most cases a particular moral viewpoint backed (for often less than moral reasons) by a political party or personage. Judaism, being the foundation of my moral existence, urges me to a certain position—but it is not an abstract "Jewish imperative," it is *my* imperative based on *my* understanding of what Judaism demands of me. There are many who read the divine script differently, but that may be my error, not theirs.

Could then a "good Jew" (I am not sure what this means) be a Communist or a Fascist? No, if such political conviction endorses the policy of preventing a man from fulfilling his potential; if, for instance, it means to make it impossible for a Jew to live as a Jew; or if the Communist or Fascist state declares the striving after God to be an antisocial pursuit. No, if being a Fascist or Communist means favoring the abridgment of human rights in any form; if the interests of the community by definition and practice submerge the liberties of the individual.

Yes, if Communism could denote, as it does for some, merely economic or political ideas which deal with the ownership and distribution of wealth and its administration. Such separation of theory from practice is hard to maintain nowadays, which makes the Yes rather theoretical, if not academic. As for Fascism, I am unaware of any acceptable description of its system which does not contain approval of violence as a means of obtaining and maintaining power, and of justice supine before the state.

(5) "God is dead": Any discussion involving man's idea of and relation to God has relevance for me. There were and are many to whom God was dead at Auschwitz; there are many today who, while they consider themselves to be Jews, yet cannot bring themselves to affirm the God of Judaism. No rabbi I know deals lightly with this contemporary dilemma. Nor is it the first time Jews have faced it.

Haskalah and post-Haskalah wrestled with it and so already did the talmudic sage who had God say of Israel: "Would that they had forsaken Me but had kept My commandments!" There is a strong implication here that Israel, as long as the *mitzvot* are recognized and kept, could conceivably get along without God. The separation of God from man has been repeatedly contemplated as a divine (and human!) possibility.

The Jew, of course, was never caught in the narrow confines of a triune affirmation. He had a hundred different terms for God, fitting every mood and every divine aspect, and in a way also fitting most philosophies. God was Father, Friend, Husband. As "Master of the Universe" He might seem far removed from man, yet He was ever so close to him in the equivalent Hebrew appellation, *Ribbono shel olam.* He was King of the Kings of Kings, and He was also *Du;* He was and is Presence, Place of the World, God of the Fathers and, always, God of Israel.

I suspect that the "God is dead" philosophers face a primarily Christian problem. For the Jew, God, Israel, and Torah are one, hence the absence or denial of God undermines also one's existence as a Jew. Theology and peoplehood dwell close together in Jewish life, while the *mitzvah-*directed, this-worldly orientation of Judaism gives all matters of belief and faith a less than central position. Jews have been occupied for a long time with the problem of survival. The time has not yet come when this preoccupation appears antiquarian.

The most serious challenge to Jewish belief is neither this particular constellation of thought nor philosophy and science as disciplines. It is, rather, *scientism*, the elevation of science to the position of arbiter of all human enterprises, the yardstick of thought and action. In this conflict with scientism, Judaism can have the devoted assistance of men in universities who themselves are scientists and yet are rigorously opposed to all dogmatic asseverations, scientific or religious. Scientism has become the pied piper of our younger generation whose hearts and minds we stand in danger of losing unless we can learn to speak to them with words and concepts they can understand, and face them with human tasks to which they can wholly give themselves.

Chaim Potok

*Editor of the Jewish Publication Society
of America.*

℄ Every theological endeavor is in essence a personal response to privately experienced tensions. Theology has its origins in the anguish that is felt when one's commitment to a particular religious model of reality is confronted by new knowledge and experiential data that threaten the root assumptions of the mode. Thus it is the problems that are of paramount importance, for the problems generate and determine the nature of the tensions and become elemental strands of the fabric that forms the ultimate response. Further, the fruitfulness of a theological response is often a function of the extent to which the initial problems reflect the general tenor of one's own age; a twentieth-century theologian preoccupied with eighteenth-century problems speaks only to ghosts of the past.

Until my late teens my religious model of the universe

was essentially formed of a fundamentalist view of Judaism. As new knowledge began to accumulate along the periphery of the model—knowledge born of my encounter with the sciences and symbolic logic—I found myself confronted with the choice of having to alter some of the basic assumptions of the model, or of rejection the new knowledge out of hand, thereby sealing off the model. For a variety of reasons, I chose the former course—and the model disintegrated. My Judaism hung in the balance for a long, anguished year, until in the end I made another choice. I chose to retain my Jewish pattern of behavior and at the same time to live suspended in a theological void until such time as I could construct another religious model—and, motivated by an intense intellectual curiosity and by what I now believe was a real love for my people, I chose to make that effort from *within* Judaism. I wanted very much to understand the dynamics of Judaism, its shades and tones, its inner texture, the warp and woof of its commingling of principles, ideas, and institutions. I gambled that once I had achieved that understanding I would be able to construct another model. There was no guarantee of success. There was only the commitment to make the attempt.

The problems that troubled me then have been resolved by the very disciplines—modern historiography and the scientific approach to the sacred texts of Judaism—which others regard as an open threat to religion. These disciplines are not an issue as far as I am concerned. They are the spectacles through which I study Jewish sources. They give the sources a form, a focus, a vitality which is impossible within a fundamentalist stance. They have made Judaism come alive for me, so that I can see it now from the inside outward.

Two things have resulted from this method of study. First, I have come to understand the unusual degree of sophistication that has gone into the shaping of Jewish source material and to realize that what best characterizes these sources is their almost obsessive preoccupation with the problem of meaning and structure. Secondly, I have come to reject completely any attempt to splinter the universe into separate domains of religion and science. I see only one world, one organic interweaving of the totality of the human experience, each element of which acts upon and reacts to every other element. Further, the theoretical scientist is as much governed by attitudinal commitments as he is by the laboratory experiments that test his constructs. And my attitudinal commitments, the commitments which form the essential fiber of my being and through which I structure reality, are as much affected by the findings of the sciences as they are by a new understanding of the nature of God. To splinter the world is to engage in twentieth-century Zoroastrianism.

As a result of all this, there has come a decision on my part to forge a religious life out of what I call provisional absolutes. There is a tendency among some of the more advanced logicians today to view even the most hallowed of logical principles as potentially alterable in the face of impinging data. Though one's attitudinal existence is not altogether comparable to a system of logic, the analogy is not without significance—for I find it impossible to live an intellectually viable existence without at the same time accepting the working premise that I must constantly be prepared to alter my basic religious assumptions should the need arise. This constitutes for me an open-minded way of living along the frontiers of knowledge, where both the theologian and the scientist stumble together in the darkness, each committed to a given set of premises, each aware of the provisional nature of his absolutes, each eager for new knowledge even though the price paid for its acquisition might be the alteration or the abandonment of his absolutes. This is not the place to explain how one can be *totally* committed to *provisional* absolutes, for that would take us into a complex discussion concerning the nature of commitment. My answers to the questions, however, might give some indication as to how this can be accomplished.

(1) The assertion that historical events or a body of doctrine are somehow linked to an ultimate ontological cause is an expression of the essential nature of the endless human attempt to find unity and meaning in the raw data of experience. Nothing is more typical of the collective Jewish mind, heart, and soul than the preoccupation with this endless search.

Biblical and talmudic sources differ as to the precise

nature of the events at Sinai. But the common denominator of these sources lends credence to the view that what they confront us with is a picture of a people voluntarily committing itself to a then unique and value-charged model of reality. (I say "voluntarily" despite the fact that there is at least one talmudic source that indicates the contrary; it is, to my mind, an atypical view.) The commitment was renewed a number of times in subsequent generations. The only record we have of the first of these collective commitments is given to us in terms of the revelation at Sinai. There the Israelites felt that they had inextricably linked themselves and their way of life to God.

The Israelite model of reality developed out of the collective experience of the people. It had its origins some time in the misty, pre-desert-experience past, achieved a singular coherence under the leadership of Moses, and underwent further development during the period of the First and Second Commonwealths. It had sufficient latitude to permit a wide divergence of opinion insofar as its detailed theological and legalistic interpretations were concerned. The theology of the priests was not that of the prophets; the theology of the author of *Koheleth* (Ecclesiastes) was not that of the author of Job; and there are legalistic differences even within the Bible itself, together with a nebulousness as to the precise details involved in the actual working out of ritual prescriptions. These differences achieved a rich and fully orchestrated quality during the period of the Talmud, when a complex variety of conflicting interpretations and traditions were able to coexist with a rather remarkable degree of harmony. This kind of coexistence, operating from a base of intelligence and commitment, I take to be the essential characteristic of a living and creative Jewish tradition.

All these differences of interpretation, however, have two characteristics in common: the commitment to a value-charged universe that is intrinsically meaningful, and the assumed need for a pattern of significant activity that can concretize this commitment and infuse it into the everyday activities of man. From this I draw the inevitable conclusion that mechanical religious acts go against the grain of Judaism, and commitments to meanings that are not translated into acts are essentially futile.

A ritual act which is not charged with meaning, which does not qualitatively enhance my existence, is drained of value and cannot become part of my acting-out pattern of religious behavior. This refers to *all* ritual, not only to the prohibition against clothing made of linen and wool. The criterion of selectivity is my own inner being, my own awareness of the fundamental principles underlying Jewish law, but the selection is always made—and this is a vital point—from a base of knowledge and not out of ignorance or for reasons of personal convenience. Further, each separate act is embedded in its own separate contextual situation and involves a separate act of thinking. It is often an exhausting procedure, but the rewards seem infinite when real contact is made between value and act. It is the only way I know to live.

My claim that intrinsic meaning and the acting-out of this meaning are fundamental to Judaism is in the nature of a provisional absolute. If for some reason I ever became convinced that it was untrue, it would be discarded and the entire structure of my religious thinking would be subjected to alteration.

(2) As a quasi-empirical inductive hypothesis with a rather limited range of probability, the notion of chosenness might be used to account for the perplexing question of the continued existence and vitality of the Jewish people. We choose to be chosen by linking our lives to the history and destiny of our people. Each generation must make its own commitment based upon whatever it finds in Judaism. We continue to exist only by virtue of these renewed commitments. And we do not choose to be racially superior—a notion that would have been absurd to the prophets and the rabbis of the Talmud had they ever conceived of it. We choose to be the bearers of a tradition which we feel enhances human existence. It is an assumption of responsibility, not superiority. That the notion of chosenness may have been the basis for various theories of national and racial superiority indicates to me nothing more than that all

ideas are potentially corruptible when taken up by small minds. That does not mean that those with great minds should cease thinking.

(3) Judaism is one configuration of thought and action. There are many others. Judaism is the responsibility of the Jew. As such, it makes no claim to being the only source of salvation for the world. Its sole criterion for the worth of one who is not Jewish is whether or not he observes the universally applicable Noahide Code. Such observance, in the talmudic terminology of approbation, makes the non-Jew worthy of the world-to-come. Some of the rabbis of the Talmud went even further: a moral non-Jew is more worthy in the eyes of God than a sinful high priest.

Those Jews who are not fearful of coping with realities still have a great deal to say from a position within Judaism to a twentieth-century world that is grappling with the problems of meaning and meaningful behavior. It may well be that much of twentieth-century humanism has caught up to the basic values of Judaism. I am not fearful of that development; I embrace it—and make my commitment to join in the attempt to forge *new* Jewish ideas. I am as much a part of the future of my people as I am of its past.

What is universal to all men is held in common by all religions. Buddha, too, enjoined his followers to love their neighbors. But the behavior patterns which embody ideas and the subordinate ideas which flow from the universal ones are essentially particularistic and the result of a complex conjunction of forces and events. The richness and complexity that characterize the totality of human culture constitute the greatest gift each generation gives to its youth. Any idea that enhances my being is openly accepted. My criterion for enhancement is the totality of what I am at the moment of contact; one knows soon enough whether or not a new idea will be a grain of sand or a flood of light. But I very much want Judaism to remain a vital element in the pool of human culture because of what I take to be its intrinsic worth. In the end I am a Jew, and it is as a Jew that I choose to serve the world.

(4) In the rabbinic tradition, the purpose of government is to maintain harmony, keep the peace, administer justice, and

thereby restrict man's aggressive nature. The yardstick for the evaluation of a government is ethical, not political. The essential criterion is its degree of conformity to certain basic ethical principles. There is no commitment to a specific political-economic governmental structure. A government is a good government if its people regard it with respect and if it acts in behalf of the people with care and concern and with a consciousness of their needs and welfare. Further, it must not be forced upon the people but brought into existence at the request of the people. Finally, its leadership must be subject to the same laws as the people. A Fascist government would have been an abomination in the eyes of the rabbis of the Talmud. Communist governments do not seem to follow a single pattern and each would have to be separately investigated in the light of the above criteria. But Communism's general commitment to materialism and to an economic dialectic of history would have repelled the rabbis.

(5) I regard Nietzsche's assertion that God is dead as having been more in the nature of an anguished empirical observation than a peremptory, categorical statement. In his contacts with human beings Nietzsche saw that man's basic day-to-day decision-making apparatus was in no way related to his worship of a living God. To assert God and to conduct one's life without Him is for all intents and purposes to make the claim that God is dead. For Nietzsche, the term "God" in the proposition "God is dead" was meant to designate intrinsic meaning.

Now, if by the term "God" in the proposition "God is dead" present-day theologians mean to designate an anthropomorphic diety, an old man with a long, white beard who dwells in some distant heaven, then this statement has little relevance to Judaism, for the essential vitality of Judaism is not dependent upon such a notion of God. If, however, they mean that the universe is in its very essence *totally* blind and meaningless, then their assertion has considerable relevance. For it is the problem of meaning that constitutes the root problem of our age. Out of the nineteenth-century came man's awareness of his model-making activity. For the first time we were able to achieve a kind of overview of the way we structure reality. The result of this knowledge was the casting out of man from his Eden of absolutes. Thus we are at grips today with an ultimate ontological problem: Is meaning real and intrinsic or fictitious and extrinsic? There does not seem to be any way at present of resolving this problem, for we are not dealing here with facts but with attitudes. Judaism, obsessed as it is with the search for meaning, a search that has engaged not only its leaders but its people as well, takes its stand on the side of an ontologically meaningful universe, a qualitatively significant universe charged with value. When the human being can live his life without the trauma of severe stress situations, this seems a plausible enough position to assert. But in moments of chaos, when normalcy disintegrates and man becomes a feather tossed about in seemingly blind storms, the mind collapses. Man then faces a choice. He can extend the pockets of meaninglessness to the universe at large and claim that all existence is absurd, or he can by dint of his own efforts engage in a search for meaning and seek to find some significance in seeming meaninglessness. Judaism makes the second choice.

The assertion of emptiness, blindness, essential meaninglessness as an inherent characteristic of the totality of things seems to me to be an inadequate response—for there is after all much around us that has apparent meaning. I would rather live in what I take to be a meaningful world and be staggered by moments of apparent absurdity than in an absurd world and be troubled by instances of meaning. I would rather try to discover some light in the patches of darkness than extend the darkness to wherever there is now light.

The notion that the universe is intrinsically meaningful is, for me, a provisional absolute. At the present stage of my thinking I am thoroughly committed to that absolute. Were this commitment ever to be shaken, the entire structure of my thought would have to be reshaped and my pattern of religious acting-out might well undergo alteration. For I am also committed to the notion that theology and behavior must be organically related. A theology that is not linked directly to a pattern of behavior is a blowing of wind and a macabre game with words. And a pattern of behavior that is not linked to a system of thought is an instance of religious robotry.

This is *my* personal response to *my* privately experienced tensions.

Emanuel Rackman

Rabbi of Congregation Shaaray Tefila (Orthodox)
in Far Rockaway, New York.

℃ (1) Perhaps, like Socrates, I corrupt youth but I do teach that Judaism encourages doubt even as it enjoins faith and commitment. A Jew dare not live with absolute certainty, not only because certainty is the hallmark of the fanatic and Judaism abhors fanaticism, but also because doubt is good for the human soul, its humility, and consequently its greater potential ultimately to discover its Creator.

This point the Bible conveys—according to Maimonides— when it tells of God's refusal to let Moses see anything but His back. God's back, needless to say, is not physical, nor can it be, without violent distortion of the meanings of words, God's negative attributes or the effects of His being rather than His essence as cause. It signifies, rather, the absence of face-to-face encounter. Recognition from the rear does not yield more than a relative amount of certainty and that is the maximum we humans can expect vis-à-vis God. God may have had His own reasons for denying us certainty with regard to His existence and nature. One reason apparent to us is that man's certainty with regard to anything is poison to his soul. Who knows this better than moderns who have had to cope with dogmatic Fascists, Communists, and even scientists?

Yet, though I remain a creature of doubts, I believe not only that God is, but that He revealed His will to man, to Jews and non-Jews alike. My belief is quite different from, let us say, the beliefs of Hobbes and Locke with respect to the social contract. To them it mattered not whether a contract had ever in fact been consummated. What mattered rather was the precise terms of the contract as spelled out from the hypotheses which were basic to their philosophical structures. In my commitment, what matters is the fact that God did actually contact man—patriarchs and prophets—and covenant with them. How He did it will continue to be the subject of both conjecture and interpretation, but that He did it in history is the crucial point for me. As creation is a fact for me, though I cannot describe the how, so is revelation a fact, though its precise manner eludes me.

The most definitive record of God's encounters with man is contained in the Pentateuch. Much of it may have been written by people in different times, but at one point in history God not only made the people of Israel aware of His immediacy but caused Moses to write the eternal evidence of the covenant between Him and His people. Even the rabbis in the Talmud did not agree on the how. But all agreed that the record was divine and they cherished it beyond description, even as they cherished a manner of exegesis which Moses simultaneously transmitted to his colleagues and disciples. In their ongoing relationship with God they sought to fathom the meanings—apparent and concealed—of every word and letter of His revelation. And that quest has not yet ended. Even as He willed that man be His partner in the conquest of the earth, so He willed that man proclaim His holiness and help history ultimately to vanquish nature. For this purpose the Law was given.

Not all the commandments are applicable to all persons, places, or periods. Nor are all of equal importance. The written and oral traditions provide the norms for their hierarchical evaluation, but each commandment has its purpose, even when its rationale cannot be explicated in purely humanist categories. The least that the least important of them must do is to make the observant conscious of God's will in all that he does—even in such trivial affairs as buying a garment or having a haircut. In interpersonal and communal relationships, the Law is even utilitarian in emphasis, and where God and man's perfectability are concerned, the teleology is unmistakable. Even its deontological character serves the teleology.

The Jew who has not made the Law the principal preoccupation of his life may not be able to make his own decisions with regard to it. On some matters everyone must sub-

mit to authority lest anarchy be the state of the Jewish community, and the people qua people fail to fulfill their mission.
Thus, for example, it is imperative in connection with the
fixing of the calendar that the will of the Sanhedrin be
imposed on dissenters. On most matters, however, the Jew
who has mastered the Law can engage in the quest himself.
He must be honest with God and himself and seek to ascer-
tain God's will, not his own. That is why consultation with
others is a desideratum. But Moses prayed that the entire
congregation might consist of prophets. In periods of overwhelming Jewish illiteracy—as when the Hasidic movement
emerged and today—there was and is an undue amount of
unquestioning reliance upon *"Rebbes"* or so-called *Gedolim*
(great men). I regard this phenomenon as unfortunate.
When Jews become more knowledgeable in their Jewishness,
I hope they will recapture in their personal lives a great
amount of autonomy, interpreting and applying cherished
source materials even as they continue to rely on centralized
authority in most matters affecting persons other than themselves.

(2) My belief that God chose Abraham and his seed for
the covenant is no warrant for any feeling of superiority
over my fellow men. Abraham, according to the record, was
selected because God recognized him to be one who would
transmit to his posterity a sense of mission with regard to
justice and righteousness. His seed had only the merit of the
fathers—especially Abraham's. In Abraham's case, the merit
was not that of Terah. Certainly neither Moses in Deuteron-
omy nor the prophets anywhere were enamored of Israel's
virtue. Yet my existence has been ennobled because of the
mission I have inherited and which I seek to fulfill. I cannot impose it on anyone other than my children—but anyone who wants to share it is free to do so. Even as a Jew, I
cannot volunteer to share the burden of the priests—I cannot
volunteer for their special role. My burden is heavy enough
and I fall short of its accomplishment. Therefore, I will not
attempt to persuade non-Jews to join me, but if they seek it,
my burden is available to them in the same measure as it
is to me. Perhaps they should be content to achieve excellence with regard to the seven Noahide laws (which are

actually many more than seven, since one of them covers the entire gamut of what we call "justice"). But I must be the "commando" in God's service and attain holiness vis-à-vis God and man. That various theories of national and racial superiority derive from a Jewish idea troubles me. But I cannot abandon a conviction because of its perversion by others, any more than I would outlaw sex because some men practice sodomy.

(3) The first mandate to Abraham involving his "chosenness" was a command that was paradoxical—to withdraw from his surroundings that he might bless them. This became the model for Jewish existence. It did not necessarily spell exile—one does not have to wander to bless. But it did make for separateness and alienation, at the same time as it prescribed involvement with, and participation in, the world. Oriental religions denied the worth of reality as we know it naturally. The daughter religions of Judaism broke with the mother religion also by denigrating the realm of the material. Judaism sought to sanctify and perfect all of it—men and beasts, matter and energy, time and space.

In that sense alone do I regard Judaism as the only true religion. Truth for me is God's name, His total being. It must address itself to my total being. Much I may never be able to explain, but the explanation exists. It exists in God. And to His will I deliver myself—or at least aspire to deliver myself.

This message is still distinctive. There is not an area of life for which Judaism does not have a distinctive message. But my Judaism provides me with the one integrating approach—I must fathom God's will on every issue. I am, for example, grateful that I have been able to formulate a position for myself regarding antipoverty programs. I wish I had enough knowledge of the facts to formulate a position on the war in Vietnam and the threat of Red China. All through life I find myself knowing the right at times, but just as often I suffer travail and doubt. That is the human situation with which I must make my peace.

I have no argument with anyone who does not share my religious commitment. I argue only with those whose ideas or deeds are a threat to the messianic vision and the this-worldly *olam haba* which is the end toward which creation moves. The secular humanist is not my enemy. The Birch Society is. So is the Buddhist who will affirm the meaninglessness of life or history. So is the Christian who will induce inordinate feelings of guilt with regard to the natural. So is the Moslem who glorifies war. But none is my enemy as a person. I must resist such of their views as I find objectionable to my commitment. Yet I welcome their challenge. My Judaism only becomes richer as I encounter challenges from other cultures.

(4) During the Jews' millennial history, their encounters with various political, economic, or social systems have usually evoked a tendency to seek in their tradition some validation of the particular establishment encountered. Thus, American Jews in the South justified the institution of Negro slavery by resort to biblical texts even as modern Jews find warrant for capitalism and socialism in the same sources. I think it incorrect to identify my heritage with any one viewpoint. My faith institutes rather a certain way of beholding and appraising all institutions in the light of God's will for man. No one system is divinely ordained—the one that was divinely ordained was never implemented and perhaps never could be. Like Plato's Republic, it only furnishes me with ideas and criteria by which to judge. Therefore, racial segregation is unthinkable for me as a Jew. It runs counter to my basic norm—the equality of all men created in the divine image. Similarly, a good Jew cannot be a Fascist. Yet, my Judaism tolerates and even stimulates the most extensive experimentation with sundry economic programs. Vested interests in property play a very minor role, for only God has divinity—not the owners of goods.

(5) When I fail to view a situation as I believe God would want it viewed, or when I fail to act as He would want me to act, He is dead for me. In this sense the question which is agitating Christian theologians has validity for me. However, much of their discussion is, I suspect, meant to make Jesus, rather than God, central to the Christian's commitment and behavior. The humanism to which they aspire may be noble. But if Jesus is deified as a son of God,

I rebel against the notion that any creature can replace the Creator. And if Jesus is a man beyond whom there is naught, than I cannot let any man be for me the measure of all things. Here I agree with Emil Fackenheim that man as the exclusive source of right and wrong is self-destructive. At the same time, my stature as a man is only enhanced, and my existence ennobled, because God willed both that I live and how I live. Yet it is precisely from the humanism which Judaism encourages that there emerges the greatest challenges to Jewish belief and behavior. As a Jew I must know the world in which I live, for I am God's partner in furthering the process of creation. Man, too, is a part of nature. Thus social and behavioral science as well as natural science must be my concern. And since God is One and all creation is His, I must synthesize all of this with my religious outlook. Can I combine the subjectivity of my faith with methodologies that are objective? Can my mind function with fixed ideas on the one hand, and, on the other, with an openness that makes for an unrelenting relativism? Even when I can achieve this for myself after years of anguish and travail, can I develop the educational techniques to transmit this to the young who I hope will share the same commitment? And when my commitment involves so much autonomy of the soul, can I join with others in the creation of institutional apparati that by their very nature make for less autonomy? Yet without such institutionalization I cannot conserve and transmit the heritage and hope for fulfillment of the mission.

Perhaps these are also the problems of all freedom-loving peoples. As a Jew, I have them too—only more so.

Max J. Routtenberg

*Rabbi of Temple Bnai Sholom (Conservative)
on Long Island, New York.*

❲ Milton Steinberg, in *Basic Judaism*, divided religious communicants into two broad categories, the traditionalists and the modernists. Both approach the Jewish religion with reverence, accept its broad postulates concerning God, the universe, man's relationship to God and the universe, and man's relationship to man. They differ, however, in their understanding and interpretation of the basic concepts and institutions of Judaism as formulated in the official literature. The traditionalists generally adopt a literalist approach to the heritage as it has been transmitted and accept only such changes in interpretation and such modifications of practice as are projected by teachers who are themselves traditionalist and whose authority is on the whole unquestioned by them. The modernists, examining the literature in its historic context, approach it with a critical eye. Armed with the insights and findings of various disciplines, they permit themselves much greater freedom of interpretation, and are given to reevaluation and reformulation of the doctrines and practices of the heritage. For purposes of identification, the author classes himself as a modernist, with a marked predisposition to strengthen and validate the major thrusts of the tradition in its historic development.

(1) Revelation, in its simplest terms, means God's direct communication with man. This communication may take place in a dream, a vision, a trance, or even in a waking state. Traditionally, it involved the use of words by God which the receiver heard, understood, and then recorded or repeated to others. It is in this sense that God revealed Himself to Israel at Sinai, speaking the words which are recorded as the Ten Commandments, and revealed Himself privately to Moses to whom He dictated the Torah.

I do not subscribe to this view of revelation. I do not believe that God makes His will known to man verbally, though I am sure that men have believed they were hearing God's voice and have imagined they were hearing His verbal communication. Nevertheless, I cannot abandon the use of the term "revelation." It is part of the vocabulary of religion. It is an indispensable tool for religious pedagogy; it is a link with all religionists who, through the ages, have regarded revelation as a central, crucial article of faith. It is the familiar and secure word which reinforces loyalty to the religious heritage.

It is necessary, therefore, for a modernist like myself to

reinterpret the term "revelation" to correspond with his belief as to how God does communicate with man. For those who regard God, as I do, as the sum total of those forces in the universe which make for goodness, for truth, and for beauty, any and every manifestation of these qualities is a revelation of God. When man becomes aware, as he frequently does, sometimes even in a blinding flash, of what "the Lord doth require of him" and it becomes consuming fire in his bones so that he must do something about it, he has received a communication from God. Man himself may verbalize this intuition and ascribe it to God, but it is divine inspiration nevertheless. Every impulse to goodness, every quest for truth, every search for beauty is a communication from God; every deed of goodness, every discovery of truth, every expression of beauty is a fulfillment of God's commandments.

Viewed in this light, the 613 commandments of the Torah do not have the same compelling force for the modernist as they have for the traditionalist who regards the Torah literally as "the word of God." The modernist must, of necessity, be selective. The commandments must be for him, as they were for his forebears, the instruments through which he achieves a heightened awareness of the divine imperative in his life. They must be related, in some way, to his desire and will to achieve goodness, truth, and beauty as he understands them. He will, therefore, give special weight to those commandments which have the power to stir these impulses within him. Those ethical commandments which have universal applicability and enduring relevance will be given the highest priority in his system of values. Ritual observances will be judged in terms of both their present worth and their powers of evoking historic associations. He will want to retain those rituals which induce a sensitivity to the ethical dimensions of human life, a deep mood of reverence for life, and a sense of the mystery of the created universe. He will find meaning in those religious rites which provide him with a sense of oneness with Jews of all times and of all places; which link him to great events and great personalities in history, to their sacrifices and to their aspirations. On the other hand he will reject, or permit to fall into obsolescence, those commandments in which he cannot discern any divine purpose, or which have become totally irrelevant to his religious quest. God no longer speaks to him through these commandments and he cannot respond. He may well replace them with new rites and rituals which are in harmony with his spiritual needs.

(2) For the traditionalist, the doctrine of the chosen people is a religious concept grounded in historic fact. It is not something which can be accepted or rejected at will. The Jews entered into a covenant with God, one of the terms of which was that Israel was to be His chosen people. The modernist, while he may question the literal account as recorded in Scripture, does not doubt for a moment that Jews have always believed themselves to be so chosen and have regarded this as the *raison d'être* of their existence. It is for this that they came into being as a separate people.

Does this concept still have meaning and validity in our day? It may, at one time, have implied that the Jews were a superior people, that they were God's darlings, and enjoyed special favors and privileges. It may have meant this to our people in their long, historic agony, serving as a soothing balm to their crushed and wounded spirits. But in their best moments and in the highest reaches of their understanding, the idea of chosenness meant special responsibility, mission, vocation. We find this in prophetic teaching where Israel is said to have been chosen to be "a light unto the nations," to be "God's witnesses," to help establish His sovereignty over all the earth. To be sure, it was a privilege to be so selected, but it imposed a heavy burden. Other peoples could defy the commandments of God and not be held accountable. Not so Israel; Israel would have to pay heavily for any violations because it had accepted God's mandate. I believe we find this idea further developed in a daring *midrash*. The rabbis picture God approaching all the nations of the earth with His Torah, seeking to make a covenant with any one of them; but all refused. Only Israel declared its readiness to accept the Torah and to assume the responsibility and burden of the covenant. Are not the rabbis saying that God did not choose one special people, but that one people chose God, chose to dedicate itself to a special vocation? Israel was not chosen, it was a volunteer in the service of God.

It is this view of chosenness as responsibility which has compelling validity for Jews today. To excise this concept from the body of Jewish thought and belief is, literally, to perform a surgical operation on a vital organ. Jews simply cannot be content with mere existence for its own sake. The view that every existence is self-justifying runs contrary to the whole thrust of the Jewish experience. The Jews are a people with a purpose, with a mission "to fashion the world as the Kingdom of the Almighty." The fact is that every nation which has some degree of self-consciousness seeks to formulate some "national purpose" both to rationalize its existence and to give its collective life content and direction. I would regard all nations with a formulated purpose as "chosen," provided the various national purposes are "for the sake of Heaven."

Obviously, there can be, as we so tragically know, nations with evil purposes which are recognized as evil by their contemporaries or by the judgment of history. They, too, have regarded themselves as "chosen," as performing a special mission for mankind, and have wreaked untold havoc in human society. This, however, does not invalidate the idea of chosenness; it represents its corruption. It is the task of men in every age to combat the evils which emerge from the distortion of useful ideas, not to discard the ideas. It is clear that when a people is wedded to noble purposes, its whole moral, social, political, economic life is raised to lofty levels and redeemed from mere automatic existence. When a nation has lost sight of its purposes, when it is no longer informed by them, or when it has betrayed them, it ceases to be "chosen." The Jewish people have had some bad moments in their history when it appeared that God had rejected Israel—wnen, by their own testimony, they had betrayed the covenant, had abandoned their vocation, had ceased to carry out their national purpose. But by and large, the Jewish people have remained faithful to their historic mission, have never repudiated the covenant, and have even accepted the role of "suffering servant" as one of the elements of their chosenness. It is the task of Jewish teachers to refine and

purify this grand concept of national purpose, and to summon the Jewish people to be its exemplar in the diaspora and
in the land of Israel.

(3) Judaism is a religion of truth. In the words of a
medieval prayer, "He is a God of truth; His Torah is truth;
His prophets are prophets of truth; He aboundeth in deeds
of goodness and truth." But God, in the classical Jewish
view, did not speak to Israel or to Israel's prophets alone.
To the degree that He communicated with other peoples and
prophets, Judaism is not in exclusive possession of the truth.
God's truths are, by definition, universal in nature and hence
accessible and available to all peoples of all faiths. Judaism is
a true religion because it is rooted in God's truth. It is not,
however, the one true religion in the sense that no other
religion possesses God's truth.

In the modernist view, God's revelation of His truth is
an ongoing, developing process, dependent upon man's
capacity, awareness, and zeal for uncovering and understanding His truth. This varies from age to age and from
people to people. Some periods in history have been more
"religious" than others and have produced brilliant dis-
coverers of God's truth, while other ages have been static
and sterile. Some peoples have displayed a greater aptitude
for religion than others, have been more preoccupied than
most with the religious quest, and have consequently discovered a greater portion of God's truth than their neighbors.
In this sense, I believe that Judaism has approximated the
truth of religion more than any other religious system. For
the Jews, religion has been their main business, their grand
obsession. They have produced a remarkable number of
religious geniuses who have spread God's truth to the four
corners of the earth and have supplied the great religions of
mankind with fundamental teachings. Surely they qualify as
experts in the field of religion and their discoveries must be
taken seriously by all earnest seekers after the truth. There
are, of course, religious truths discovered by other religions
which can change or modify some of the views held by Jews.
Until the present age, there has been very little opportunity
for fruitful interchange of religious ideas among the various
faiths. Whatever exchange has existed has been largely

polemical in nature. Today there is a much greater disposition to engage in religious dialogue, in a spirit of inquiry and honest search, which should once and for all dispel any notions of "one true religion" and help create a kind of symphony of religious beliefs which, in their harmonious totality, express God's truth.

In this symphony, each religion will sound its distinctive note. Judaism will contribute not only its unique system of rituals and ceremonies, its *sancta*, but its peculiar view of religion as embracing the totality of life and its special technique of transmitting religion through law. To make religion a matter of legal procedure; to regulate the ethical life according to legal norms and procedures; to turn every "ought" into a "must" through the application of legal sanctions—all this constitutes one of the great and unique insights of Judaism. Thus, there is no distinction between civil and religious law in Judaism. It is as much a religious duty to pay the laborer his hire as it is a civil ordinance; and it is not simply a religious duty to observe the Sabbath, it is also a civil requirement. It may seem strange to apply the canons of law to the ethical life, but it has worked in Jewish life and has succeeded in translating vague and nebulous ideals into concrete and specific patterns of conduct.

(4) It is generally believed that Judaism can, as history may indicate, flourish under any system of government. Its life depends not so much upon the particular form of government under which it finds itself, as upon the manner in which a government treats its political and religious minorities. Thus, in the ancient Roman Empire, there were emperors who were "good for the Jews" and those who were bad for them. Under Moslem and Christian rulers, the determining factor for the welfare of the Jews was not the "system" but the ruler. In Fascist Italy, prior to the days of the Rome-Berlin axis, Jews enjoyed complete freedom in the exercise of their religious life and many of them were, no doubt, loyal Fascists.

We must, however, make a distinction between the kinds of Judaism we are talking about. When we think of Judaism purely in its religioritualistic aspect, then it is probably true that a Jew can support almost any kind of political system; he can be a monarchist, a Fascist, a Communist, so long as he is given the freedom to practice his religious rites in accordance with his conscience. But there is another aspect of Judaism—to many of us the crucial one—which is religio-moral-social in nature and which envisions a certain type of ideal society that man must fashion. It is a society in which not only religious freedom is provided, but where political, economic, and social freedom is equally guaranteed. It must be a society in which the state exists for the welfare of the individual, not the individual for the state. It is a society in which freedom is guaranteed to all its inhabitants and where no discrimination is tolerated against any minority group. From this point of view, it is not possible to fulfill one's religious obligations in a totalitarian state, or in any other kind of political system in which the individual is made subservient to its welfare. Conversely, it should be noted that in a democratic state like Israel it is not possible for a Jew to fulfill his total religious commitments according to the dictates of his conscience. There, he enjoys full freedom to express himself in the religio-moral-social aspect of Judaism, but he is denied the freedom to practice the religioritualistic aspects of Judaism which correspond to his views and beliefs. One can lead a full religious life only in a system where both freedoms obtain.

(5) Judaism is a theistic religion and finds no place for any system of belief which says that there is no God, or that God is dead. It has dealt, and is still dealing, with different views of the God-idea. It reckons with various levels of belief in God, from the childish to the most sophisticated, and has been, at its best, hospitable to all of them. Every religious system in Judaism, from Philo to Mordecai Kaplan, has included the belief in God as a living force in the universe. There are Jews who do not believe in God, but they do not claim to be religious Jews. They accept the fact that there can be no religion without the concept of God at its center, unless we change the meaning of religion so that it is exactly the opposite of what, by general consensus, it has always meant. There simply cannot be any religious dialogue

without the tacit assumption that the participants have a center of orientation which they call,. God, whatever their particular view of God may be.

The challenge to Judaism comes neither from atheists nor from "God is dead" theologians. It comes from the ethical humanists. They are nontheistic but they subscribe to many of the same values as religionists, especially those of us who regard the core and essence of Judaism to lie in its ethical tradition. The fact is that ethical humanism has approximated, without religious ritual and without a belief in God, the deepest and noblest insights of Judaism. Why, then, the ritual, why the belief in God? Briefly, the religious answer is based on the belief that man is too fragile a reed to serve as his own sanction, as the authority and justifier of the ethical life. There are times when man is weak, when he is uncertain, when his own springs of idealism have run dry. The religionist is, at all times, sustained and nourished by the conviction that he is performing God's will. When he is in doubt, uncertain, confused, he turns to those whose task it is to reinforce his spirit by interpreting the word of God to him. It goes without saying that the religionist can have no quarrel with those whose lives are patterned on great moral principles and whose deeds are deeds of goodness and truth. For himself, he prefers to anchor his life in the great traditions of his religious heritage and to spin the web of his life with the filaments woven by the Divine Weaver.

Richard L. Rubenstein

Director of the B'nai B'rith Hillel Foundation and chaplain to Jewish students at the University of Pittsburgh.

❧ (1) I believe the entire Torah to be sacred but not divinely revealed. It is the authoritative document out of which the inherited corpus of Jewish religious myth and ritual is ultimately derived. I find it impossible to accept any literal conception of divine revelation. I do not believe that a divine-human encounter took place at Sinai, nor do I believe that the norms of Jewish religious life possess any superordinate validation.

Nevertheless, I do not regard the tradition of divine revelation as meaningless. It has psychological truth rather than literal historical truth. Something happened at Sinai and in the experience of the Jewish people. Somehow the Jewish people structured their personal and group norms by objectifying the parental image, projecting it into the cosmic sphere, and interpreting these norms as deriving from the objectified group-parent. I believe religion to be the way we share the decisive times and crises of life through the inherited experiences and norms of our community. The Torah is the repository of those norms. Because of its origins in the psychological strivings of the Jewish people, it is largely appropriate to its function.

All 613 commandments are equally binding, but our existential situation is one of total freedom to accept or reject any or all of them. There is no agency, human or divine, which can compel our response. I suspect that, in our times, the response to a large proportion of the commandments will be negative. I am, however, opposed to any contemporary Jewish group legislating its historically circumscribed reaction to the 613 commandments for generations to come. I hope it will be possible for subsequent generations to confront all 613 commandments in the light of the insights of their time in order to decide what sector is meaningful for them. I seriously doubt that they will respond as we have. They may very well be ritually more compliant. Since we are totally free before the commandments, no two people will respond in the same way. I suspect that all attempts to construct a set of guiding principles to determine what type of commandments remain meaningful are doomed to failure. I think it is wisest, both theologically and practically, to recognize *both* the binding character of all the commandments and our total freedom before them.

I believe some of the commandments lacking ethical or doctrinal content are among the most meaningful. We must distinguish between the *latent* and *manifest* content of the commandments. By proclaiming the continuing relevance of only those rituals with an explicitly ethical content, we tend to ignore rituals which dramatize our feelings concerning enormously important areas of life. At the manifest level, a ceremony such as *bar mitzvah* has little ethical significance. Nevertheless, something very important takes place. The young man passes through a puberty rite. He is confirmed as a male and a Jew at a crucial moment in the timetable of his life. The real question we must ask about ritual is how it *functions* in the life of the individual and the group. Vast areas of Jewish ritual are deeply rooted in our psychological needs. Religion's primary function is priestly rather than prophetic, insofar as we can separate the two categories. It is excessively difficult to effect ethical improvement through religious instrumentalities. Most rabbis function largely as priests. Their role is to help the individual pass through the crises of life with appropriate rituals which have the power to alleviate the conflicts inherent in the worst moments and heighten the joys of the happier times. People aren't going to change much. Moralizing rituals have a severely limited potency. Rituals which help us pass through such crises as birth, puberty, marriage, sickness, the changing seasons, and death are indispensable.

(2) I believe that my Jewish identity is an absurd given. It is the way I have been thrust into the world. This identity involves having been born into a community with an inherited mythic tradition. That *mythos* includes the doctrine of the election of Israel.

I find it impossible to believe in the doctrine of the chosen people, yet I know of no way in which Jews can be entirely quit of this myth. The Jewish people made a fantastic claim for themselves, that their traditions and destiny were peculiarly the object of God's concern. Ironically, the Gentile world took them seriously, so seriously that the Christian Church to this day asserts the election has passed from the "old" Israel to the Church, the "New" Israel. Too frequently, Judaism is criticized for its "chauvinistic" chosen-people doctrine, as if Jews were the only ones with such a doctrine. In actual fact, Christianity cannot be understood apart from its chosen-people doctrine, the claim that the Church has replaced the Synagogue as the New Israel. The real problem implicit in the chosen-people doctrine is not Jewish ethnocentricism but the two-thousand-year-old sibling rivalry of Jew and Christian over who is the Father's beloved child.

When I recite the prayer "Praised be Thou O Lord our God . . . who has chosen us from among all peoples and given us the Torah," I assert the appropriateness and sufficiency of the Torah as the authoritative document of Jewish religion in the face of the continuing claim of the Church that my religion remains an imperfect anticipation of and preparation for Christianity. I do not see how a believing Christian can avoid claiming that he is a member of the New Israel, the truly elect of God. Even Jewish and Christian death-of-God theologians cannot avoid this Law-Gospel conflict. It has an Antigone-like quality. There is no way out, save moral and psychological modesty in recognizing that the Christian has been thrust into his religious identity as absurdly as the Jew into his.

I see no inner resemblance between the chosen-people doctrine and modern doctrines of racial superiority. The chosen-people doctrine has been the source of millennia of pathetic and unrealistic self-criticism by Jews. Because Jews felt under special obligation to fulfill God's covenant, they have been convinced since the prophets that their religious performance was never good enough. They have interpreted every Jewish disaster from the destruction of Jerusalem in 586 B. C. E.* to the hideous disasters of the twentieth century as God's attempt to punish His errant children in the hope that they would be restored to perfect fidelity to Him. This contrasts with modern ideologies of racial superiority. The racial doctrines are totally devoid of any shred of self-criticism or the feeling of unworthiness before God. On the contrary, these ideologies lend respectability to the most vicious kinds of self-aggrandizement by the nations involved at the expense of their neighbors. The bitter irony of the Jewish doctrine was that its effect was to magnify beyond all realism Jewish guilt-feelings before God. There can be no comparison between the chosen-people doctrine and modern ideologies of racial or national superiority.

(3) I believe that all the major religions are psychologically true for their believers. As such, they are deeply con-

* Before the Christian era.

196 / THE CONDITION OF JEWISH BELIEF

gruent with the needs and identities of their participants. In terms of psychological function, Judaism is no "truer" than any other religion.

I believe that Judaism continues to make a unique contribution to the world, more in terms of the quality of its men and women than in terms of any special insight absent from other religions. Judaism will continue to make a distinctive contribution so long as it develops men and women who function as an element of creative discontent before the regnant idolatries of any given time or community. I also believe that Judaism possesses a peculiar sanity which ought never to be overlooked. Judaism is largely a this-worldly religion. It focuses attention upon the requirements of I and Thou in here and now. In this context, the old Law-Gospel controversy retains enormous contemporary relevance. Two thousand years ago, the Christian Church claimed that some of the tragic inevitabilities of the human condition had been overcome through the career of Jesus. Before this claim the rabbis preferred their sad wisdom that the human condition had not been altered. They focused Jewish attention of those norms which could make life's limitations more viable, rather than on a savior who promised to overcome the limitations. The fundamental Jewish posture is one of realism before existence rather than one of seeking an escape from the world's necessities.

There is a sense in which I am forced to assert that Judaism is "truer" than Christianity. The Christian Church makes certain claims about the way the career of Jesus changed the meaning of the Synagogue and its traditions. Christianity does not assert that it is an entirely different religion from Judaism. It claims that the full meaning of Israel is finally revealed through the Christ. That is why Vatican II could only go so far in resolving the Church-Synagogue conflict. I regard the claim of the Church vis-à-vis Judaism as inherently mistaken. Insofar as Christianity is compelled to define the ultimate meaning of my religious community in its own special perspectives, I must be a dissenting partisan. I find myself in the paradoxical position of asserting that Christianity is as true psychologically for Christians as Judaism is for Jews, while maintaining that the manifest claims of the Church concerning Israel and Israel's Messiah are without foundation.

I find your question about the distinction in the ethical sphere between the believing Jew and the believing Christian the most difficult to answer. I honestly don't know. As a this-worldy religion, Judaism stresses the ethical more insistently than does Christianity, the only realistic alternative in our culture. I might almost be caught saying that a truly believing Jew would be more fully committed within the sphere of I-Thou than others. I find that I have to pull back. I wish it were so. Certainly, Jewish ethical standards are no worse than others. I doubt very much that one could demonstrate that unbelievers have a lower standard in behavioral matters than believers. I am convinced that any attempt to establish the current uniqueness of Judaism on the basis of the special virtues of its believers is doomed to failure.

Finally, I would caution against the tendency in contemporary Judaism to overstress the moral and the ethical. Admittedly, Judaism seeks to inculcate high ethical standards, but one of the most important functions of a religious community is the *sharing of failure*, especially moral failure. We turn to the sanctuary less to be admonished to pursue virtue than out of the need to express and share our inevitable shortcomings in that pursuit.

(4) In the absence of a biblically ordained theocracy—which few contemporary Jews desire—Judaism has much to say about justice but very little about politics. It would make little difference whether a practicing Jew was a Republican or a Democrat provided the area of disagreement concerned the political means whereby an equitable society could be achieved. However, the problem of Judaism and politics cannot be divorced from the historic experience of the Jewish people. I do not see how Jews could possibly feel at home in right-wing groups or parties. Their underlying appeal is for the supremacy of a particular racial or ethnic community. Inevitably, such groups must turn anti-Semitic or at the very least yearn to "put the Jews in their place." That is why Jewish opposition to the Goldwater compaign

was so overwhelming. Jews understood instinctively that the half-Jew Goldwater was seeking to harness the irrational forces in American political life which were striving to assure white supremacy. They knew instinctively that the Goldwater campaign, if successful, would ultimately become anti-Semitic. Jews have fared best in multiethnic communities in which the ties between citizens were rational and contractual, rather than emotional and based on real or imagined membership in a primary group. For that reason, Jews will usually favor that party which fosters a rational, contractual conception of citizenship and is neutral in religious and ethnic matters.

I do not believe a religious Jew can support racial injustice or enforced segregation. Nevertheless, Jews do believe in a measure of religious separateness. We do not favor intermarriage. Hence we tend to be cautious about a host of social arrangements which can lead to it. I am convinced that the Jewish community will continue to be an ally of the Negro community in its quest for political justice. There are, however, important areas of conflict between the two communities. The Negro community's goal seems to be the ultimate obliteration of the voluntary as well as the involuntary kinds of segregation in America. The Jewish community is not prepared to heed that call. To do so would be to destroy the religious and communal basis of Jewish uniqueness.

I see no impediment to a believing Jew's being a Marxist, but he cannot, I think, be a Communist. As a Communist, a believing Jew would have to endure an insupportable conflict between party discipline and loyalty to his religious community. I can never forget the way in which Communists of Jewish origin insisted that Hitler's war was of no concern to them until the Nazi attack on the Soviet Union on June 22, 1941. These people were indifferent so long as Hitler was murdering Jews, but not when he attacked the Soviet Union. After the Hitler experience, I fail to see how any believing Jew could be a Fascist.

(5) I am convinced that the problems implicit in death-of-God theology concern Judaism as much as Christianity. Technically, death-of-God theology reflects the Christian tradition of the passion of the Christ. As such, the terminology of

the movement gives Jewish theologians some very obvious problems. Nevertheless, I have, almost against my will, come to the conclusion that the terminology is unavoidable. The death-of-God theologians have brought into the open a conviction which has led a very potent underground existence for decades. Death-of-God theology is no fad. It is a contemporary expression of issues which have, in one way or another, appeared in embryo in scholastic philosophy, medieval mysticism, nineteenth-century German philosophy, and in the religious existentialism of Martin Buber and Paul Tillich.

No man can really say that God is dead. How can we know that? Nevertheless, I am compelled to say that we live in the time of the "death of God." This is more a statement about man and his culture than about God. The death of God is a cultural fact. Buber felt this. He spoke of the eclipse of God. I can understand his reluctance to use the more explicitly Christian terminology. I am compelled to utilize it because of my conviction that the time which Nietzsche's madman said was too far off has come upon us. There is no way around Nietzsche. Had I lived in another time or another culture, I might have found some other vocabulary to express my meanings. I am, however, a religious existentialist after Nietzsche and after Auschwitz. When I say we live in the time of the death of God, I mean that the thread uniting God and man, heaven and earth has been broken. We stand in a cold, silent, unfeeling cosmos, unaided by any purposeful power beyond our own resources. After Auschwitz, what else can a Jew say about God?

When Professor William Hamilton associated my theological writings with the death-of-God movement in his article on radical theology in *The Christian Scholar*, I was somewhat dubious about his designation. After reflection, I concluded that Professor Hamilton was correct. There is a definite style in religious thought which can be designated death-of-God theology. I have struggled to escape the term. I have been embarrassed by it. I realize its inadequacy and its Christian origin. I have, nevertheless, concluded that it is inescapable. I see no other way of expressing the void which confronts man where once God stood.

I am acutely aware of the fact that Christian death-of-God

theologians remain fully committed Christians, as I remain a committed Jew. As Professor Hamilton has suggested, Christian death-of-God theologians have no God, but they do have a Messiah. Christian death-of-God theology remains Christocentric. I affirm the final authority of Torah and reject the Christian Messiah, as Jews have for two thousand years. Professor Thomas J. J. Altizer welcomes the death of God. He sees it as an apocalyptic event in which the freedom of the Gospels is finally realized and the true Christian is liberated from every restraint of the Law. I do not see that awful event as a cosmic liberation. I am saddened by it. I believe that in a world devoid of God we need Torah, tradition, and the religious community far more than in a world where God's presence was meaningfully experienced. The death of God leads Altizer to a sense of apocalyptic liberation; it leads me to a sad determination to enhance the religious norms and the community without which the slender fabric of human decency might well disappear. In the time of the death of God, Christian theologians still proclaim the Gospel of the Christ; Jewish theologians proclaim the indispensability of Torah.

I believe the greatest single challenge to modern Judaism arises out of the question of God and the death camps. I am amazed at the silence of contemporary Jewish theologians on this most crucial and agonizing of all Jewish issues. How can Jews believe in an omnipotent, beneficent God after Auschwitz? Traditional Jewish theology maintains that God is the ultimate, omnipotent actor in the historical drama. It has interpreted every major catastrophe in Jewish history as God's punishment of a sinful Israel. I fail to see how this postion can be maintained without regarding Hitler and the SS as instruments of God's will. The agony of European Jewry cannot be likened to the testing of Job. To see any purpose in the death camps, the traditional believer is forced to regard the most demonic, antihuman explosion in all history as a meaningful expression of God's purposes. The idea is simply too obscene for me to accept. I do not think that the full impact of Auschwitz has yet been felt in Jewish theology or Jewish life. Great religious revolutions have their own periods of gestation. No man knows the hour when the full impact of Auschwitz will be felt, but no religious community can endure so hideous a wounding without vast inner disorders.

Though I believe that a void stands where once we experienced God's presence, I do not think Judaism has lost its meaning or its power. I do not believe that a theistic God is necessary for Jewish religious life. Dietrich Bonhoeffer has written that our problem is how to speak of God in an age of no religion. I believe that our problem is how to speak of religion in an age of no God. I have suggested that Judaism is the way we share the decisive times and crises of life through the traditions of our inherited community. The need for that sharing is not diminished in the time of the death of God. We no longer believe in the God who has the power to annul the tragic necessities of existence; the need religiously to share that existence remains.

Finally, the time of the death of God does not mean the end of all gods. It means the demise of the God who was the ultimate actor in history. I believe in God, the Holy Nothingness, known to mystics of all ages, out of which we have come and to which we shall ultimately return. I concur with atheistic existentialists such as Sartre and Camus in much of their analysis of the broken condition of human finitude. We must endure that condition without illusion or hope. I do not part company with them on their analysis of the human predicament. I part company on the issue of the necessity of religion as the way we share that predicament. Their analysis of human hopelessness leads me to look to the religious community as the institution in which that condition can be shared in depth. The condition of finitude can only be overcome when we return to the Nothingness out of which we have been thrust. In the final analysis, omnipotent Nothingness is Lord of all creation.

Herman E. Schaalman

Rabbi of Emanuel Congregation (Reform)
in Chicago.

⦅ (1) Revelation is the event in which the divine breaks into the human sphere and discloses an aspect, a fragment, of its being. It is thus an encounter, at His initiative, between God and a human partner of His choice. The event is self-validating in that its experience is so unique, overwhelming, and transforming that the human partner emerges from it reconstituted in his own being and certain of its meaning.

It is this meaning, this interpretation of the revelatory event, which the human partner then puts into words. It is his understanding of it, his pouring into language of the re-lived and now structured and ordered recall of the encounter which a Moses and others set down as Torah, instruction.

In other words, Torah is the human record of the revelatory moment. Torah is the transcript into human language of man's always limited capacity to understand what the presence of God in the encounter was to mean. The only safe-guards against major error arising from man's limited capacity to grasp anything about God fully lie, first of all, in God's selection of the human partner and, secondly, in the nature of the encounter itself. It is such as to leave man no choice but to respond and to use his unique means of communica-tion, words, to express its contents, i.e., to structure its mean-ing. *Dibra Torah bilshon b'nei adam*—"The Torah speaks human language."

As a part of the Torah, the 613 *mitzvot*, the command-ments, whose exact number and content were matters of con-troversy until well into the Middle Ages, are, then, the results of the process of revelation as described. Never were all of them binding on or practiced by the Jews; e.g., a number were specific to the King or High Priest. In fact, since the period of the greatest faithfulness to Torah and its *mitzvot* began after the destruction of the Temple, when the center of Jewish population shifted away from the Holy Land, addi-tional hundreds of *mitzvot* could not be, and were not, per-formed by our ancestors. (It seems unlikely, for instance, that most believing Jews today would worship God by animal sacrifices, even if the Temple were rebuilt in Zion.)

Moreover, as the statements and discussions in Pirke Avot, Yoma, etc. indicate, there was a clear awareness in talmudic times that the *mitzvot* differed in weightiness. Thus we are admonished to observe a "light" one as zealously as a "weighty" one (on the ground that their ultimate results in divine providence are beyond human ken). Obviously, at least in talmudic times, Jews were discriminating concerning the importance of various *mitzvot*.

The situation today, however, differs radically from that of even the most recent past, in that the seat of authority and hence of decision has shifted almost completely to the will of each individual. The nearly total disappearance of a functional Jewish community of the kind that in premodern times exercised and enforced a very large measure of control and compliance makes the performance of any *mitzvah* dependent on each individual's response to tradition, upbringing, education, belief, and whatever other factors may from moment to moment shape such response.

Starting from the assumption that contemporary Jews have the will to confront the issue of *mitzvot* and to familiarize themselves with the commandments, I would propose that they keep all those *mitzvot* which to them become openings, channels, means toward sanctifying life through heightened awareness of God. The purpose of *mitzvot* is to dedicate a moment and an act to God, thereby transfiguring life. Any *mitzvah*, then, which has the power, regularly or occasionally, thus to become a window on the divine, a meeting place with God, ought to be observed by the Jew who believes in the "Commander," God.

(2) The concept of the "choice" of the people of Israel is related to and inseparable from the covenant. "To be chosen" means to be covenanted to God. To speak of the choice of Israel is to say that this is the people with whom God entered into the covenant, the terms, experience, and history of which are recorded in the Bible. The covenant is the very basis of Jewish existence, and the only sufficient explanation for the presence of the Jewish people on the stage of the world then and now. Hence the fact of God's initiative in making the covenant as expressed in His "choosing" the people of Israel is equally basic to being a Jew today.

The choice lay with God. It was His initiative. As such it was then, and still remains, a mystery. It was an act of His grace. It began undeservedly with Abraham, whose progeny Israel is, and it was reaffirmed in Exodus and at Sinai, among other occasions. That this election was puzzling already in biblical times is evidenced by such attempts at explanation

as the idea of the "merit of the Fathers" which benefited un-
deserving later generations, or by the reference to the "love
of thy youth" when Israel proved its faithfulness for the moment. But these efforts carry little conviction and rather point
up than solve the problem.

Jewish tradition again and again has understood this inexplicable "choice" not as an unmitigated blessing but in
fact as a rather difficult, if not painful, task. Israel is like an
olive which yields oil when pressed, Midrash Exodus Rab-
bah states, giving voice to the fact that the choice entailed
obedience to the demanding voice of God. To be chosen
means to be His servant—a lot which is amply described in
the well-known passage in Isaiah. While there was and is joy
in performance of the *mitzvot* as the sign of the covenantal
relation, these same *mitzvot*, the evidence of the choice, are
also understood and accepted as a yoke.

There were times, undoubtedly, when this idea of the
choice was distorted by Jews and particularly by Christians.
The latter especially, in possible ambivalence over their claim
to having inherited the election, were likely to impute meanings to the concept which were neither intended nor authentic. Despite this risk of distortion, it seems to me that
the concept has such profound theological and existential
value that it should not be discarded by us.

(3) The claim of any religion to exclusive possession of
truth seems to me untenable. This position arises from the
fact that the major object of truth in any religious system is
God, who by definition and nature is knowable only frag-
mentarily to man. Even Moses, who according to our tradition shared the supreme relationship of intimacy with God
attainable to man, understood that one could never see "the
face of God" but only as it were "His back"—i.e., that all
human knowledge of God, including his, must always remain
limited. Moreover, how much truth, how much value a given
insight into the nature of the divine would contain depended
on the condition of the human being who sought to understand something of God.

All knowledge of God, all truth concerning Him, is relative. No one person nor any religion may, therefore, claim
to have the truth about God and thus to be the one true

religion. Each system of religious thought and each experience of God's presence contain splinters of truth. It is the same God who was sensed and encountered and understood incompletely by all who were open to His presence or call. Different traditions developed their partial insights, each in a way adequate and acceptable to those who professed allegiance to the particular tradition. The consequences of their insights, particularly in the sphere of human behavior, permit judgments as to their relative values. But I am not particularly interested in proving that Judaism is best. It's mine; it's sufficient for me. It has virtues such as its resistance to philosophic definition of its tenets, its irresistible thrust into the ethical, its undeviating involvement in history and the world, its sensitivity to human values, its unshaken recognition that the eschatological moment has not yet come, and others. It may have defects, such as its occasional overemphasis on legal detail, its occasionally too rigid reverence for the past, and perhaps others. What is important, it seems to me, is not so much to "sell" Judaism as to know it, not to draw up its balance sheet as to begin taking it seriously. For to him who sets out with the proper teacher on the voyage to its discovery, it will reveal depths and beauty sufficient to address meaningfully and manage the questions of one's identity, one's relation to others, and to God.

There are differences, of course, in the manner of thought and life among believers of various religions and also those who hold no religiously identifiable position. But it seems to me that a statement of such differences is basically so much less fruitful than study that it becomes virtually a wrong question to pursue. To the Jew the most important, the right, question is: How do I start learning?

(4) As a system of religious thought and practice, Judaism inculcates, when successful, a very intense degree of sensitivity toward one's fellow man. Both he and I are "made in the image of God." He is constituted in his humanity through his response to God, just as I am. Or to put it differently, the only effective motivation for ethical living derives not from some calculation of "advantage" or "disadvantage," from anything which involves power relations, but from the initial recognition of the other as a "child of God." It is the ac-

ceptance of accountability to a power other than oneself or society which alone enables one to avoid the pitfalls of the attempt to establish ethical demands and motivation on a nontheistic basis.

To anyone who thus takes seriously the relevance of God to ethical norms and behavior, racial segregation, persecution, humiliation of another are unacceptable and ought to be impossible. That they may occur also among those who start from such basic assumptions is evidence of human fallibility.

The Jew thus sensitized to his fellow man's existence and rights cannot without inner contradiction subscribe to any political program or ideology which includes in principle recourse to violence (such as class warfare) as a necessary means to its ends, or a perpetuation of inequality of power (such as the acceptance of political or economic dictatorship), or a denial of the existence of God as necessary to a universe conceived to be totally materialistic. Neither Fascism nor Communism, then, is a possible form of political and social structure to a believing Jew.

(5) The problems raised by the "God is dead" theologians have virtually no relevance to Judaism. At least according to Altizer, it is an exclusively Christian concern. As he sees it, the once transcendent God in an irreversible thrust decided to become totally immanent, a process symbolized in the historic incarnation in the person of Jesus of Nazareth. God willed to die as transcendental Being and henceforth only to incarnate in man. "Christ" is where life is lived to the fullest.

Indeed, Altizer almost aggressively, perhaps even too aggressively, declares that the transcendental God of the Jews can be believed in and encountered only by Jews whose condition of exile removes them from the involvement in real history. Apart from the fact that this implies to my mind a distortion of the meaning and experience of exile as conceived by us, it leaves no doubt that Altizer understands God's "death" and now different existence in incarnation to be acceptable and relevant only to Christians.

Quite apart from this consideration, Jews cannot apply the term "death" to God in any meaningful way whatever because such application is only possible when traces of mythology are allowed to be attached to God. To the Jew who knows of God as the totally Other to whom man can relate only by the mystery of a divine grace, ascriptions of "death," "becoming," et al., are repugnant. Human understanding of God's Being changes and we may discover and then formulate new insights into His Being, but these are reflections of our, and not His, changeability, contingency, limitation. These are verbalizations of our groping for proper images to describe what essentially is wordless. Perhaps all we can ever say of God ultimately is only that He is, which here also means that He is beyond time. Hence no "death" or "incarnation" as a historic event is conceivable or acceptable to us.

If, however, such terms as "death" and "incarnation" were to be taken purely symbolically, they could have a certain relevance to the Jew. "Death" could be used as a warning not to take any verbalization concerning God's Being as ultimate truth—i.e., it would mean that the time had come to discard past formulations and start thinking and speaking in an updated vocabulary; and "incarnation" could be used as an emphatic declaration that the only way to God is via man. The latter idea is so basic to Jewish tradition that it hardly needs stating, but the former could be a wholesome corrective for any and all who are too sure that they know what God is and how He functions. It is debatable, however, whether Altizer and company would be content with such an interpretation and use of their terminology.

The most serious challenge of modern thought to Judaism comes from the radical consequences drawn from the assertion of man's autonomy. Instead of helping to establish man as a "partner" of God in an uninterrupted dialogue, it has misled him into self-idolization. Thinking that he is totally self-sufficient and self-explanatory, he denies any meaningful and useful statement concerning the existence of God.

Zalman M. Schachter

Head of the department of Judaic studies at the University of Manitoba in Winnipeg, Canada

❲ Shammai was a great Zen master. The person who sought to learn the entire Torah while standing on one foot did

not get the message. Shammai in good *Rinzai* fashion had hit
him over the head with the builder's rod. Had he gotten the
point he would not have had to go to Hillel, who managed
to hook him and hold him to "the rest now go and learn."
The symposium questions beg the writer to hit the reader
over the head in twenty-five hundred words or less, to en-
lighten him abruptly. But the questions also hit the writer
over the head and here are the sparks he saw. He who needs
more must go to Hillel and learn the rest.

(1) Orthodox, perhaps better "orthoprax," is a definition
I'd like to have of myself—that and Hasid. In this, the assertions I make about Torah and *mizvot* must be in consonance
with the normative standards of Orthodoxy—only being modified by Hasidism. However, if only this were the case, my
personal reply would not be quite relevant. By aligning myself with normative opinion I would not do more than give
witness to a series of acts of faith without stating what they
are and how and why they are made. That would make only
another vote for tabling the issues at hand. It would also not
be honest because, if I left it at that, it would not be quite
true.

The questions that initially brought me during my teens
into opposition to Orthodoxy, and Hasidic answers I received
which reconciled me again with it, have now shifted. The
dialectic of my inner life has exchanged vocabularies and
focused on different problems but—thank G-d*—the noise is
still great with question and answer clamoring for the floor
of my awareness. What is disquieting is that the tenor of the
"shegetzy" questions—the kind asked by outsiders or unbelievers or skeptics—is often more serious, more devout, holy,
prophetic, and divine than the patness of the *Sha!* be-quiet-
and-gorge-yourself-with-the-answer stance of the righteous one
in me. At best I can sigh with R. Moshe Kobriner's Hasid,
"Halevai she'ani ma'amin—Would that I believed."

Standing on such shaky ground, how can I address myself
to the question of the bindingness of the Law on others? Let
them suffer their own suffering and let them as honestly as
they can answer their questions. But this attitude I cannot
permit myself either. Before I talk to another Jew about his

* See footnote p. 104—*Ed.*

bond with the 613 commandments of the Pentateuch and the seven of the Rabbis and the many of the rabbinic fence-making plus the Gaonic institutions and the many beautiful and not so beautiful customs—before I talk to another, I must see how I talk to myself.

I want to be included in G–d's normative plan for souls and thus in the normative statements of our tradition. All the *oughts* that my master, the Lubavitcher Rebbe (*Shalita*)*, my repository of the faith, prescribes for me are my *oughts*. Thus all the commandments of the Shulhan Arukh are equally binding on me (and my fellow Jews) as *oughts*. This is without distinction of ethical or doctrinal or deuteronomic content. In fact I believe that the *hukim*—those commandments inaccessible to my own ethical and doctrinal apologetics—are more filled with heteronomic divine content because they ask for a more total surrender to G–d's will than *edot* (doctrinal commandments) and *mishpatim* (ethical commandments). The latter two give wider scope to inspirational motives.

The reason I believe this is that the *hukim*, as I have sometimes experienced them, touch much deeper, preverbal, levels in myself than the more easily verbalizable *edot* and *mishpatim*. Therefore they bring me closer to the realization of G–d. But this is on the level of the *ought*.

I know also how terribly far I am from the *ought* level and how recalcitrant my nature, my crooked heart, is from G–d's taught and revealed will. I could, I suppose, make the leap to full obedience, to the *ought* that I know of, but there is something not quite unholy in me that stays on the level of my *is*, with all its hang-ups. Being vulnerable to world and persons, to inner and outer conflicts, I believe that there is a sliding hierarchy in which I move from *is* to *ought*. It is so dynamic that it defies analysis and justification by reason. The metatheory behind the calculus of this hierarchy, which sometimes makes me lax in the service of something more immediately compelling and of higher priority than *Avodat Hashem*—the service of G–d as defined by the tradition—other times makes me forsake the subjective standards and scramble back into the objective standards of the

* A Hebrew acronym meaning, "May he live a long and good life"—*Ed*.

consensus of the pious, is not accessible to my own defining. Rather is it rooted in the subjective self that makes these decisions as part of the calculus of its covenant with G–d. Yet it has the power not only of shrewd calculation but also of reckless love of G–d. This recklessness is closer to the great Maggid's "now that I have no more part in the world to come, I can serve You the more lovingly," than to Calvin's being damned for G–d's greater glory. Some of R. Zussia's readiness to go to hell because "in this I can fulfill one more *mitzvah*" is stronger than a Kierkegaardian suspension of the ethical.

This metatheory is inaccessible to my own critique. If I get pushed very hard I take refuge in some vague and despairing outcry that this constitutes not the normative rule but the more and more invading "teaching of the hour" which demands exception to the rule. The rule applies to those times when the majority is ready to live by it, and it demands the excommunication of those individuals who want to dissociate themselves from the majority. However, in our day when the majority of the 11.5 million Jews do not see themselves as living under the rule, it seems the teaching of the hour has become more the rule than the exception. It is for this reason that it becomes necessary for me to realize how the dynamics of the teaching of the hour operate to me. The rule in a sense convicts me by its *ought*; it becomes so pressing that I have difficulty in locating even half of my *behavior* within it. The teaching-of-the-hour clause threatens in all reality to supplant the rule as a guide. I often see that I err in the teaching of the hour, that there is more wisdom (considering the probabilities) in the normative rule than in my own deviations. The tension between *ought* and *is* makes me wish for the unthinking and unstruggling repose that can be won by conforming to the consensus of the pious. Yet as soon as I yield to the consensus of the pious and to unthinking repose, I miss the pain of striving and the very intimate guidance of Him who imparts the teaching of the hour.

In the end I find that the sliding scale does have a rhyme and reason to it and it presents itself not in the antinomian abrogation of all Law—but in a not so antinomian way of keeping it.

When someone who eats in a nonkosher restaurant orders beefsteak instead of pork chops because he "keeps kosher," I can no longer laugh at him. His choice was occasioned by a sort of low-level, yet very genuine, concern not to eat of "impure beasts." When he asks that his steak be well done— so that he can obey "eat no blood"—I respect him even more. When he refuses butter on it and milk with his coffee because of "seethe not the kid in its mother's milk," I respect him still further. And if he orders a scale-bearing fish instead of meat, I see him struggling honestly to do G–d's will.

Now I notice that my own sliding up and down is also based on a continuous scale rather than on an abrupt break. The deviations of the hour are not aimed against the structure of the Law. They represent the accommodation of a struggling person to a poor but living compromise. This is not hypocrisy in the usual sense. There is no pious pretense in public, with a frivolous breach of law in private. On the contrary. In private, where the environment which I create helps me to deepen my observance, I often do more than in public. The sliding scale works the other way.

In making a rule for others, I must be guided by the same scale. If the other is informed, committed, willing, and capable of observance, then the ontologically projected objectification of G–d's will in *halakha* holds to the fullest. I cannot invent theological tricks to save me or him from our moral bankruptcy. I don't want to mitigate the *is-ought* tension, I also want my fellow Jew to experience this tension, for out of it new guidance arises which informs the "crooked heart," and through the multiplication of this process, the consensus of the pious (who are by and large not immune from the same tensions) is modified. This is how the *halakha* progresses and in this lies its viability. I must insist on the bindingness of the 613 commandments as an *ought* and yet with the compassion of one whose *is* is far from the *ought*, I must feel with others and I must not lessen the tension.

The questions of authority and historicity are for me quite beside the real point. The covenant and the Law are what they are among the pious, and it is this that creates the real tension. I cannot live in a vacuum no matter how well documented its existence be. I need the fellowship of my fellow Jews, my fellow Hasidim, and our constant anchoring in the norms of the Shulhan Arukh and the Rebbe to produce this tension which I feel. But since this is not a verbal thing, the dichotomy between the deuteronomic and ethical as against the nonrational commandments makes no difference. On the contrary, here too the rationals become nonrational because of the nonverbal tension. But because of that tension I return to rational concern.

Let me take up some of your questions in my own order.

(5) Nietzsche's Zarathustra is glad to announce the death of G–d. Prometheus is no longer threatened and all of G–d's fires are now available for man's use (abuse?). To Sartre this is no occasion for rejoicing. Sartre must take on infinite responsibilities. There is no exit; and looking at those who take no responsibilities at all, he is filled with nausea. This is no problem for me. *Halakha* limits my responsibility. I am not infinitely responsible. In responding to G–d through the *halakha* my responsibility is finite, but once I fulfill His command He takes infinite responsibility. And when I implore Him in prayer He gives me His fires as a gift, and there is no Promethean cost involved. Yet even so, I must at times kill Him in me. When a heroic act or an act of help is required, I must, according to R. Moshe Leib of Sassow, not say, *G–d will help you, trust!* At that moment I am an atheist; G–d is dead and only I am available to help. This is not a theological, but rather a functional, way of dealing with the problem of the suffering of others and the arrogance of my offering help.

However, in this a new aspect of "G–d is dead" challenges me. G–d's will having been so clearly defined as to be capable of being printed in a Shulhan Arukh, He is no longer necessary. It is all cut-and-dried. And a cut-and-dried G–d is dead. To be overly concerned with Him who commands rather than with the product of His commandment is generally not *de rigueur* in the circles of the shapers of the consensus of the pious. Only by deviating from this consensus do I admit G–d to live in my tensions, to shape the mute still voice that issues from my subjectivity and moves me up and down the sliding scale. Where the halakhic behaviorist kills G–d, so that He need no longer live among His subjects (except to keep score), the crooked heart revives Him in the battle to please and love Him. *T'shuvah*—repentance—the tension between *ought* and *is*, is the arena of His manifestation in me. In a circle of others who struggle in the same way, He becomes palpably present. A *minyan* praying, "Pull us back to You, oh Lord and we will come back," makes Him manifest.

Speak to those who either by their fulfillment of the Law or by their complete disregard of it ignore Him, mention His blessed name to them and there is no movement, no vital reaction. In this sense "G–d" is dead indeed like any other word of power that has become impotent. No longer does the word "G–d" compel moral choices; often the words "*halakha*" and "Shulhan Arukh" still do. Civil rights and Vietnam are alive and G–d is dead in this sense, a dead issue for too many of us.

G–d is also Death. Where He fully lives I do not. To see Him from the inside is to see His face—no one can survive this. Even a short glimpse of G–d's own atheism is an immense shock from which one can hardly recover. He has no G–d: no one to judge Him and, alas, no equal to relate to. To feel G–d's absolute loneliness is to despair absolutely. I help Him bide His eternity by contending with Him. He helps me by playing G–d to me. And I in return reflect back to Him my trembling fear and longing love—"for all is in the hands of Heaven but the fear of Heaven" and *"what does the Lord,"* so bored by His Supremacy, *"require of thee"* —*"but to"* borrow some *"fear."* This deuteronomic covenant we promise one another, "The Lord bespake you" and "You bespoke Him." We agree to play a cosmic game.

The most serious challenges to Judaism posed by modern thought and experience are to me game theory and psychedelic experience.

Once I realize the game structure of my commitment, once I see how all my theologizing is just an elaborate death struggle between my soul and the G–d within her, or when I can undergo the deepest cosmic experience via some minuscule quantity of organic alkaloids or LSD, then the whole validity of my ontological assertions is in doubt.

But game theory works the other way too. G–d too is playing a game of hide-and-seek with Himself and me. The psychedelic experience can be not only a challenge but also a support of my faith. After seeing what really happens at the point where all is One and G–d immanent surprises G–d transcendent and They merge in cosmic laughter, I can also see Judaism in a new and amazing light. The questions to which the Torah is the answer are recovered in me. There is a new and transcendental luster on the answer, and having seen that there is little else I can do except play this game or another, having seen that this is the game to which I was chosen, I choose it in return and decide to play it with delight—what else am I going to do? Hope and despair are end-game moves.

(2) For Judah Halevi chosenness implied being the "pick" of the nations, the best: the *Kuzari* has strong racial leanings. To Samson Raphael Hirsch it was something quasi-chemical induced by kosher food. Whenever there is a group that survives in its ethnic character one can make a case for chosenness on evolutionary grounds, and an application of the Jungian collective unconscious can help locate chosenness even there. To me chosenness implies a part in the game—the play of history. When the play is over both villains and heroes are eligible for applause.

For me the problem constitutes itself as follows: Is it possible to raise people to high levels of religious intensity without the accompanying fanaticism? My working hypothesis is that this is possible—against all the evidence of the past. This means holding to a view of the cosmos as a stage for many actors. The "villain" who opposes me, "the hero," is also deserving of love since my own role is utterly dependent on his. Knowing that behind the phenomena portrayed on the stage there is a dressing-room comradeship, I can manage to oppose him on stage and love him too. "He who separates the holy from the profane . . . Israel from the nations" makes each dependent on the other. I can't do away with my chosenness, nor can I permit that violence "acted" out on the stage to be real and fatal. My mission is to convince my opponent that we are actors on life's stage, and while we must "act," we dare not resort to violence. My enemy and I must be able to congratulate each other for the good show we put on.

Prior to the holocaust we lacked—and indeed still lack—a viable theology of the Gentile. Some liberals do not want to maintain the distinction between Israel and the nations, and the archaics take it too seriously. A realistic theology of *Goy*-vs.-chosen people keeps the distinction to the stage.

Once more we are involved in game theory which, in challenging us, offers us a new potential for the service of G–d.

(3) Judaism stands between the fatal seriousness of the West and the dreamy frivolity of the far East. It is not just a dream of Brahma's mind, it is a covenant—a collusion between G–d and man. There is a game in progress, and it has rules—*and here is our emphasis on Law and rules*: Every move counts and G–d is the scorekeeper, and the game has a terminal point at the end of the sixth millennium and the judgment will be offered, yet the players will all be rewarded for the way in which they played their respective roles. In Christianity there is only one player—the Christ. In Islam surrender is demanded and not covenant. There is no structure to the Hindu game and there is no scorekeeper in the Buddhist one. This, then, is our contribution: We give the world a metatheory for religion that at once moves it out of a purely objective and ontological realm and at the same time out of a purely subjective and psychological one. Buber's intuition that the message of Judaism *to the world* consists in just this—the I-Thou relationship which contains no special dialogue words—is correct once the basic ground rules of the seven Noahide laws are accepted by the nations. For Jews who have the full covenant and all the rules, Buber's insight is feeble when compared to Franz Rosenzweig's do-ability—the *could* relating to the *ought*—and growing-in-commandedness game. Rosenzweig, who includes Christianity and excludes Islam and others, is too particular. Rav Kuk saw further.

In this too the believing Jew is different from all the other knights of history, past and present. The covenantal game *ben adam la-chavero* is part of the total game and the divine scorekeeping.

(4) Therefore the political framework that will permit the greatest freedom to various constituents of the game population to play the game is the one that can claim to represent the "one Torah you shall have for the citizen and the

stranger." The citizen and the stranger do not play the same game but they have a common civic framework—a metagame that protects all games so that they do not interfere with one another. This does not mean a homogenized democracy of tyranny by the majority establishment, nor the Fascist one-game-for-all, nor the Communist one-game-for-all, nor a Western one-world-game-for-all policy. Hence a man cannot be a good Jew who will not fight for the game-freedom of all men, who will not safeguard the game-freedom for others, who will not insist on the "natural law" which makes all sorts of covenants simultaneous and compatible and which pledges itself only to one basic principle—to paraphrase Hillel: "The game you don't want to play, inflict it not on someone else."

Perhaps this is a new *ought* toward which we must flex in the tension of the *is*. In responding to the challenge of this *ought* we might be able to respond to the other challenge of "Those who say unto me day by day 'Where is thy God?'" Perhaps we *could*.

Harold M. Schulweis

Rabbi of Temple Beth Abraham (Conservative) in Oakland, California.

❡ (1) The Torah is the selective record of Israel's extraordinary religious interpretation of its collective experience during the formative period of its career. The origin of Torah lies not in an extramundane source which has cast down absolute truths upon a receiving people, nor is it the arbitrary projection of human inventiveness flung upward. Torah is rooted in the matrix of a living organism, in a people which discovers out of its experience with failure and fortune the powers of godliness residing within it and its total environment. Torah as revelation is the product of Israel's creative transaction with history. Out of this experience has been extracted the insight of a cosmic moral teleology which serves Israel as its dominant interpretive principle of history. The attributes ascribed to divinity, the act of naming that which is holy, the consecration of particular deeds and potential energies, the enunciation of prescriptions and proscriptions, are revelatory disclosures wrought out of the wrestlings of our people with idolatry, superstition, and enslavement and out of their acknowledgment of such values as compassion, justice, peace, and freedom as the forces upon which life depends for its meaning.

The sanctity of Torah-revelation lies not in the perfection of its authorship nor in its absolute finality. The Torah is holy not because it is the last word, but because it is the first self-conscious word of Judaism which reveals the direction of its moral thrust. The holiness of Torah does not require that its contents be held as infallible or immutable. In the ark of holiness alongside the whole commandments lay the "broken tablets of the law" to remind us that errors are inescapable in the evolution of Torah. Revelatory claims are time-conditioned and properly subject to criticism and revision on grounds of rational judgment and moral consequences. Auschwitz and Bergen-Belsen make it impossible for us today to read the genocidal commandments to exterminate the Amalekites as divine orders (Deut. 25: 17–19; 1 Sam. 15: 1–34).

To argue, as is fashionable among so many contemporary theological statesmen, that Torah admits of some human elements, and then to offer no way of determining where divine initiative ends and where human interpretation enters, is to avoid the heart of the question. To claim *that* revelation occurs without commitment to follow *what* revelation demands, or to proclaim the will of God without offering grounds for distinguishing true from false revelation, is to offer a vacuous form-revelation without content or criteria. In my interpretation, the divine element of Torah-revelation comes not vertically from a superperson whose will descends upon us, but horizontally from a people engaged in the process of complex interaction within history. Real events and ideal visions acting upon each other yield the *sancta* of Judaism, and these values named sacred are ever being validated in the experience of this people.

The natural reverence which observing Jews have for the Torah as the sourcebook of their being should incline them to hold the *mitzvot* as "practical absolutes." Here the layers of rabbinic interpretation upon the text of the commandments continue to offer meaningful reason for their observance. And it remains the task of Jewish leadership to offer relevant rationales for expressing one's Jewishness through the *mitzvot*. Should the ritual lose its symbolic power, as in the case the editors cite, or should it run counter to our contemporary moral judgment (e.g., the laws prohibiting a *Kohen* from marrying a divorcee or proselyte), then the convinced religious leadership should allow the commandment to be abandoned. Unless the rabbinate exercises moral sensitivity and anticipatory wisdom in cases of moral obsolescence or irrelevance, the end will only be disrespect for all religious law. The acceptance of religious pluralism, which is a fact of Jewish religious life, and the encouragement of responsible group decision as to ritual observance are the only valid alternatives to the extremes both of authoritarianism and anarchy.

(2) "Chosen people" is an example of a doctrine believed to be of divine origin which can no longer be accepted in the light of our experience and ethics. The doctrine presupposes a superpersonal diety whose inscrutable will chose to inform a particular group of His truth and ways. To be exclusively chosen by God is to have a special metaphysical status. Such supernatural selection remains inviolate. The elected may be punished for not properly witnessing to the truths it is specially given, but its status as elect remains eternal. Under no conditions will a people admit that its election has been nullified, and no prophet has dared so to proclaim even in the midst of his fiercest denunciation of Israel.

While one can understand the psychological value of such belief during years of isolation and humiliation, one cannot on such pragmatic grounds justify its morality or truth. Modern attempts to hold on to the concept of "chosen people," but to redefine its contents, remain unconvincing. There are those who explain that God-chosenness does not establish political superiority but only results in a *noblesse oblige* directive to lead a life of holiness; but this fails to recognize that such a claim to higher spiritual obligation remains an aristocratic conceit which demeans all other peoples by lowering our moral expectation of their behavior.

The effort at compensatory parceling-out of divinely designated racial or national gifts—e.g., philosophy to the Greeks, administration to the Romans, religious genius to the Jews—both caricatures nations and peoples and presumptuously offers the greatest prize to Israel as God's witness on earth.

The modern suggestion that God's choosing of Israel really means Israel's choosing of God is as valid a translation as turning X's owing Y money into Y's owing X money. The propositions are clearly not symmetrical. Moreover, if to be chosen means to choose, then which group holding a concept of God is not equally chosen by God?

The traditional "chosen-people" idea fosters a crude way of thinking whereby people and traditions are elevated or denigrated in wholesale fashion. The principle of God's election tempts its complementary form into being. The tragedy of Christianity's use of the rejection of Israel's election illustrates the dangers and arrogance of either claim.

Rejection of the doctrine of chosenness in no way denies the uniqueness or value of a people, its style of life in theory and practice. Uniqueness must not be confounded with the theological claim that one people is distinguished by God from all others as He distinguishes light from darkness, the sacred from the profane, the Sabbath from the weekday.

It is presumptuous to hold or to argue that the Jewish idea of chosenness is a model from which racist or national ideologies of superiority are derived. The effort to trace complex systems back to an idea which functioned quite differently is at best a highly speculative affair. Religious and secular chauvinism requires no antecedent models, though if one is looking for precedents one usually can find whatever one wants to in history.

Judaism, however, now has an opportunity to make a major moral contribution to the world by pioneering the rejection of all religious claims to exclusive divine revelation, its own included. It can once again offer the world the power of its moral directive.

(3) The application of "truth" as a criterion for judging revelatory claims of religion is misleading. Religions are neither true nor false in the same sense that these terms are used in cognitive discourse. The "truth" of any religious doctrine admits of no falsehood and religion offers no method of disconfirmation. Articles of faith are not espoused as hy-

potheses, theological propositions are not seriously subject to public tests of verifiability, nor are they meant to be merely analytically true.

Loyalty to Judaism does not demand that it possess exclusive truth. Should it happen that other religions or cultures are found to contain insights or values of significant merit lacking in Judaism, the alternatives for the Jew lie neither in abandonment nor in conversion and self-denial. Alien values which may enrich Judaism can and have been absorbed and Judaized throughout Jewish history.

Three unique interrelated religious perceptions of Judaism have conditioned its distinctive response in the sphere of ethics:

(a) The world is created imperfect and incomplete. Consequently, Judaism is not given to counseling conformity with the world as it is, or to proposing acquiescence in natural law. Nature is not God's teleological order which men must accept and imitate. The conquest of nature, human and physical, far from being considered a tampering with divine order, is sanctioned as an opportunity and indeed an obligation for man.

(b) Man is assigned the role of ally of God in perfecting and repairing the incomplete world (*tikkun olam*). Man is not helplessly fallen but endowed with an *imago dei*; he is called upon to exercise his moral freedom and responsibility in this world. The high status conferred upon man as a morally competent partner of God produced and still cultivates a social consciousness and activism in the knowledgeable Jew. The Jewish moral hero, from Abraham to Yossel Rakover, is gifted with a religious audacity unique among religious traditions. God Himself is challenged by moral man without man's being accused of heresy or hubris. From this a significant moral a fortiori follows: if one dares confront even God on moral grounds, shall one be afraid to challenge the tyranny of kings or the fury of the mob?

(c) The entire people of Israel is entered into the moral covenant with God. Social involvement is not the concern of some individuals but of the entire community. The individual, in turn, cannot function without the community. His very communion with God can be achieved only through his community. Neither the solitariness of individual salvation nor the rootlessness of abstract universalism fulfills the terms of the covenant.

The ethical consequences of such a people-centered covenant theology cannot be ignored. For one, theology is wedded to the total concerns of the community and its this-worldly efforts to realize the aims of the covenant. For another, it encourages in religion an openness to those interests—economic, social, and cultural—more often relegated to the secular in doctrinally-centered theology. Equally important, the particularity of peoplehood roots the universalism of Judaism in the social concreteness of Jewish reality. The vague generality of humanitarianism is offered the flesh and blood of Jewish specificity. Judaism knows that "the attempt to speak without any language in particular" is doomed to voicelessness.

(4) Jewish religion cannot be said to endorse any particular political viewpoint. Such political endorsement would in any event lose for Judaism the critical function which enables it to select and reject in any or all political ideologies those particular elements supportive of its moral vision. This role of religion does not imply an aristocratic aloofness from social movements but a transcendence of partisanship which frees Judaism to judge without the pressure of political expedience.

When one sees Judaism as something more than a body of definitive texts and decisive positions from the past, one can appeal to the collective experience of the Jewish people as an index of Jewish moral attitudes toward political ideology. Thus, the Jewish opposition to Fascism, Communism, or theocracy is arrived at through experience, not scripturally. Such principles as religious pluralism, the democratization of Jewish life, the separation of church and state have become *sancta* for a great many Jews more through the testimony of historic experience than through textual examination of biblical or rabbinic literature. Similarly, the dominant religious position in American Jewish life in favor of birth control and in opposition to capital punishment is a moral decision arrived at through the transaction between the social and behavioral sciences and the wisdom and ethics of tradition.

Thus, knowledgeable Jews can argue that racial segregation is irreconcilable with the cumulative power of religious tradition based on the massive evidence of Jewish law, lore, and liturgy, and the millennial tragedy of Israel's persecution at the hands of prejudiced men and their systems. Both Jewish ethics and experience have sensitized the Jews to the sameness of bigotries and the kinship of suffering.

(5) The most recent theological rebellion among the younger Protestant theologians ought not to be dismissed as sensationalistic or faddist. After the intended shock therapy of the obituary has subsided, there remains the searching concern to restore relevance and effectiveness to religion. Of special interest to Judaism is their reliance on and utilization of authentic Hebraic motifs in calling for a humanistic theology of melioristic behavior. Not to be dismissed is the figure of Dietrich Bonhoeffer, whose writings and exemplary life loom large over this post-holocaust theology. For the new theology is as much as anything else a reaction to the irresponsibility of institutional religion which rationalized passivity and silence on the grounds that the church had more transcendent interests than attacking the social evils of the state and defending the rights and lives of those outside the religious establishment. As in the case of too many German Christian theologians in that critical period, activist involvement of the church against the barbarities of the state was judged a violation of *Obrigkeit* [authority] and a meddling with divine *Schöpfungsordnung* [the order of creation].

The new theologians' dissatisfaction with both metaphysical and supernatural theologies has turned them to the moral theology pronounced in the Jewish prophetic tradition. Especially interesting is their receptivity to the values of secularity traditionally disdained as inimical to the religious life.

Ironically, while the Christian descendants of an otherworldly salvationist tradition are turning toward social involvement and the adoption of the values of the secular city, some younger Jewish religious thinkers, children of the Hebrew prophets, are assuming a transhistoric posture and forming a common platform against secularity, humanism, naturalism, and liberalism. We are witness to a historic turnabout of roles: the Protestantization of Judaism and the Judaization of Protestantism. An older Christian vocabulary has crept into some Jewish religious writings and with it a new agenda focused upon sin and salvation, redemption and eschatology. This new approach is accompanied by a weakening of Jewish communal consciousness in favor of personal encounters, a growing anti-intellectualism, and a paternalistic glance at social and political activism.

The theological effort to purge Judaism of "Jewishness" poses one of the serious threats to Jewish self-understanding and conduct. For beneath the attack upon Jewish "ethnicism" lies the threat to the unifying role which peoplehood plays and to the civilizational character of Judaism.

The theologization of Judaism fits especially well into the social condition of fourth-generation American Jews. The latter are less attached to the claims placed upon them as a world people by the covenant; they prefer native and nonsectarian philanthropies to overseas need, are embarrassed by Zionist demands and by the "secular" conflicts with the Christian majority over school prayer and federal aid to parochial schools in which they have to side with secularists and agnostics. The social advantage of making Judaism a religion like all other religions is the newest mode of unhealthy collective assimilation which threatens the uniqueness and authenticity of Jewish religious civilization.

Seymour Siegel

Professor of theology at the Jewish Theological Seminary (Conservative).

❡ Judaism has its ground in the divine-human encounter, which is ordinarily called "revelation." This encounter occurred between the divine and the people of Israel. The divine self-disclosure to the community of Israel resulted in the covenantal obligation assumed by our ancestors. They were to be a "kingdom of priests and holy people," living their individual and communal lives in the presence of God.

The record of this divine-human encounter is contained in the Torah. The Torah (and the rest of the sacred literature of the Jews) is the result of revelation; it is not identical with it. It is the human writing-down of the divine word.

Therefore, the Bible is not infallible. It does not reflect scientific truth (though it may contain it); and it may reflect historical inaccuracies (though it may, and almost always does, reflect historical truth). Both the divine and the human are bound up inexorably in the Torah and cannot be separated or distinguished by means of some formula.

The process by means of which the community of Israel reads the Torah so as to know what is demanded of it in the concrete, historical situation is the process of interpretation called *midrash*. The history of Judaism is the history both of revelation and of the interpretation of revelation. Indeed, "Judaism is based on a minimum of revelation and a maximum of interpretation" (A. J. Heschel). Talmudic literature is basically an attempt on the part of the rabbis to reexperience the original revelation and then to confront their own time, to formulate what must be done. This is the meaning of the rabbinic assertion that both the written Torah and the oral Torah are products of revelation.

One of the most important elements of the revelation is the system of *mitzvot* (commandments) culminating in the system of *halakha*. The purpose of this system is to make concrete the divine demand to be holy and to pursue justice. It is the natural result of the acceptance of the covenant. As the Mishna puts it, first one accepts the yoke of heaven and then one accepts the yoke of the commandments. Through the performance of the *mitzvot*, the Jew acts out his being set apart as a priest people and opens himself to the experience of the divine. Thus, all the *mitzvot* (usually counted as 613—though in effect many fewer are binding since a good many presuppose the existence of the Temple) are theoretically obligatory upon each Jew. However, through the process of interpretation, the tradition has discarded some commandments and added a host of new ones in response to changing conditions. The process of reevaluating the *mitzvot* through interpretation goes on in the living community of the people of Israel. The *mitzvot* are not to be seen as a group of Platonic Ideas existing for all time in their perfect and unchanging character. They are the demands of God upon the community of Israel, which lives in time, and they are therefore subject to change, growth, and (all too frequently) decay. Thus, we do not believe that the Bible's toleration of slavery is to be seen as normative. In a real sense the *halakha* is constantly reevaluated by the *aggada*. The community reinterprets and changes its structure of obligations in the light of their ability to express our faith and by their power to evoke faith. Some commandments are legislated out of existence (for example, the canceling of debts in the year of *shemitta*); others fall by the wayside through neglect (such as the prohibition against eating "new" grain before Passover).

The individual Jew, insofar as he is an active member of the believing community, is guided in the Law by those whom he accepts as its interpreters. He is also guided by his *ability* to observe the Law, and this is dependent upon his education and his spiritual preparedness. So long as he is serious about his responsibility and concerned about his Jewishness, he is doing the right thing in the sight of the Lord. But he should always aim to incorporate more and more of Jewish obligation into his life. The entire corpus remains as an obligation and a demand. But each Jew seriously and prayerfully should move as high as possible up the "ladder of Jewish observance" as he gains in sensitivity and understanding. What I have been saying is a restatement of Franz Rosenzweig's thoughts on the question of Jewish observance. Actually, I have little to add beyond his formulation.

From what has been said, it is clear that to make sense of Jewish existence it is necessary to affirm the belief that the community of Israel is not a "natural" community. It is a community founded by the divine in order that it be "His people." The doctrine of the chosenness of Israel involves three motifs—*covenant, responsibility* and *suffering*. "Chosenness" is not for privilege, but for covenant with God. It involves a relationship with the divine which imposes responsibilities and obligations. This idea is in direct opposition to ideas of inherent wisdom or natural superiority. The Bible is clear in stating that the Jews were not chosen because they were wise or gifted. Israel Zangwill has said that the Bible might almost be looked upon as an anti-Semitic book —because it so frequently and so bitterly criticizes the Jews for their shortcomings and failures. It was the prophet Amos who expressed the motif of responsibility most eloquently: "Only you have I known among the nations of the earth—

therefore, I will visit upon you your iniquities." This responsibility means that the Jew by his very being offends totalitarians of all kinds. The Jew—even if he be a non-believer—is perceived as the enemy of those who want to make the nation or the party the sole arbiter of value. It is uncanny that this feeling of chosenness should be found in the deep recesses of the consciousness of most Jews, even if they are indifferent to Judaism. "I have yet to find a Jew who does not in some manner or form exhibit this profound sense of difference and special vocation" (Will Herberg). It is possible, of course, to misunderstand the doctrine of chosenness and transmute it into the mad theories of national and racial superiority. It is also true that some Jews have been guilty of such misunderstanding. But for those who understand the meaning of chosenness in its biblical and rabbinic sense, comparing it to the Nazi abomination or to white supremacy is like comparing a man to a monkey.

Judaism has recognized that the experience of the divine is not limited to Jews. One of the most striking features of rabbinic Judaism is the idea of a covenant made with the children of Noah (that is, before there were any Jews) wherein they too were obligated to observe the seven commandments known as the Noahide laws. These represent a kind of natural religion and ethic. Judaism is the one true religion for the Jew because it is the content of the specific covenant made with the children of Israel. Every Jew is a member of the covenant by virtue of his having been born a Jew or because of voluntary obligation, through conversion. Other peoples have their covenants. I find most cogent and meaningful the double covenant theory of Franz Rosenzweig which sees Christianity as the "Judaism of the Gentiles": through it they establish their relationship to the divine. These religions, based on the Bible, "carry the word of God to the far islands" (Moses Maimonides). As long as the non-Jew is true to the seven laws of Noah, he is fulfilling his obligation. Judaism has wisely postponed the universal acceptance of Judaism until the end of time—that is, it has recognized that in historical times, men will have different religions and worship God in their own way. Judaism and the other religions are like parallel lines which will meet in eternity.

The Jew has much to contribute to the world. His long history and his long attachment to humanistic values and rationality have trained him to extraordinary sensitivity and resulted in phenomenal achievement. The values which inhere in Judaism are important, even vital, for our civilization. But over and above this, the Jews have an obligation to continue to exist as a community, and as such, to stand witness against themselves and against others who are tempted to worship false gods. The Jew waits patiently for the redemption of the world—though he is bidden to be active in helping to bring it about.

Judaism has accumulated great wisdom which can be applied to the solution of ethical dilemmas. It is lamentable that Jewish scholars and thinkers have not done more to make this known to the wider community. But in terms of ethical obligation, all men are judged by God. We must, therefore, work together with all men of good will in the promotion of humanistic values. There is a basic difference in viewpoint between the believer who sees his ethical obligation rooted in the divine demand and the humanist who knows no outside source for his duty. The latter lives on the so-called unearned increment of the capital invested by his forefathers, who derived their morality from their relation to God. It is possible to start with new axioms such as "peace is war" (as is being done in some totalitarian countries and as might be done in 1984). This does not mean that non-religious people are ethically inferior to religious people. All too frequently the opposite is true. But the moral principles of the religiously committed man are more reliably anchored.

Judaism possesses a particular ethical viewpoint. It cherishes the individual as created in God's image. It commands the pursuit of justice and the practice of mercy. It is realistic about the weakness and the potentiality for evil found in human nature. The demand of Judaism is to put these principles into practice in all spheres of human concern. The precise application of the ethical demands of Judaism may be subject to differing interpretations. Jews may thus be Democrats or Republicans, socialists or capitalists. But they cannot at the same time be true to their religious responsibility and be partisans of movements or systems of government which are founded on the supposition that human worth is subservient to the state and that some human beings are not entitled to the dignity which is theirs as beings created in God's image. Thus, Fascism, Communism, racism, and other personality-denying ideologies are antithetical to Judaism.

For a long time, Jewish theology followed Christian theology. Today, in several significant ways, Christian theology is returning the compliment. Christian thinkers are beginning to understand the importance of the theological notion of *galut*, of the believing community as the people of God, and of the importance of the world as the arena where God and man meet. The Jew is not a tourist in the "secular city." He finds himself on familiar ground. The thrust of the system of *halakha* was to move the area of concern out of the sanctuary into the place "where the action is." In regard to the "death of God" controversy, the Jewish thinker should be impressed by the sincerity and the acuteness of the demand of those who want to make us explain in understandable terms what we mean when we say God. It is also important to realize what tasks we as people must be willing to undertake, what problems we must solve without thrusting the burden on God. "We solve problems one by one; we rely on the One to conquer evil finally" (A. J. Heschel). Insofar as the death-of-God writers have called for clarity and demanded action in the midst of the "city," they are welcome. But though the Jew has known, only too well, the eclipse of God, he cannot admit His complete absence. Though God may be a *hiding* God, He is not a hidden God. Of course, the idols whom we sometimes call God must be smashed. The fuzzy ideas we hold about Him must be clarified. From Philo through Maimonides until our own day this has been seen as a religious duty. But as Rosenzweig and others have stressed, the reality of the divine is a *datum* of experience—a reality different from the world of man. He who does not share this experience has not opened himself up to it.

The aspects of modern thought which are most disturbing are those which lead either to a Prometheanism in which the achievements of man are celebrated, or to a radical anomie in which all standards of value are reduced to human whim or historical accident. The first seems to be present in those who have been overwhelmed by the success of technology; the latter is most prevalent among the social scientists. There are many problems to which Jewish thought must address itself. First and foremost, Jewish thought must try to fathom the meaning of the European holocaust. To many it has meant that faith in God and man vanished in the smoke of Auschwitz; for others, it was a tragic confirmation of the special character of Jewish existence. But for all Jews (and non-Jews as well) it remains the most agonizing question of our age. I believe very strongly that when we wrestle with these awful facts with deep conviction and with open souls we will understand better the meaning of Jewish existence and the majesty and awful grandeur of God.

Ezra Spicehandler

Teacher of Hebrew literature at Hebrew Union College (Reform) in Cincinnati; he is presently on leave in Israel.

℃ (1) The questions posed by the organizers of the symposium on Judaism and Jewish belief reflect an essentialist view which turns Judaism over on its head by proceeding from doctrine to practice. Historically, Judaism moved in the opposite direction, arriving at doctrine through practice. While it is true that Jews believed that the Torah (or parts of it) were revealed at Sinai, I doubt whether any generation of Jews performed *mitzvot* because of this belief, even in those rare Jewish communities where theologizing was in vogue (medieval Spain or nineteenth-century Germany). Jews observed *mitzvot* because for them *halakha* was a way of life, a discipline of acts under whose yoke one was placed from the moment of his birth. The machinery of rationalization was brought into play only after the act was accepted and performed. This explains why, although the act remained constant, the rationale for it was altered with every change in the social and intellectual milieu.

The real crisis in Judaism, I suspect, grows out of the fact that following the Emancipation, the religious *act* itself was put into question: Jews stopped observing *mitzvot*. The decline of Jewish practice has more to do with history, economics, and sociology than it has to do with theology. It is the cause, rather than the result, of the failure of modern Jewry to develop a generally accepted intellectual scheme by which to justify Judaism. Attempts to do so have floundered because they could not be grounded in the concrete reality of a practicing community.

But even if the reverse were the case, it is doubtful whether we could possibly arrive at a new Jewish theology in a world which has also rejected secular ideologies. The anachronistic attempts of a number of Jewish theologians to construct academic theologies by adapting existentialist jargon to Judaism represent a case of understandable arrested development (after all, they are for the most part products of the European *Bildungsschicht* and the German *Gymnasia* of the 1930's). These precious existentialist speculations will probably receive a decent burial in the many departments of "Jewish studies" which are now being established at American universities. They do not and will not have much relevance for most Jews.

Judaism may survive the current crisis if it can find its way back to the *mitzvah*—the concrete act. Only after—and not before—the establishment of the *act* will it find the authority for its observance. Here it need not begin *ex nihilo*. Even today, two Jewish facts exist: (1) there are Jews; and (2) many of these Jews practice various *mitzvot*.

The failure of most Jewish theoreticians to come to grips with the bare facts of Jewish existence and Jewish practice constitutes the greatest anomaly in contemporary Jewish life. As a Reform Jew, I have often wondered why my prayer-book, with all its pretensions to relevance and modernity, almost ignores the European holocaust, has not yet formulated an adequate prayer about the relationship of diaspora Jewry to the State of Israel, and speaks only in the vaguest terms about such great American Jewish enterprises as the United Jewish Appeal and Jewish welfare programming. Orthodox and Conservative Judaism have, incidentally, no better record.

Stranger still is that most of these theoreticians not only ignore but usually display hostility toward those few practices and customs which many American Jews still observe. Blatant examples of this attitude are the many rabbinical barbs which are aimed at institutions such as the funeral, the wedding, and the *bar mitzvah*. Granted that these institutions have frequently been vulgarized, but their very persistence (and even their elaboration) testifies to their vitality. As practices which are tied to the life cycle, they are *real* and deeply rooted in the Jewish psyche. Their reality supersedes any intellectual or aesthetic formulations of Jewish creed. To these we might add many other Jewish practices and sentiments: the persistence of Rosh Hashanah, Yom Kippur, and Passover, the fear of intermarriage, the feeling of Jewish solidarity in the face of anti-Semitism, preoccupation with Jewish welfare projects, the involvement with Israel and world Jewry, and the deep sensitivity to social justice. I make bold to suggest that for the contemporary Jew a contribution to a Jewish Welfare Fund, attendance at a Bonds for Israel dinner, participation in a demonstration in behalf of Soviet Jewry have become *mitzvot*. Both the compulsion (social as well as moral) to observe such *mitzvot* and the satisfaction derived from their discharge have a religious significance which is often greater than that engendered by many traditional *mitzvot*.

Given the context of a practicing community, one may perhaps move to the sort of conceptualization which seems to attract the organizers of our symposium. For obviously, if Jews perform *mitzvot* which grow out of deep religious and historical needs, the Jews would wish to relate them to Torah and God. In the course of this process the very meaning of Torah and revelation will change to fit the needs of the practicing community.

(2) History has turned the "myth" that Jews are the chosen people of God into a reality. By rejecting the majority religions, Jews remained "exiles" in the Moslem and Christian world, and by this choice their fate has been determined. As a minority people, they became and still are the touchstones of history, marking by their own prosperity or adversity the high and low watermarks of Western civilization. Victimized as Jews often were, they learned in the flesh

to empathize with the persecuted and the exiled and thus were reinforced in the ethical views which they already had accepted in biblical times.

Individual Jews have escaped this burden of history by assimilation, but I doubt whether they can do so as a group —even in Israel. Jewish achievements in Western culture are a byproduct of the Jewish historical situation. While I reject any attempt to justify "exile" or the death of a single Jewish child at the hands of a Nazi butcher, there is some consolation in the fact that despite his historic situation, or perhaps because of it, the Jew has contributed so much to Western civilization.

It is a calumny to assert that the "doctrine of choice" serves or served as a model for various theories of national or racial superiority. The "myth of choice" insists that God chose Israel even though Israel hardly merited such a choice. The Jew received no privileges but a burden of moral and religious obligations. Like their neighbors, Jews sometimes displayed religious chauvinism. Toynbee's assertion that they were the first to do so is an error in historical fact, which was probably spawned in some unconscious mire of prejudice. Intolerance toward human beings who are outside the group is a primitive evil, shared by almost all societies. Certainly Judaism, with its repeated stress on obligations toward "the stranger," often rejected xenophobia. Racialism and nationalism are nineteenth-century concepts which were beyond the cultural world of ancient and medieval man. Traditionally, any Gentile could become a Jew if he followed certain prescribed rituals and if he was willing to assume the burdens of Judaism.

Among certain Christians and Jews there seems to have developed a morbid compulsion to blame everything on the Jew—even the very racialism and anti-Semitism which almost destroyed him. Jews ought not to permit Gentiles or fellow Jews to confuse a theological and ethical doctrine of choice with such biological superstitions as Nazism and to employ such a false analogy as a ready device to relieve them of responsibility for the death of six million Jews.

(3) Judaism is certainly not the one true religion. Even according to the Talmud, all who observe the Noahide laws

have a share in the world to come. In the nineteenth century, essayists played charming games in which they defined differences between their own religion and others, attributing all sorts of unwholesome doctrines to the latter while reserving the noblest doctrines for their own. I do hope that we have moved beyond such games.

Certainly Judaism contains a fascinating blend of ethnic particularism and universal religion—so does the Greek Orthodox Church. Compared to certain Christian sects which believe in the incarnation of God, Judaism posits a more pristine monotheism which defines God as wholly other than man. But there are many Christian groups which agree with this view. Judaism is comparatively free from the doctrine of original sin and the rather morbid view of man and of sex which sometimes is derived from it. Many Christians also reject original sin or, at least, the distasteful consequences which may spring from it. Finally, Judaism seems to give greater emphasis to law and to lay stress upon mercy and love. But, then, there are the Hasidim and the Calvinists to consider.

What distinguishes the modern Jew from his Christian neighbor is his historical, sociological situation rather than a set of theological beliefs. To be sure, this distinction sometimes reflects itself in differences in theology, but that is a result rather than an effect.

(4) Judaism is neither conservative nor liberal in its political point of view. It opposes any political philosophy which destroys the image of man as a child of God or places *Realpolitik* above God's ethical commandments. Judaism would therefore reject racialism and racial segregation, Fascism and those forms of Communism which find their theoretical bases in dialectical materialism.

Jews are individuals and as such hold all sorts of political views—even anti-Jewishness.

(5) The "God is dead" theology has relevance for contemporary Jews. The critique of conventional religious attitudes propagated by this "new" theology might serve to clear both the Synagogue and the Church of much deadwood and cant. In a sense both Reconstructionism and Reform Judaism

proclaimed the old God "dead" almost half a century ago. The God to whom such Jews pray is a "natural," a "symbolic" God and not a "supernatural" or "anthropomorphic" God. The masses of Jewish worshipers even in liberal synagogues tend to confuse the traditional God with the new God. Yet the suggestion by an American rabbi that we eliminate the historical terminology of religion from the synagogue service violates the sense of religious continuity.

Ultimately we are brought up against two diametrically opposed views of Jewish history: an analytic view which would read Jewish history as a chronological sequence of otherwise disconnected events, and a synthetic view which conceives of Jewish history as a unified structure. Advocates of an analytic approach would argue that the contemporary view of religion is radically different from the traditional one and that therefore the continued use of the term "God" is misleading and inaccurate. Those holding a synthetic view would insist that the God of contemporary Jewish theology is linked by history and by tradition to the God of the past and that modern man perceives with greater clarity what ancient man saw dimly and inaccurately.

My own prejudices lie with the synthetic view. In the history of man, concepts undergo metamorphosis but they reach back to antiquity. A sense of history unites the present with the past, giving a symbolic unity to the strivings of man. I am happy to see that at least one Christian advocate of the new theology shares this view (Harvey Cox, *The Secular City*).

The greatest danger to Judaism is that so many Jews have lost their sense of Jewish particularity. Judaism's contribution to Western culture has been its synthesis of Jewish particularism with universal ethical values. The Jewish people are one of the *realia* out of which Judaism springs.

Several years ago I undertook to translate into modern Hebrew an essay by Karl Shapiro in which he discussed, among other things, the relationship between Jewishness and Judaism. At that time, I was struck by the fact that modern Hebrew used a single word for both concepts, *yahadut*, and that this word also denoted Jewry. I had to construct a new and awkward word—*yehudiyut*—for Jewishness (I was somewhat surprised to discover that others had independently used it before me).

The point is that Jewishness and Judaism, until recently an inseparable whole, have begun to go their separate ways. It is doubtful whether this process can be arrested, but if the breach widens, it bodes ill for the future of Judaism and of Jews, both in Israel and in the diaspora.

Jewishness, like the Jewish religious act, is the concrete reality from which Judaism arises. Ultimately it is the *mitzvah*-performing Jewish community which will determine the nature of that abstract scheme of values which men call Judaism.

M. D. Tendler

Professor of biology at Yeshiva University (Orthodox) and teacher of Talmudic law at its theological school.

❦ Avtalyon says: "Sages, be most careful in your teachings . . . lest your students who succeed you, drink thereof and die—and thus the name of God be profaned" (B. Avot I).

The errorless transmission of the truths of our faith requires meticulous care in choice of words and idioms. The personal *rebbe-talmid* relationship is the main guarantee that errors due to faulty student comprehension do not blemish the perfection of the Torah concept.

This attempt to state some of the most fundamental beliefs of Judaism through the impersonal medium of a published article is fraught with danger. The written word lies naked on the page with all its inadequacies exposed for all to see. Can I possibly prevent the false impression, the mistaken connotation, the erroneous deduction, in this attempt to teach the Torah "while standing on one foot"? Unfortunately, I cannot hope for such perfection of idiom. I can, however, beseech the reader of my words to remember that my inadequacies are not those of our Torah whose words are "absolute truth complementing each other in their righteousness" (Ps. 19:10).

(1) The literal interpretation of the theological doctrine of divine revelation differentiates Torah Judaism from the organized faith communities that have arisen as deviants from the traditional form. The development of Christianity during the last nineteen hundred years and the development of Reform and Conservative Judaism during the last hundred years represent similar deviations from the literal interpretation and application of the divinely revealed code of human conduct—the prophecy of Moses; the Torah.

It is the foundation of our faith that God spoke unto Moses as a teacher instructs his pupil. Unlike other prophets, Moses did not receive his instructions while asleep or in a trancelike, physiologically abnormal state. Moses heard and recorded the word of God while mentally alert and intellectually responsive. Only Moses received a Torah—a code of human conduct. The later prophets did not simplify or "liberalize" the Torah. Their sole contribution was to instruct the Jewish nation and to exhort them to observe the Torah without modification. This prophecy, the Torah, was received by Moses accompanied by the necessary explanatory details. The actual words and sentence structure of this divine revelation are recorded in the Pentateuch—the Five Books of Moses.

There is yet another record of divine revelation—the oral tradition, comprising the explanatory notes and details of the biblical ordinances recorded in the Pentateuch. The oral tradition is now recorded in the Talmud along with the later man-made rabbinic edicts. Thus the Pentateuch and the oral tradition are of equal authority, are equally obligatory on all Jews as the direct instructions of God to His nation, Israel.

The Torah (written and oral) records our duties at times in great specific detail, at other times in broad principles. The Talmud presents for study the differing opinions of our sages with respect to the application of these principles to specific legal or ritual circumstances. These discussions, pro and con, enable us to encompass intellectually the full intent of the God-given principle and thus give us the understanding to apply it to new situations not discussed in the Talmud. Thus, in this age of scientific, technological, and sociological advances, the divinely revealed Torah principles serve as the objective yardsticks by which all new concepts and actions are measured. The vital and vibrant biblical scholarship of the Orthodox communities in all the countries of the diaspora, as recorded in the staggering number of *responsa* publications dealing with every aspect of human endeavor, bears irrefutable testimony to the greatness of our Torah. Rather than stultifying and mummifying our lives by lists of obligations and prohibitions, our Torah, as given to us by God on Mount Sinai thirty-three hundred years ago, has proven applicable to all societies throughout our nation's history.

The vast majority of these applications of Torah principles has been codified in our law books—the writings of the *Geonim, Rishonim* and later sages. These applications serve as precedents, simplifying our task of applying the Torah principles to modern-day problems. These secondary sources have, through centuries of usage, been accorded the greatest allegiance by the Torah community. The renown of the Shulhan Arukh, authored by Rabbi Joseph Karo, earned for it the role of final arbiter in all disputed matters upon which he commented.

The role of the rabbis as lawgivers must also be mentioned. We are careful to distinguish between the divinely revealed oral tradition recorded in the Talmud and the later man-made edicts. The rabbinic edicts were mostly designed to protect the biblical law—to serve as "fences around the law." For example, the present-day observance of dietary laws necessitates the use of separate dinnerware for meat and dairy meals. This is a result of a rabbinic injunction proclaimed to protect the biblical law against cooking mixtures of meat and dairy products. When, in response to the religious needs of our people, the rabbis promulgated new laws and edicts, occasionally unrelated to biblical ordinances, these rabbinic laws became obligatory on every Jew after they proved themselves useful and practicable. The Bible specifically sanctions the rabbinic right to make such ordinances. Thus in actual practice, every traditional Jew accepts these rabbinic laws as no less obligatory than the biblical laws.

All the biblical commandments are binding on every Jewish male when he reaches thirteen years of age. Women, who assume their religious obligations a year earlier, are exempt from some of the 248 positive commandments. Likewise, those commandments specifically ordained for the *Kohen* or Levite apply only to these classes of Israelites. There are no significant distinctions between the sexes with respect to the obligation to abstain from the 365 biblical prohibitions.

Because of the destruction of our Temple and the exile of the Jewish nation from the land of Israel, many of the commandments governing the Temple service and priestly conduct are not in effect today. Only 77 of the 248 positive commandments and 194 of the 365 biblical prohibitions play any significant role in the conduct of the Jew living outside of the land of Israel. The others await the coming of the Messiah and the reestablishment of the theocracy in Israel.

All the Torah commandments are given to the Jew for his ennoblement. There are none "lacking ethical or doctrinal content." The *mishpatim* are those commandments whose purpose and utility are clearly understood. The *hukim* are those whose full intent is not known. It is axiomatic that our omniscient God did not give us arbitrary or purposeless responsibilities. All of them have ethical or doctrinal import. King Solomon boasted that he knew the true reason for the *hukim* of the Torah except those governing the sacrifice of the red heifer (Num. 19:1–13). Our failure to devote adequate time and effort to the study of our Torah has drawn a veil over some of God's commandments.

Throughout the ages, the dictum "The study of the Torah equals all else" has encouraged our rabbis to search for and to postulate reasons even for the *hukim*. The dangers that are inherent in this search are obvious. A human reason for a divine edict may be in error. The refutation of this man-given explanation can weaken the integrity of the biblical commandment in the mind of the uncritical layman. A prime example of this pattern is the health-code explanation for the Jewish dietary laws offered by the early writers of Reform Judaism. To many laymen who accepted this explanation as the true one, the efforts of the U. S. Department of Agriculture and the Public Health Service exempted them from the obligation to observe these tenets of our faith.

Thus the search for reasons (*taamei hamitzvot*) has been rejected by some of our scholars as unnecessary, if not essentially destructive. However, to many of our sages, exercising their right and responsibility to search for new insights as valid reasons for all Torah commandments best fulfills their obligation "to teach them diligently to thy sons" (Deut. 6:7).

The specific example of the questioner concerning the prohibition of wearing clothing woven of a mixture of wool and linen fibers is explained by Maimonides (in his *Guide of the Perplexed*, 38) as a denial of idolatrous practice and a reaffirmation of our monotheistic belief. In his study of the idolatrous religions that were once the dominant cultures, Maimonides noted that the priests wore, as a talisman, clothing of wool and linen while holding in their hands a mineral object. The symbolic intent was to encompass the entire material world during their idolatrous service and thus invoke the blessings of the many gods on the main industries of man: agriculture (linen), animal husbandry (wool), and mining (mineral).

This reason of Maimonides is meaningful to me now. Even my garments proclaim the oneness of God! However, the key reservation must be understood. Maimonides discerned this reason through his intense study of our Torah and his understanding of the secular world of his day. If he be proven totally in error, the Torah commandment against the wearing of clothing woven of wool and linen threads (*shatnez*) is in no way either less binding or less acceptable to us.

(2) There are two aspects of Israel's unique status as the chosen people. The first and foremost is the fact that the nation Israel chose to accept the Torah way of life. The Talmud is careful to point out that the same choice was offered to all other nations of the earth. Only Israel agreed to accept the discipline of the 613 commandments. To this day, any convert to Judaism joins in this "chosenness" by dint of voluntary choice. No Semite was ever given the choice to become an "Aryan" by the racists who undertook to destroy the chosen people.

Does the fact that Israel is the chosen people demean other peoples who have not chosen to follow the Torah way of life? No one even casually conversant with biblical and tal-

mudic literature can doubt that this superiority is uniquely
different from the chauvinism and racism abounding in the
secular world. It is—and this is the second aspect—a uniqueness of responsibility, an assumption of obligations that casts
no aspersions on those who chose not to assume them. It is
the divine scheme for humanity that only if the Jew observes his Torah, and the non-Jew his Torah, will the world
survive. If there is synergistic benefit in this association, it is
as it should be.

The Talmud sums it up most beautifully (Talmud Bavli,
Berakhot 17a). The wise men of Yavneh were the chosen of
the chosen. The nation Israel had just suffered the near-
fatal blow of the destruction of the Temple and the desola-
tion of the land of Israel. In the hands of the wise men of
Yavneh rested the destiny of the nation Israel. Never before
had any group more reason to feel superior. Never before
had the crown of Israel, the Torah, become the sole property
of so few. Yet "they were wont to say, 'I am but one of God's
creatures just as is my unlearned friend. My labors are in
the city, his in the fields. I arise early to my work just as
he does. Lest you say I accomplish much and he but little,
note. Whether much or little, it is all the same if one but
intends to do his work in the name of Heaven.' "

Judaism is a world religion. It is not a compilation of local
tribal customs. It speaks to Jew and non-Jew. It is a Torah—
a code of conduct for all humanity. It is the only "true"
religion.

God promulgated different obligatory behavior for Jew
and non-Jew, just as He differentiated between man and
woman, and between *Kohen*, Levite, and Israelite. The seven
Noahide laws are binding on all humanity. They have served
as the basis for all civilized codes of conduct. They are the
Torah of the non-Jew. In this sense there is but one true
religion. There is one true record of the responsibilities demanded by God of man created in His image.

The concept of a "true religion" is often intertwined with
the requirements for "salvation." The 613 *mitzvot* are the
means by which a Jew earns salvation. The non-Jew can
achieve the same goal in seven giant steps, the Noahide laws.
If the non-Jew observes these fundamental laws, his religion
is equally true.

Despite the influence Judaism wielded in forming most of our present concepts of man-God and man-man relationships, it still remains basically unique and distinctive. The broad brush strokes on the canvas of all the great religions testify to their Judaic heritage. The fine art work bears little resemblance. Even the concept of one God, monotheism, is not equally shared by Judaism and Christianity. The total negation of the "other gods" is found only in Judaism. Negation of intermediaries in prayer to God, denial of all superstitions and astrological influences as opposed to the conscious will of God, is the basic tenet only of Judaism. The monotheistic belief in a personal God who knows and cares, who ordains and instructs man even in every mundane human activity, evolved in a practical, not theoretical, code of conduct only in Judaism.

Our greatest "contributions" to humanity have yet to be taken over by other religions. For example, let us analyze the Sabbath concept in Judaism. Its socioeconomic value has been properly recognized. However, in the age of man, this contribution fades in significance when compared to the main concept of the unique Jewish Sabbath. It is a day reserved for vigorous toil in the uniquely human sphere and for a rebalancing of the spiritual and material influences on man. For six days we share with the beasts of the field a common goal—material sustenance. Only on the Sabbath day, when we proclaim God the creator and man as one created in His image, do we assume truly human proportion. To rest by lying on a hammock, ruminating on a large meal, would be a further mimicry of the animal world. To "rest" by spending the day in intellectual disquietude, by mind-wracking study of God and man, by fatiguing examination of the children's studies that week, is a uniquely Jewish concept hardly understood, let alone shared, by other religions. The manifold Sabbath prohibitions that serve to negate man's role as a creator in opposition to God, coupled with the obligation to make of the Sabbath meal and dress an occasion for material pleasure, serve to establish the golden mean for every Jew. God decries both asceticism and hedonism. He has given us a way of life fit for mortals who aspire to human existence.

Similarly, in the ethical sphere of man-man relations, Judaism remains unique despite the espousing of the Judaic heritage by other ethical systems. Our Torah stands on the two legs of man-man and man-God relationships. Our system of ethics cannot be "taught on one foot" because it is the intertwining of the man-God relationship that guarantees the appreciation of the Torah concept of ethics. The famous response of the Great Sage of Israel, Hillel, to the request of the non-Jew that he teach him our Torah while "standing on one foot" best summarizes this thesis. Indeed, it can be summarized by the simple dictum: "That which is hateful to thee do not do unto your fellow man," but the understanding of this dictum requires you "to go and finish your studies of the man-God relationship."

Empathy, charity, kindness are the results of observance of the Torah commandments governing our mutual responsibilities. They are not the motivations of these observances. I feed the poor because the Torah so ordained. This permits me to absorb in my personality both sympathy and understanding for the needs of others. If my feeding of the poor depended upon the preexistence of a sympathetic soul, as presumed by ethical systems without religion or by those of other religions, the poor would all too often go hungry if I were not at that moment emotionally attuned.

In most ethical concepts, our differences with other religions far exceed the similarities. Indeed, we have much to contribute to all nations. The lack is only that of suitable and articulate exponents to serve as "prophet unto the nations."

(4) Judaism is a total code of conduct. No sphere of human endeavor is neglected. Most certainly there is the "opinion of Torah" (da'at ha-Torah) on the great political, sociological, and economic issues of the day. A Jew cannot observe our Torah commandments and at the same time be a Communist, or a racist, or a Fascist, any more than he could at the same time be a Shintoist or Buddhist. The Torah governs how much profit he may make on a sale, as well as how much charity he must or may give. The law of the land is given Torah support to make it binding on every Jew—but only if it does not require the Jew to violate the ethical teachings of his religion. If men band together to

establish a democratic welfare state, or a monarchy, the Torah then adds its authority to the need for observance of all the laws of the kingdom. If, however, taxation is imposed inequitably; if the integrity and worth of the individual are denied; if due process of law is violated, the Torah cries out with divine authority—"Cease and desist, lest I turn the world to ashes!" A racist doctrine, promulgated by the governmental authorities, is as hateful to the Jewish citizen as the promulgation of the classical anti-Semitic ordinances so familiar to the Jew of history.

(5) Our living God "dies" in many ways. The "God is dead" theology has been our bitter enemy since God descended on Mount Sinai to give us a Torah. To proclaim God the Creator every Friday eve, and to declare him King every Rosh Hashanah, is hardly proof that He is not "dead." If we literally proclaim, *The Heaven is the Lord's*," and "*the earth is given unto man*" (Ps. 115:16), then we have a "God is dead" theology. Only when we recite at the Friday eve *kiddush* that in addition to making the heavens and the earth, God also redeemed us from Egypt do we proclaim, "The God of Israel liveth forever." God who is too exalted to care about the daily activities of man is a "dead God." God who is too liberal to restrict man by the issuance of a code of human conduct analagous to the code of natural laws He proclaimed for the rest of creation is a "dead God."

When a Jew discusses the great problems of our age—race relations, world population control, international relations—from a purely sociological, political, or economic point of view, he proclaims that the God of Judaism is "dead." The Torah has a point of view. The Torah is a repository of progressive, feasible solutions to the problems of mankind that dare not be overlooked. God lives and speaks anew to us each day. Would that we listened!

The great challenge to Torah Judaism has always been the same. Ignorance of the teachings of our faith is our only worthy adversary. Appreciation of the relevance of Torah concepts is directly related to the time devoted to the study of our Torah teachings. Ignorance of what we say and what we believe can mislead our youth into assuming that the Torah does not maintain its role of guide and mentor of human conduct. With man appearing more and more in the central role of master of the physical universe, the omnipresent danger of declaring man as creator and master assumes new proportions.

The invasion of the uniquely human area, that of memory, intellect, and emotion, by psychotropic pharmaceuticals which put the veneer of mechanistic behavior on this last vestige of uniquely human attributes, points up most sharply the need for a Torah system of human values. The Jew recites each morning in his prayers, "Although the preeminence of man over beast is naught . . . we, the children of Thy covenant can truly say 'How goodly is our lot, how beautiful our heritage.'"

Dudley Weinberg

Rabbi of Congregation Emanuel B'nai Jeshurun
(Reform) in Milwaukee.

❡ A symposium like the present one is inevitably governed by a set of ground rules which are none the less effective for their apparent unobtrusiveness. This is not to suggest that any limits other than those of space are placed upon the range or the substance of the discussion. The unwritten ground rules grow out of the very questions which are offered for consideration. The presentation for serious discussion of precisely these questions comes very close to being a tacit declaration that there is a core of abiding validity in Judaism's traditionally characteristic view of the people Israel and of Israel's Torah. The questions seem almost to rule out the possibility of completely negative replies.

These preliminary remarks are not meant to imply either that the questions have been rigged or that it is time to rejoice over the impending victory of religion over secularism. What does seem clear is that the questions reflect, at the very least, a certain disillusionment with insistently "secular" accounts of the specific Jewish experience in history and of the human enterprise in general. The climate which produces this set of questions for discussion here seems to welcome Jewish *religious* affirmations.

The hospitality of the climate does not of itself, however, make it easy to produce crisp formulations of such affirmations. Not even a Jew who earnestly accepts the discipline of the Shulhan Arukh can glibly say why he does so if he has kept his mind and his spirit open to the flow of history as our generation has experienced it, and to the terms in which so many contemporary men of goodwill have expressed their understanding of the human situation. How much less easily, then, can a Reform Jew who does not accord equal a priori validity to all of the carefully defined traditional disciplines offer precise answers to the crucial questions posed here. Questions as large as these require volumes for proper reply. Perhaps the only ultimately convincing answers are not those which are given verbally at all, but those which are given with one's whole life. In any case, the verbal attempt must be made, however clumsily, in the hope that it will point to what escapes words and perhaps does not need them.

Two assertions of faith seem to me to be indispensable and unavoidable. The first is that the people Israel has been and is addressed by God. The second is that Israel responded and responds to that address; its corollary is that Torah is at least a partial record of Israel's apprehension of the divine address and of Israel's response to it.

The divine address belongs to the "givenness" of Israel's experience; so, in all likelihood, does the essence of Israel's response. Both address and response lie in that area of human experience which escapes all efforts to describe and contain it within a systematic and logical construction. To say this is not to mount an attack on systems or on logic. It is only to say that the logic of life as we experience life is larger than the systems of logic which our rational powers can construct. It is also to suggest that when we admit into our conscious concerns only what can be contained and managed in our logical systems, we do violence to ourselves and deprive ourselves of precious and sometimes awesome sources of meaning and joy.

Does it follow that no people other than Israel is addressed? There is no reason to assume so. Nor does our tradition make such an assumption. On the contrary, the ancient *aggada*, speaking in its own culturally conditioned idiom, declares that the Torah was offered to all the nations and peoples of the world before it was offered to Israel. To be sure, it also adds that the response of the non-Israelite peoples was negative and that Israel alone replied in trustful obedience. Whether or not contemporary Jews would still pronounce such a pejorative judgment on non-Jewish peoples or would feel any need to do so is open to debate. What is *not* arguable, even in the narrowest construction of the tradition, is that the divine address is not and never was limited to Israel. The seven Noahide commandments are by their very designation directed to the entire human race. And, of course, it was never maintained that the initial wholehearted response of Israel was very durable. The golden-calf incident followed distressingly hard on Israel's eager acceptance of the Torah, and ever since, the people has described itself as a community of sinners in need of the merciful forgiveness of God.

What then distinguishes Israel from the other peoples of the world? Certainly not that they alone are addressed by God. The difference lies in their apprehension of the address and in their grateful and dutiful response to it. The two together produced the fruit which is called Torah: the scriptural text and all the subsequent texts which flowed from the persistent and continuing efforts of the teachers of the Jewish people to understand the divine address and to know what it requires of them. The struggle to do and to be what was and is understood to be required is the story of Israel's career in history.

This is not the place to attempt to "demonstrate" that the divine address occurred and occurs. That it did and does is unabashedly offered here as a prime article of faith. Without it, the emergence of the human enterprise in what we experience as an utterly nonhuman universe is totally incomprehensible. What human beings do when they write poetry, paint pictures, or make music—even badly; what they do when they organize the enormous variety of their sensory impressions into the truth-seeking systems they call science— even inadequately; what they undertake when they attempt to establish such relationships between persons and peoples as will produce what men call justice, love, peace—however tragically they fail: none of this is understandable in a universe which seems otherwise unconcerned with beauty, truth, and goodness apart from a "word" which is spoken to man, which man "hears" and to which he responds. God "speaks" and man has a task—and it is precisely this divinely given task that constitutes his humanity. The "speaking" is surely addressed to all men. What differs from person to person and from people to people is the apprehension of the address and the response to it. Ultimately, both are set down in terms which embody the unique characteristics of specific persons and specific peoples. This too our tradition seems to understand and recognize when it says, "The Torah speaks in human language."

It remains to be added that as Jewish tradition sees it, the address, the ability to "hear" the address, and the capacity to respond to it are all divinely given gifts. They may be used and enjoyed, but they are never merely *quid pro quo* rewards for labor commendably performed. They are gifts, conferred out of the overflow of what in our "human language" we call God's love.

Ah yes, the questions! Certain answers emerge from the foregoing. Their editorially enforced brevity should not be misunderstood as a claim for their unassailable validity.

(1) The Torah is surely divine revelation insofar as it reports Israel's apprehension of and response to the divine address. Without the address which is "absolute" and "eternal," the historically conditioned human apprehension and response could not have occurred.

Rabbinic tradition says that the ultimate response was expressed in 613 commandments. However many they actually are at any given time, the effective commandments can never be truly understood apart from the concrete situation in which a specific Jew or a specific community of Jews is located. Accordingly, even in traditional terms many of the commandments are inoperative since their actual performance depends upon circumstances which do not obtain, e.g., the existence of the Jerusalem Temple or residence in *Eretz Yisrael*.

Jews, like anyone else, can respond genuinely only in their specific living situation. To be sure, that situation includes memories of responses which were made in former situations. Such recollected responses (commandments) may continue to be observed as precious reminders of yesterday's loving reply to the divine love and as stimuli to today's continuing response. It is precisely the loving human response to the divine love that is expressed in the nonethical and nondoctrinal commandments. These, like genuine prayer, are truly devotional acts. But it happens in the course of time that the concrete situation changes so radically that the recall of *some* earlier responses no longer evokes present responses. In that case, the repetition of the earlier response is no longer loving; it is merely nostalgic. Worse still, it may express a preference for the habitual and certain ways of an old remembered love rather than a willingness to risk the uncertain demands of a renewed and living love.

For the vast majority of contemporary Jews, the prohibition against the use of clothing made of a mixture of linen and wool is surely neither a vital memory of loving response to the divine address nor a present response to it. The prohibition is therefore for them inoperative as one of the duties which love imposes. Jews should observe both those commandments which are genuinely and immediately expressive of their responding love and those other commandments which can effectively remind them that love once was and still can be.

A warning is required here. Before a Jew or a group within the Jewish community decides that any traditionally inherited precept is no longer obligatory, it must give that precept and the possible implications of its cancellation more than hasty and cavalier attention. Such cancellations indeed have often been appropriate. But it is also true that the abolition of what is traditionally received may proceed from crude ignorance, from unworthy desire not to be distinguished from the surrounding multitude, and from sheer unwillingness to "hear" the divine address.

(2) The Jews experience themselves as the chosen people of God not because He addressed them alone, but because over the long stretches of history they responded to His address ardently, responsibly, and, as nearly as they could, totally. Whatever they could bring as offerings of love they brought, even and perhaps especially the stuff of their common everyday life. Thus their diet, their dress, their mar-

riage customs, their business procedures, their legal systems, their forms of communal and political organization, their worship—all were invested with heightened and holy significance because, specific and transient though they may have been, they were transformed into vehicles through which their own love of the loving God was expressed. What other people has redeemed even the lowliest functions of the body for exquisite meaning as did the pious Jew for whom those functions became the occasion for a prayerful meditation on the wonder of the human body and the sustaining wisdom of the Creator? Jews knew themselves chosen for God's love because they opened themselves to it by their own carefully cultivated response.

If others see this glory of lover and beloved as a perverse assertion of "national and racial superiority," we can only pray that they too—together with those in the household of Israel who have closed their hearts to the pure love of God —will one day also dare to "hear" the divine address and by their loving response in *their* situations and with the stuff of *their* lives also learn that they are chosen. Every beloved knows himself to be chosen; nor does his awareness of election require that no other should be elected. Faithful love rejoices that others are also beloved. If this means that God "makes covenants" with other peoples, then that is what it means. A doctrine of multiple covenants would in no way damage the uniqueness of the covenant with Israel. Every covenant, every relationship of mutual trust and love, is unique.

(3) Certainly Judaism is "the one true religion"—*for Jews.* It is *their* love and *their* life and the length of *their* days. It is their response out of their personal and collective history to the God whose address they "heard" within that history. And this is what Judaism always has to contribute to the world, for whatever else Judaism is or may become, it is the persistent paradigm of the way in which man in all his finiteness becomes aware of the infinite and of its summons to him. It calls persons and peoples *where* they are and *as* they are to listen, to hearken, and—in grateful awe—to respond, to do the *mitzvah* which love *commands.*

It is the response that makes the difference. Ethical acts

are ethical acts, no more and no less, no matter who performs them. But an ethical act is not yet of itself a *mitzvah*, a commandment. A *mitzvah* is an act, ethical or "ritual," deliberately performed as loving response to the divine address. Does it matter, then, whether an act of justice or of peacemaking is only ethical or is ethical-*mitzvah*? It matters indeed, because the ethical act as often as not fails to achieve what it intends. Repeated failure brings disillusionment and cynicism, and often results in abandonment of ethical values and goals. In the real world, non-*mitzvah* ethics almost invariably needs success in order to persist from generation to generation and even through a single lifetime. It requires a pragmatic demonstration that "honesty is the best policy." The *mitzvah* response does not depend upon success for its validation. Honesty may not always be the best policy in the ambiguous world of business and politics. It is the only possible policy in the unambiguous world of the *mitzvah*. Success and failure are not at issue here, even though their consequences are keenly felt. A man's faithful response to faithful love is at issue—and that is quite a different matter. To put it a bit differently, political "liberals" often grow tired. The man who does his *mitzvah* in loving trust grows stronger in the doing. Perhaps that is why our rabbinic teachers said, "Greater is he who does because he is commanded (*m'tzuveh*) than he who does and is not commanded."

(4) Judaism as a "religion" entails the perfect human response to the perfect human apprehension of the divine address. Man's very inability to achieve perfection in this primary endeavor must render the Jew critical of all other human endeavors for which claims to perfection are made. Judaism requires that a Jew give his utmost loyalty to the *malchut shamayim* (the Kingdom of God), whose corpus of ideal purposes and disciplines would emerge from the perfect "hearing" of the divine address and the perfect response to it. The *malchut shamayim* is *the* standard in terms of which all political standards and systems must be judged and toward which all of them must be moved. Ultimacy belongs to the Kingdom alone even though our comprehension of it is marred by the inadequacy of our human understanding

and therefore involves the risk of grave error. Ultimacy does *not* belong to any historically and socially conditioned political system. The very claim to ultimacy which is inherent in totalitarian political theories and institutions renders them unacceptable—even idolatrous—to the Jew. That is why Judaism is incompatible with Communism and Fascism and why the Jew must resist them and, when possible, struggle to redeem them from their dangerously destructive absolutism. But if it is correct to say that no political view or system may claim the ultimate loyalty of a Jew, then the political system called democracy must also be held to be subject to judgment according to the standards of the *malchut shamayim.*

Since Judaism teaches that all men are equally addressed by God and that the response of each man and each people is equally invited, any political, social, or economic stance which attempts to overrule the divinely conferred equality is contrary to Judaism's requirements. Jews therefore are obligated to resist racial segregation and to seek its elimination from any political entity. Certainly the authority of Judaism may not be invoked to justify racial discrimination of any sort.

(5) The "God is dead" question is not one question but several. All of them are relevant to the Jewish enterprise if only because all questions which are earnestly raised deserve serious consideration by Jews. But these questions are not now being confronted for the first time in Jewish experience and need not frighten us as they might if Judaism had not realistically dealt with them before.

Some of the "God is dead" theologians are concerned with the problem of language. They doubt—and they are entitled to their honest doubts—that the strictly "religious" vocabulary —and especially the word "God," which is so confidently employed in the religious traditions and institutions—has any referents in reality. Others express concern in various ways about the irrelevance of religion to the tormenting flesh-and-blood problems of the world and of this living moment in human history.

These are not Jewish problems. The doubts and the certainties of Judaism are precisely the reverse of those whose difficulties with language prompt them to proclaim the death of God. We are certain about the reality to which our vocabulary about God refers. We are and always have been doubtful about the adequacy of the human language with which we refer to God. We never quite forget that the Torah after all does speak in the language of men and not, if one may say such a thing, in the language of God. The "language of God" is precisely the mystery we struggle to penetrate and to comprehend in our effort to "hear" the divine address to us.

Nor is the problem of relevance to the here-and-now of this world a Jewish problem, for it is in just this world that we believe we are addressed and in which we are called upon to respond. Whatever Judaism may teach concerning what is "beyond" this world, it holds stubbornly that the human task is to labor and to hope for the redemption of this world.

The "God is dead" problem arises primarily from disillusionment with the precise validity and reliability of language on the one hand, and from an essential uneasiness with or even contempt for the world on the other. These attitudes are the most serious sources of "challenge to Jewish belief."

The first arises, at least in part, from intellectual habits which were nurtured by prenuclear physical science and which in turn encouraged the false expectation that human language could achieve a perfect and total expression of reality. That is exactly what scientists once believed science —which is after all simply a human language—would ultimately do. Some scientists still cling to that outmoded belief. The more thoughtful scientists have come to understand the inherent limitations of the scientific vocabulary and no longer make quite such sweeping claims for it. But the older intellectual habits persist and lead to the equally erroneous conclusion that if a vocabulary cannot express all reality perfectly, it expresses no reality at all.

Contempt for the world is an attitude which constantly cries aloud for correction. It is a persistently recurring attitude, perhaps because the world is not easy to manage and is too frequently uncomfortable for human beings. This viewpoint inevitably carries with it either the assertion that any reality genuinely worth knowing lies "beyond" the present world or that no worthy reality is to be found anywhere. Such despairing cynicism springs from non-Jewish sources, religious and nonreligious. The Torah which records the fruit of the Jewish response to the divine address declares that "God saw everything that He had made, and behold, it was very good."

Herbert Weiner

Rabbi of Temple Israel of the Oranges and
Maplewood (Reform) in South Orange, New Jersey.

❐ First a general word—perhaps defensive—about belief and believers. The capacity for belief is a gift, a form of talent which with some can reach the level of genius. Then it can build and move worlds. It can also destroy them. Maybe it is just as well that most of us are given this talent in small —and therefore safe—amounts.

Anyway, the image I fall back on when questioned about my own beliefs is appropriated from Rabbi Abraham Isaac Kuk, the first Chief Rabbi of Palestine (d. 1935). He was a man who wrote much about the desirability of *vadaut*—certainty—and he had much talent for belief, but not so much as to place him out of reach for those of us who are less certain and less talented. Somewhere in his commentary on the prayerbook, Kuk compares the joy that can encompass a believing Jew to waves of shimmering, pulsing, heavenly light. I'm not sure that he was thinking of the aurora borealis, but that is the picture which comes to my mind when I try to recognize my own beliefs about God, Torah, Israel, and, indeed, most of the matters projected for discussion in this symposium. I find that these beliefs have about them an "aurora borealis" quality. There are moments when they can glow with a brightness that lights up the heavens. There are other moments when they become dim, or vanish completely into the darkness.

I wish it were different. That is, I wish that my "waves" of belief were somewhat brighter and more constant. But I do not envy those for whom the blackness of the night has been completely and permanently obliterated by a clear and unwavering brightness. I have met such people. Usually they have a glassy stare. I have the feeling that the smile of com-

passion with which they regard those who do not see their
light can quickly freeze into a grimace of hate for those
who persist in their "blindness."

Actually, I think that the "aurora borealis" type of believer
is quite characteristic of Judaism—a fact which may distinguish it from some other religious faiths. Moses, the greatest
of Jewish "seers," begs God to reveal more of His "ways,"
but is told that "man shall not see Me and live." Abraham
had difficulty perceiving God's justice. The prophet and the
psalmist speak of a "God that hides." Levi Yitzchak summons God to a lawsuit, challenging Him to justify His ob-
scure behavior toward Israel.

I would even venture a definition of religion along these
lines. In Judaism, at any rate, it seems to me that a believer
is not just one who has faith, but one who is always *trying*
to have faith, to see and "reveal" more and more of the light,
both to himself and others. In this enterprise, he uses the
help of "seers" more talented than himself. He uses a wisdom
and a technique which help to sensitize the inner eyes so
that they can penetrate the darkness and reveal that half-
hidden and evanescent light which he hopes and assumes is
the ultimate truth of the universe. I like so much the reply
given me by the Lubavitcher Rebbe when I was complaining
about the inability of modern man to believe. What makes
you think, said the Hasidic Rebbe who once studied electri-
cal engineering at the Sorbonne, that faith is something
which one achieves and then possesses—like a ten-dollar bill?
"Like the body, faith must be continually fed."

Religion is, then, a structure of life and thought which
helps one to "feed" faith. One's beliefs about God, the Torah,
the *mitzvot*, cannot be static. They will, like the lights of
the aurora borealis, tend to strengthen, weaken, or altogether
disappear. Much depends on the "feeding."

The prime instrument for feeding the faith of Jews—for
strengthening and making more obvious the evidence that
behind the seeming impersonal darkness of life's events there
is a design and a mind and a heart—is the Torah, with its
claims and commandments. In traditional Judaism, the very
existence of the Torah has been taken as proof that light—
goodness, justice, and mercy—is the ultimate reality, and that
this light can occasionally be revealed with a brightness that

will convince the most skeptical eyes. Such a revelation, says tradition, occurred at Sinai.

Personally, I have no trouble in believing that there have been individuals and even generations whose eyes were better sensitized than ours for the enterprise of seeing that light which we call God. I can also believe that there were moments in time—perhaps an unusual confluence of nature, historical event, and talented "seers"—when waves of light which to us seem dim and evanescent, appeared brilliantly clear. That there was such a moment at Sinai seems to me a plausible premise. Or rather, I would say with Ludwig Lewisohn that it is far more reasonable to think that *something* unusual and unforgettable took place at Sinai than that nothing at all occurred.

Would an understanding of divine revelation in this sense satisfy the demands of Orthodox Judaism?

I doubt it. On the other hand, there are many Orthodox interpretations of the happening at Sinai. Readers may remember an article by Gershom Scholem in *Commentary* [vol. 38, no. 5, November, 1964] where he quotes the suggestion of a Hasidic Rebbe that all which was "heard" at Mount Sinai was the first letter of the first commandment. That letter is an *aleph*—a silent consonant. The fact is that Judaism does not demand and indeed discourages any attempt to diminish the mystery of Sinai by making it more explicit. Even at Sinai, God is pictured as descending "in a thick cloud." The full nature of the revelation at Sinai is relegated by Judaism to that category of "hidden things which are reserved to God." It is the "revealed matters that are given to man," and by "revealed" Judaism refers mainly to the *mitzvot*—the commandments. Deeply Jewish is the startling invitation which the Talmud attributes to God. "Abandon Me, if you will, but keep My commandments." The implication later suggested is that the keeping of the commandments will in its turn "sensitize" the eyes so that they will be better able to "see" God.

It is, then, to the *mitzvot*—the commandments—that Judaism would direct our attention. And here there is less room for talk about mystery, darkness, and evanescent lights. Here intuitions and feelings can be buttressed by historic facts, even if these facts seem to confront one with an insoluble dilemma. Let us then proceed both to the facts and the dilemma.

A Judaism without *mitzvot*, without a "yoke" of command-ments—laws, not just folkways or pretty ceremonies—is his-torically inauthentic, and lacking in both the reason and the capacity for long-range survival. Of course there are "good" Jews who do not assume this yoke—among them the bulk of American and Israeli Jews, many Jews of the "liberal" religious persuasion, many Jews who are not religious. But it is a fact that from its beginnings, and for more than three thousand years, "normative" Judaism has been completely identified with an elaborate system of law. If there were Jew-ish communities which did not abide by this halakhic legal Judaism, they do not seem to have survived the passage of time.

It is also clear that a Judaism which is uncommitted to the "peculiar" aspects of its law will have a hard time finding its *raison d'être*. The idea of one God, the call for justice, the insistence on man's essential worth and dignity—these may have been Jewish contributions to civilization. But the contribution has been made. And one need not be Jewish today in order to share the historic Jewish attitude toward God, fellow man, and community. Civil-rights activities, an-tagonism toward the John Birch Society, liberal economic and political legislation—these may make up the bulk of pro-gram and activity for our major national Jewish organiza-tions. But they are obviously not a Jewish monopoly and in most instances they could be carried on more effectively out-side an exclusively Jewish framework. Where then can we look for reasons for Jewish survival if not to those laws which confessedly make us a people apart, "different from all other peoples"—that is, to those laws and commandments which cannot be readily interpreted along broad ethical and uni-versal lines? Commandments calling for the truth, mercy, and justice can certainly be observed without commitment to a Jewish or even a religious faith. It may be that religion can buttress the case for morality—though there is enough evi-dence for morality or immorality in both the religious and nonreligious camps to make the claim highly debatable. In any event, one cannot be "bribed" into a belief in God or Judaism by the promise that it will pay off socially.

If, then, we seek those aspects of Judaism which cannot be found either in other faiths or in commonly accepted social and moral principles, we will have a hard time finding them outside the commandments which we usually think of as parochial or anachronistic. I mean commandments which deal with matters like kosher food, phylacteries, the Sabbath (not just as a day of rest but in its peculiar Jewish expression), and the *agunah*.

An *agunah* is a widow whose husband's death cannot be ascertained by the testimony of witnesses, and who, according to Jewish law, may therefore not remarry. I use the example of an *agunah* rather than the prohibition against wearing a mixture of linen and wool, because it is a much more important and real problem in Jewish *halakha*, especially in a land like Israel, where these religious laws have state sanction and apply to non-Orthodox as well as Orthodox residents. So is the problem of a divorced woman marrying a *Kohen*, a descendant of the priestly family, for whom this kind of marriage is forbidden. So are many other laws relating to the use of electricity or transportation on the Sabbath.

And here we have the dilemma. Judaism without law—and religious law means a structure that cannot readily be bent or dissolved under the impact of man's will—is inauthentic and incapable of survival. A Judaism which insists on observance of all the laws is unthinkable—except to a small minority who even in the state of Israel work out many of their problems on the assumption that other Jews will be willing to break religious laws in order to guard borders, run electric plants, and perform other necessary tasks. We thus come to the question—indeed the major question of modern religious Judaism: how do we select? How do we choose what to observe and what to neglect?

To this question I have a short answer. I don't know.

But then I don't know the ultimate answer to so many important problems—like inflation, Vietnam, integration, or what I'm really doing here on earth. That doesn't stop me from trying to carve a little bit of meaning and life out of the mystery. So it is with the *mitzvot*. I find pleasure, meaning, and much chaos-dissolving structure in the observance of dietary restrictions, the donning of phylacteries, the saying of No to creative work on the Sabbath and Yes to its rich intricacies of mood, prayer, and ceremony. If pressed for explanations as to why I observe this or that commandment, I can come up with a variety of reasons—depending, I suppose, on the waxing and waning of those aurora-borealis beliefs at any particular moment. Usually, ethical or intellectual content is the smallest part of my explanation. I prefer the hint of the Hasidic Jew who reminded me that if a person wears tight shoes he can get a headache—that is to say, the "somatopsychic" approach to *mitzvot*, the idea that if you eat kosher, you think and feel "kosher." Or sometimes I think of the whole business as a game—the kind of game described in Hermann Hesse's *Magister Ludi,* which can, through being played, bring one into contact with the deepest strata of thought and life. Most often and basically, however, I think of the *mitzvot* as the visible extensions of the Jewish collective soul. They are the means by which a Jew can connect himself with this soul and through this soul with the wellsprings of life, ultimate reality, God, or whatever you want to call it. And the more *mitzvot,* the more connections. And the more connections, the greater the infusion of life juices. And the more life juices, the more sensitivity, pain, joy, consciousness. In other words, "the more Torah, the more life." So I pick eclectically from those commandments which seem to be, as the Kabbalists would put it, the particular "diet" for nourishing the roots of my soul. My reason for observing Jewish *mitzvot* is not that they give me a better religion, or make me more just and ethical. They fit the needs of my soul, which seems to be more alive when it is connected with the Jewish soul. As to the dilemma—I'm afraid I must just leave it to the fermenting, changing, but wonderfully stubborn life of that Jewish soul to come up with future answers to problems I cannot solve.

And now, having spoken of the collective Jewish soul, we are on to the question about the chosenness of Israel. But why the question? Of course Israel is chosen. Here is a belief that needs no ultrasensitive eyes to probe the darkness. The heavens light up with this fact, light up with a glow that comes both from Sinai and from the fires of Auschwitz. Work it out on any level—statistically, in terms of numbers and contributions to every aspect of civilization; historically, in terms of sheer longevity of existence; culturally and spritually, in terms of the faith and ideas that have come from this little group of wanderers. Obviously there is something unique about the destiny of Israel.

Shall I deny this obvious chosenness because some other peoples have also spoken of chosenness and made of their mission a curse and abomination? Every great idea has its devilish caricature. There is no apology needed for the Jewish concept of chosenness. It is plainly stated in the Bible for all to see and judge. It is a chosenness which affects the genes, but it is open to people of every race. It is a chosenness not for privilege but for burden; a chosenness to be a "light unto the nations"; a chosenness to set an example of mercy and righteousness so powerful that it will transmute the nature of man and beast so that "nations will no longer learn war, . . . tears will be wiped from every cheek and death be swallowed up forever." Apologies, explanations? Let all peoples of the world feel so chosen. This is indeed the ultimate purpose of Jewish chosenness.

No. On this question I cease being an aurora-borealis type of believer. If Judaism has any dogmas, it is that one dogma suggested by Judah Halevi—the tragic and glorious belief that Israel is a seed which may be crushed, but in being crushed releases the power to transmute the soil around it into a tree of new life for all mankind. This I believe—and yet. For there *is* an "and yet" to the Jewish concept of chosenness which must be remembered, lest it end up as a petty and constricting bit of boastfulness.

Chaim Greenberg recounts a fascinating conversation with the great Hebrew national poet, Chaim Nachman Bialik. The poet meets a little blond Aryan girl on the train, and muses out loud about adopting her. He jokingly speculates that this little girl, if brought up in his house, would become a fine Jewish lass, just as the Vilna Gaon, idol of rabbinic Jewry, would have grown up to be a good Tartar if kidnapped as a child by the Tartars. Greenberg is shocked by his light treatment of the essential Jewish soul, and Bialik tells him that he must learn the "mystery of rhythm." He illustrates his point by telling how Sholem Aleichem's Tevye the Dairyman repudiates his daughter when she marries out of the faith. One day, Tevye sees his daughter waiting on the

road but, his heart breaking, he drives his milk wagon past
her without a word. Then there comes a summer twilight
when Tevye is again riding in his wagon and speculating,
"Why did God create a divided world—Jew, Gentile, my
faith, your faith? Wouldn't it have been better if we were
all alike?"

"Tevye understood the mystery of rhythm," said Bialik.
He understood that one must not be reconciled with a
daughter who is an apostate, and yet that it was necessary
from time to time to pass into a sphere of thought where all
these things "aren't worth a plugged nickel." Any Jew, con-
cludes Bialik, who is incapable of "ridding himself of his
nationality from time to time and then returning to his roots,
to his environment, and its spirit—to his tribe if you please—
such a Jew is a sick person."

It does seem to me that any statement about Jewish
beliefs—beliefs about the chosenness of Israel, God, Torah,
morality, etc.—is incomplete without a sense of that "mystery of rhythm" which is itself part of an attempt to free
Judaism from any fixed and unalterable set of beliefs and
definitions. And this brings us to the last two questions of
the symposium.

"Every definition of God," wrote Rabbi Kuk, "involves
us in idolatry." It substitutes a man-made and age-condi-
tioned idea for reality which transcends all such limitations.
Something like this could be said about all attempts to identify Judaism with pat systems of attitudes toward soul, body,
and society. We should be even more suspicious of attempts
to identify Judaism with any current political, economic, and
intellectual issues.

It would seem to me that even a brief exposure to the
variety of belief in historic Judaism would make us cautious
about such easy identifications. Take the principle of the
separation of church and state. I really think that the bulk
of the American Jewish community has come to believe that
this principle is to be found not only in the Constitution,
but in the Torah. I don't know how they overlook the fact
that a wall of separation between religion and politics is
just what the Torah and the prophets seem to abhor. But
the will to believe in a way which fits one's environment
is very strong. Thus, in lands which did not know of

Jeffersonian democracy, Jews found ample support in their tradition for praising monarchy as a system of government. And a Southern segregationist can do at least as well as a Northern liberal in bolstering his case with biblical and rabbinic quotations.

That does not mean that Judaism lacks convictions about the dignity and value of man, or standards of truth and justice, or personal and family ideals, or conceptions of holiness. But Judaism has always used these principles and intuitions as a measuring rod by which to judge the worth and moral health of a society, whatever be its form of organization. Jewish leaders and organizations should take a stand on vital and concrete issues of the day—integration, Vietnam, etc. They should strive for such commitments as human beings and citizens. I think that Judaism would ask for such involvement. But individual and organizational commitment is one thing; the attempt to put their pronouncements in the category of "thus saith the Lord" and read out of Judaism those who do not agree with them is quite another.

I believe that this refusal of Judaism to be confined within any limited system of ideas, and its capacity in history to encounter and digest an immense variety of intellectual fare, means that it is not going to be seriously challenged by any particular aspect of modern thought. If anything, a believing Jew might see in the "God is dead" controversy an attempt to reach out toward Judaism's basic premise—that God is too alive to be captured in any set of theological doctrines. But truthfully, I don't think that all the theological and philosophical discussions of our time have as much influence on religious beliefs as the fact that we buy our meat in frozen packages at the supermarket, or spend the time we are alone looking at television. A style of life which succeeds in insulating us from a vital consciousness of death and loneliness, which tranquilizes both our griefs and our joys by exposure to "healthy-minded" counseling, brightly painted hospital chambers, and endless quantities of entertainment, has much more to do with the withering of the religious sense than the intellectual turmoil of a Tillich, a Buber, or a Sartre.

I remember a discussion about problems of prayer in

Israel where people cited one or another intellectual failing of the old prayerbook. The discussion came to an end when one person rose to say, "Gentlemen, the main problem of prayer in our day is—that it is no problem."

The main problem of religious belief in our day is not the discovery of any new insight into the nature of the universe or the reality of evil, but a way of life which has succeeded in so diverting man from the mysteries of existence that religious belief is no problem. Why struggle for glimpses of evanescent aurora borealis-like lights when we can avoid looking at the darkness—unless the darkness becomes too heavy for dissipation by man-made lights?

Jacob J. Weinstein

Rabbi of K. A. M. Temple (Reform) in Chicago and president of the Central Conference of American Rabbis.

❑ (1) From its very beginning Reform Judaism proclaimed that the Torah was the work of men inspired by a deep commitment to God. As the work of men, it contains the errors, limitations, and fallibilities of men as well as their true insights and judgments—some so true and noble as to merit the promise of permanence. The Shulhan Arukh is not accepted as a guide to daily conduct by Reform Jews. Many of its directives are congenial to Reform Jews because they reflect moral necessities and ethical sensitivities necessary to the good life, or because they prescribe ritual observances which are aesthetically satisfying and which strengthen Jewish identity and fellowship. Reform Jews would not consider the prohibition against mixing linen and wool as fulfilling any of these conditions.

(2) Reform Judaism has consistently interpreted the choosing of the Jews as a call to outdo ourselves morally. It has been partial to the insight of the prophet Amos, who said: "You only have I known of all the families of the earth/Therefore I will visit upon you all your iniquities."

The Jews, the prophet believed, were more responsible than any other people because of their special relationship to God; they did not have that margin of permissiveness which might be given to people who had not assumed the yoke of the Torah. This may very well be the real source of that spiritual athleticism which Freud attributes to our abiding sense of guilt for the murder of the primal tribal father—a guilt which Christians can exorcise vicariously through the Crucifixion.

While Reform Jews have not gone as far as Dr. Mordecai Kaplan, who simply eliminates any reference to the chosen people from the Reconstructionist prayerbook, we have removed most of the "superiority" connotation by translating the *bachar banu* before the reading of the Torah as "Thou hast called us from among all peoples," while we have removed *mikol ha-amim* ("from all the nations") from our version of the Kiddush and freely translated *banu vachartah* as "Thou has ennobled us." We are aware of the possible use of the chosen-people doctrine as a biblical precedent for the racial megalomania of the Germans and the Japanese, but we can only take comfort in Martin Buber's reminder "that it is the fate of every great idea that no sooner does it come upon the stage of history than it is accompanied by its caricature." Consider that "Nazi" is an elision of national-socialism, a term which Ber-Borochov had hoped would describe a far different order of reality. Reform prefers to keep the idea of chosenness as the seal of a spiritual election by which the Jews choose God more than the other way around. It is a theological expression of a call to service and sacrifice which we believe to be the true badge of the people of Israel. While it may entail the risk of spiritual snobbery, it may also be an effective antidote to feelings of inferiority which anti-Semitism, and our minority position generally, have all too often bred into our people.

(3) Even traditional Judaism has never laid claim to exclusive possession of religious truth. Its belief in the Torah as divine revelation and the supremacy of Moses among the prophets did not lead halakhic Judaism to deny that the good Gentile was entitled to his share in the world to come. We have always deliberately denied ourselves the motivation which prompted the evangelical Christian and

Mohammedan to encompass land and sea to make converts and thus save their souls. This very permissiveness, this recognition of the plurality of true faiths is a quality which few Western religions share with Judaism. There are other qualities in Judaism which may be found in the literature of other religions and perhaps in the experience of other communicants but not in the same degree or intensity. Judaism is a subtle interplay of faith and folk, of creedal affirmation and group experience. It is the way the profession washes our in the deed that counts, and it is the weighted average of the generations' commitment that makes the authentic record. Here, then, are some of the distinctions I see in the record:

The unyielding affirmation of the dignity and preciousness of man as creature and partner of God. God sacrifices a portion of His omnipotence to allow man free will. Man can most properly worship God in freedom: "I am the Lord thy God brought thee out of the house of bondage." Man is placed on earth to enjoy the good things of earth. The affliction of the body is an offense to God. Judaism is earth-oriented. No gains can be made in heaven by detouring the world. The life to come is only an extension and fulfillment of life on earth.

The exaltation of the community in the sacred fellowship of man. Social responsibility is as high a value in the Jewish ethic as personal fulfillment. The two are in fact intertwined and utterly dependent one on the other. Consider the admonition from Pirke Avot: "Do not separate thyself from the community." Salvation is impossible outside of community.

If I am only for myself, what do I amount to? Hillel's question has come down to the Jews of our day. The magnificent social-welfare institutions of the Jewish community attest to this.

The apotheosis of study and learning. Study is a form of worship in the Jewish tradition. An ignorant man cannot be pious since he has no adequate knowledge of God's world. Learning was not confined to simple truths. The mastery of numerous and complex data and their channeling into usable categories were part of the halakhic discipline, and this discipline in some measure accounts for the prominence of the

Jew, far beyond his proportion to the general population, in those scientific and administrative professions which demand a passion for intricate detail and reasoned analysis. This factor becomes supremely important as we shift from the battle to attain certain legally assured social objectives to the more difficult goal of implementing them and fixing them into the structured enclaves of our society. We in America have moved from the roomy mansion of the Bible to the crowded small print of the Talmud, from the great over-arching soul-searching of the prophets and psalmists to the meticulous inquiry of the halakhist. Judaism is prepared for this shift.

Judaism's optimism about the viability of the universe, the persistence of man, and the ultimate triumph of peace and justice does not differ from that of other high religions but it does have the added authority of a three-millennial continuity. When so many feel alienated from the universe, insignificant in the face of the scientific revelation of infinite time and space, fearful under the threat of nuclear war, it may be reassuring to have the testimony of a people and a faith that have weathered so many threatening crises in the past.

(4) Judaism does entail a political viewpoint—not in the narrow, but in the broader, sense of politics. There is no way in which we could excommunicate members of the Ku Klux Klan, of Rockwell's American Nazis, or of the John Birch Society if they happened to be Jews, but such people would have a very difficult time indeed in holding to their Judaism unless they built a soundproof compartment between their political and religious commitments. There is something in Judaism that hates a wall. Abraham was commanded to walk before the Lord and be an *ish tam*—whole-souled, all of a piece—and we have not forgotten that injunction. Fascism's theories of race and authority are uncongenial to Judaism, as are Communism's dogmatic determinism, its materialism, and its sanction of violence as a permissible instrument of social revolution. A man might be a Fascist or a Communist and be a Jew, but he could not be a good Jew and a very ardent Fascist, or a doctrinally kosher Communist.

(5) "God is dead" theology does not have much relevance for Judaism even though several rabbis have joined the ranks of these so-called "new theologians." Judaism has never placed God in the jeopardy of mortality. He is for us the Alpha and the Omega, the I AM THAT I AM, the *En Sof*—the without end. Judaism did not permit the Zoroastrians to divide God in two, nor the Christians to divide Him into three. It did not permit Him to become realized in a man. Nor did it follow Spinoza in allowing nature to swallow His transcendence and naturalize Him. Nor did it permit Marx to make Him an exalted chief of police and dispenser of opiates, nor Freud to make Him the authority figure sitting tightly on the id. Judaism was even cautious about designating a name for God, out of fear that the destruction of the name might also endanger the reality behind the name. Therefore the Jew does not actually pronounce the name of God.

The word "God" has acquired many meanings in the course of its journeying through history, but we are not semantic purists. We rather enjoy the opulent permissiveness of our sacred words. Our understanding of the prime importance of continuity encourages us to nudge new meanings out of old familiar terms rather than call for the linguistic bulldozer. Even Dr. Altizer, the *enfant terrible* of the "new theologians," allows that God is less dead for the Jews than for the Christians. We are still able to say Kaddish to Him rather than for Him. We have too long witnessed the pageantry of the gods walking across the stage of history to mistake the passing of the half-gods for the death of God. There is nothing which the new theologians aim to achieve by declaring God dead that we cannot achieve by proclaiming that He lives. Altizer may want God to be dead in order that Jesus may take His place as a fully grown successor-son. We Jews have no such motive. Nor do we have to abandon our theological vocabulary to free the humanistic values in our tradition. The superstructure has never been so heavy in Judaism as to suppress the expansion of our ethical and social values. It is our judgment that those values have been preserved and enhanced by being enclaved in a folklore and in a context of dynamic symbolism and ritual. In the prophets and in the heritage they left us, we have an adequate built-in antidote to the encysting process, to the tendency of institutional thinking to strangle the ideal.

The aspect of modern thought which most seriously challenges Jewish belief is a loose reading of depth psychology which makes religious values a consequence of infantile dependency and subjects social values to the ultimate defeat of the ever-ascendant primitive instincts. This Freudian fatalism plays into the massive uneasiness engendered by the cold war and the alienation engendered by the impersonal bigness of our urban centers (where most Jews live), and it conspires to create a cynicism toward all religious values and a special bitterness toward a patriarchal culture. Jewish youth does not have that confidence in the future which my generation had and which is a key presupposition of Judaism. In rebelling against the sexual as well as the religious mores of Judaism, Jewish youth is making a double-barreled attack both on our religious teaching and on our continuity as an ethnically identifiable group. This combination of circumstances, more than any single school of philosophy or psychology, is the source of our danger. We can only hope that channels of communication can be kept open between the generations so that we may better know what is really troubling our critics and they may look at our tradition without bitterness and prejudice. The present leadership in Reform, both lay and rabbinic, is keenly aware that we must make Judaism intellectually challenging to our young and give it a greater degree of moral integrity by committing our resources more widely and intensely than we have so far to the elimination of war, racial discrimination, and poverty.

Arnold J. Wolf

Rabbi of Congregation Solel (Reform) in Highland Park, Illinois.

℃ (1) The real problem is not that there is too little divine revelation but too much. I believe the Torah is divine revelation; I believe the 613 commandments are divine revelation; I believe Judaism is divine revelation; I believe that what I see of God now is divinely revealed, and that so is what every man sees of every god.

My problem is not the primitive, the extravagant, or the unexpected in Judaism. I should not know what to do with a religion that came on like the Boy Scout manual or like the Ethical Society. My problem is not a silent God, but a God who creates so immense a world, produces so enormous a Torah, communicates so embracing and so resonant a word that I can find no moment and no country without Him.

My problem is myself. My problem is that I cannot appropriate for myself all that God means, that I cannot comprehend it, that I sometimes cannot stand it, that I often cannot fulfill it. God is bigger than all our definitions or even than all His own revelations, while I am a good deal smaller than any of them. My evil inclination always tries to get me to set my mind above His, my pleasure above His service, my needs above my need for Him or even my need to need Him. I do not believe He is really surprised by me, though I fear He is often sorry.

I try to walk the road of Judaism. Embedded in that road there are many jewels. One is marked "Sabbath" and one "Civil Rights" and one "Kashruth" and one "Honor Your Parents" and one "Study of Torah" and one "You Shall Be Holy." There are at least 613 of them and they are of different shapes and sizes and weights. Some are light and easy for me to pick up, and I pick them up. Some are too deeply embedded for me, so far at least, though I get a little stronger by trying to extricate the jewels as I walk the street. Some, perhaps, I shall never be able to pick up. I believe that God expects me to keep on walking Judaism Street and to carry away whatever I can of its commandments. I do not believe that He expects me to lift what I cannot, nor may I condemn my fellow Jew who may not be able to pick up even as much as I can.

The various commandments look somewhat different to me. Some seem larger, some smaller, some important, some (like the linsey-woolsey *shatnez*) trivial. But there is no commandment that may not have its day, and no certainty that may not sometimes fall into doubt. I must not decide in advance what properly belongs on Judaism Street. Nor may I walk down the broad parkway only, but must follow the road even when it narrows and is no longer very easy to walk.

I do not "accord status" to the commandments. I do not feel permitted to rate them in advance of performing them. In principle, no commandment is inferior to any other. But some are in fact unavailable to me, some are dependent on a land in which I do not live, some on a world which is not my world. Some are just too heavy for me to lift. That is no reflection on them or, perhaps, even on me; it is just so. Any Orthodox insistence that every Jew must do the same thing at the same time in the same way is oblivious of human differences. Liberal subjectivism which lets every Jew be his own god forgets our deepest need to become what we are not yet by serving a very great Master. Neither Orthodox nor liberal, I try to be a Jew.

(2) God chose the Jews in history. Sometimes we can even see His work. At the time of the decisive battle of Stalingrad, Hitler was deploying thousands of able-bodied SS men to destroy a defenseless and pitiful Jewish remnant. After the war, Stalin chose Jews to represent Soviet power in several satellite countries because he rightfully mistrusted the nationalisms that would finally wrench themselves free of Great Russian domination. But soon he began to destroy precisely those Jews whose loyalty to him was their only hope for survival, because he hated Jews even more than he feared Poles or Rumanians. An American Jew who still more recently chose to be a Nazi and a Klansman ended in suicide when his profoundest wishes proved to be impossible.

Examples are, of course, no proof. Still, it is a matter of record that Jews who have chosen to support totalitarianism in any of its forms, ancient or modern, have had very hard going indeed. The doctrine of the chosen people has its secular analogue in the insane resistance of tyrants to their would-be Jewish supporters. God does not let the Jews be what they would sometimes like to be: participants in demonic power. God often causes them to be or permits them to be caused to be what no man would ever like to be: victims.

Yet the Bible holds no brief for the Jews. It is not because we were many, wise, or good that God chose us. He might with greater reason have chosen the Hurrians, the Persians, or the British. He did not, for reasons known only to Him. He chose us willy-nilly to be enemies to Pharaoh, Haman, Torquemada, and Stalin. He chose us to be victims of Sargon II, Godfrey de Bouillon, and Hitler.

The doctrine of the chosen people is a mystery, not a problem. It must be lived out, not explained away. It is irrational, implacable, incommensurate with Jewish character or competence. It entails no pride but condemns to recurrent humiliation. It is in no way self-serving. It is not a Jewish idea, but only our interpretation of historic fact. That is why it is so easy to caricature chosenness. The sacred is only a step from the absurd.

(3) All religions are "false," in the sense that they are human refractions and betrayals of God's word. The Bible itself might be defined as a record of Israel's successive evasions of what God did for them and tried to say to them. Judaism itself is both a storing-up of, and a retreat from, God's commandment. It would be nothing less than idolatrous to assert that our religion is the "one true religion." It would be invidious to judge its teachings by comparison with those of any other religion. A man who must believe his own wife is the most attractive woman in town really has no wife. That is why the last of the Ten Words forbids covetousness; interminable shopping among wives or religions for the truest and loveliest is an easy way to surrender responsibility for any one wife or any one religion. And, of course, one can never know whose wife or religion is the fairest of them all anyway, since such knowledge requires the proximity of marriage or the inwardness of faith.

The purpose of Judaism is not to "contribute" to the world's stock of ideas. Nor was "monotheism" ever Judaism's "contribution." It is a Greek word for a Greek idea which answers a Greek question. The Bible is not in the God-counting business, nor is its deity the unmoved mover (who must inevitably turn out to be "one") of Aristotle. Rather, the Hebrew Bible is a battlefield on which many gods struggle for mastery and are endlessly crucified and resurrected, while the God above all our gods longs, fights, and waits to become known to His people. Judaism is not a system of ideas nor even a way of life. It is the Jew's personal enactment and rejection of God's restless, infinite movement toward His world.

There is no "ethical" sphere. The divorce of human obligation from responsibility to God is dangerous and un-Jewish. We cannot render anything to Caesar which is not also God's. We permit no distinction between spirit and matter, between faith and morals, or between doing for God and doing for man. God is present in every human responsibility; what we owe our "nearest" is also owed to Him who is infinitely far. Any provisional distinction between *ben adam la-chavero* and *ben adam la-Makom* falls away on such decisive occasions as Yom Kippur when everything we owe man and do not pay is seen as sin against God.

What distinguishes the Jew from other believers is only that he is a Jew; his ethical sensibilities have been modified in the guts of the generations. He has never been hung up on a spirituality which evades responsibility for this world. Thus, Kierkegaard's refusal of human marriage, or the Buddha's rejection of human parenthood, or any Oriental denial of the human world itself strikes the Jew as rebellion against God. The believing Jew shares with his secularist brother an unqualified love for and commitment to the secular. His God is a God of this world (which to him is, of course, not only "this" world) ; his task is to bring this world toward God. He differs with the secularist only in admitting that he cannot save the world alone. He is more confused, more chastened, more empathetic with the transcendent than an agnostic who knows nothing in the world that is more than man.

Judaism makes contact with other religions not to compare whose God is bigger or whose theology is more coherent, but rather to try to hear what other men have heard of God. Fortunately, and not unexpectedly, what they have heard is very often the same as what we have heard: "Love your neighbor as yourself; I am God." But their problem and ours is not so much to learn what is good as to do what is good. And that requires the systematic repressive-remissive strategy of a disciplined, i.e. religious, life. Judaism is,

272 / THE CONDITION OF JEWISH BELIEF

accordingly, not so much a theosophy which discloses secrets as it is a regimen which achieves persons. I cannot possibly know whether it is a more effective regimen than, say, Zen, but I know that it is still more than demanding enough for me. I think that is all I need to know just yet.

(4) As men, Jews are free, though their freedom is limited by their being Jews. Every gift, even the gift of love, is a limitation. Jews can try to be racists or totalitarians. Individual Jews may get away with it in the short run, but the Jewish people cannot in the long run. A "good Jew" is one who embraces the long run. He affirms his chosenness.

The Jewish religion is politics. From its roots in creation to its ultimate working-out in messianic redemption, it is about the human community. Its God is no man's step-Father. Its Torah gives no man the right to own at another man's expense. In his utmost particularity, the Jew embraces the universal community and his life is a life for all men. A "good Jew" rejoices to find he is obligated to humanity, and is willing to pay what his rejoicing costs, sometimes his life.

(5) The "death of God" theologians are a specifically Christian phenomenon. They are responsive to a technical Christian problem: If the Messiah has come, why is the world as bad as it is? (The symmetrical Jewish problem may be: how can the Messiah ever come to such a world?) The secular Christian solution is radical, stimulating and, I think, mistaken. It confuses the scornful refusal or the sad inability of men to attend with the unwillingness of God to address. When the sun is eclipsed it is still not burned out, as Buber correctly insisted.

Like many Judaizers in the history of Christendom, the new theologians are often theoretical anti-Semites. They use the symbol "Torah" to stand for mindless legalism. They describe the Synagogue as an atrophied Church. They seek to reduce the living God of Israel to mere irrelevance. They systematically depreciate Jewish premises.

Still, Judaizers they are. In beginning to break down the wall between the sacred and the secular, in affirming the centrality of political responsibility, in demythologizing the Church into a *kehillah,* they make most useful contributions to Christian theology. We only wish their mythic hero were somewhat larger than Lyndon Johnson as Orestes, and their optimistic politics rather more demanding than lib-lab tokenism. These Unitarians of the second person (as H. Richard Niehbuhr called them even before they were born) are prematurely eschatological, and thus finally conformist.

The problem for the Jew is how to become a Jew. Trapped between the enormities of Auschwitz on the one hand and the ambivalences of capitalist America on the other, the Jew does not know how to turn. He seeks the bread of biblical and rabbinic Torah and is offered the stone of a dozen inadequate rationalisms. He sees black and brown men all over the world searching his tradition for paradigms, but he no longer can read it for himself. He suffers the agonized impotence of our American Jewish antiheroes, but is put off by Moses, the giant murderer, and David, the royal adulterer. He hopefully explores the involuted and inbred system-chopping of his New York intellectuals, but has no time for talmudic dialectics or the deep silences of Maimonides. Where Freud could point him ruthlessly back to Jewish anthropology, he prefers the sentimental optimism of Erich Fromm. Where Marx (or Adam Smith) could confront him with authentic Jewish choices and tasks, he chooses the vapid me-tooism of the liberal consensus. Now the Cambridge, Massachusetts country boy Harvey Cox bids fair to become his Kierkegaard!

Perhaps we, too, are not to blame. We are, all of us, the children and grandchildren of assimilation. The Jewish *polis* has long been a generation behind the times; when other Europeans were revolutionaries we were already reformists; when Americans sought reform we called ourselves liberals. And now, apparently, we begin to settle for refurbished conservatisms. Egypt always looks good to us in the wilderness.

Modern thought is no enemy of the Jew. But he must become a Jew in order to have the stamina to meet it face-on. Otherwise, as in Berkeley, the secular Jewish liberal will miss his *kairos* and fall on his face. The courage to be present to the present absolutely requires, I believe, the enormous resource of Torah. Man without God may be tragic; the Jew against God is only pathetic.

But with God, the mysterious, ancient, and overpowering

God of Israel, modern thought also becomes Torah, and the
modern Jew knows he is chosen again.

Walter S. Wurzburger

*Rabbi of the Shaarei Shomayim Congregation
(Orthodox) in Toronto and editor of* Tradition.

⊂ Conscious and unconscious strands are so closely intertwined in a faith commitment that one is hard pressed to
identify, let alone analyze, even the most significant elements of one's "ultimate concerns."

I prefer to speak of my "faith commitment" rather than
my "beliefs," because far more is involved than mere assent
to a set of metaphysical or axiological propositions. But
while religious truth is existential and not merely proposi-
tional, it does not follow that the content of one's religious
ideas really does not matter.

I am not prepared to treat religious truth merely as something functional, subjective, or relativistic. Monotheism, by
its very nature, repudiates any ideology which fails to acknowledge the absolute sovereignty of the one God.

Various religions are true to the extent that they incorporate the universally valid ideas of ethical monotheism.
But Jews, as a result of a special covenant with God, have
additional obligations. They are members of an ethnic community that was to constitute itself as a "holy people." Judaism has rightly been defined as "religious ethnicism," but
this does not form a mixture that can be isolated into two
distinct components. Instead, we are confronted here with
an organic whole that cannot be broken down into its con-
stituent parts without destroying the very life of the organism involved.

Axiomatic to Judaism is the belief that God has elected a
particular people—Israel—to serve as His "witnesses." This
election—a divine mystery beyond the ken of rational comprehension—confers, however, no special privileges vis-à-vis
others. What it does impose is an onerous mission to sanctify the name of God by virtue of exemplary moral behavior,

spiritual sensitivity, and a life hallowed by total commitment to the service of God.

This concept does not warrant the charges of tribalism or ethnocentricism. In the dialectics of Judaism, the creative tension between universalism and particularism is but one of many polarities that provide the thrust for a dynamic faith experience. Israel must form a distinctive and separate people—that "dwelleth alone and is not reckoned among the nations." Yet this very apartness is necessary for the ultimate fulfillment of the promise given to Abraham, "and through you all the families of the earth shall be blessed."

The messianic aspirations of Israel are not self-centered. It is through the redemption of Israel that all of human society will be transformed by the application of our ethicoreligious ideals. Israel plays a unique role in the drama of history, because its very existence is endowed with transcendent worth as a divinely ordained instrument for the establishment of His kingdom. It was to fulfill this destiny that Israel was called upon to bear witness to the absolute sovereignty of God and as a "holy people" to abide by the provisions of a divinely willed mandate.

Underlying this view of Israel's role in history was a conception of holiness that stressed man's responsibilities in the here-and-now. Faith in God was not to lead to withdrawal from the world and the abdication of responsibility in a spirit of submissive acquiescence. Man was not to lose himself in the eternal. As a result of the incursion of the divine into the realm of the temporal, life was to be sanctified— not dismissed as inconsequential. Human deeds were endowed with ultimate significance because God Himself provided man with specific tasks, couched in terms of "thou shalt" and "thou shalt not." It was through a vast network of commandments encompassing practically every area of life that man's actions in the here-and-now were related to the divine will.

Because of the central role which Torah and *mitzvot* play in God's covenant with Israel, I look upon many sophisticated versions of the "covenantal theology" which are in vogue today as completely inadequate to the minimal requirements of the Jewish faith commitment. I can fully appreciate the predicament of theologians who, while regarding the notion of divine revelation as indispensable to Judaism, find it intellectually embarrassing to subscribe to the belief that God actually communicated specific content to man. To facilitate escape from the horns of this dilemma, an ingenious compromise solution has been evolved. Revelation is conceived exclusively as an encounter with the divine presence. Since, on the basis of this view, there was no content to the revelation, the commandments become merely the human response to an encounter with the divine presence.

However appealing this formulation may be to the modern mind, we must bear in mind that it cannot possibly do justice to the preeminent position of Torah as the bridge between God and Israel. Christian theology may be able to operate successfully with a doctrine of revelation that "merely" amounts to the self-disclosure of God. But for Jewish purposes, revelation cannot be divested of content, for this would for all practical purposes displace Torah from its pivotal position in the structure of the Jewish faith experience. As I see it, revelation itself (through the written and the oral Torah) provides the basis of the binding character of the *mitzvot*.

In view of the fact that all the commandments represent the revealed word of God, I cannot, insofar as questions of observance are concerned, differentiate among them. In the final analysis, irrespective of the doctrinal or ethical content of a given *mitzvah*, it is observed as a *commandment* of God, ideally performed out of unconditional love for Him as an act of submission to His will.

But in spite of the central position that the Law occupies in the covenant, the charge of legalism is totally unfounded. Compliance with specific legal provisions satisfies merely the *minimal* requirements of Jewish piety. The *halakha* represents the *road* on which one travels toward the ultimate goal—the spiritual heights where "all one's actions are performed for the sake of God." The Jew always saw in Torah a channel to the love of God. Hence, "engagement with Torah" is not—as some Jewish existentialists claim—the antithesis of the authentically free personality which is truly open to God. It is rather through Torah that man is to be liberated from his bondage to self-centeredness, and that he becomes ever more qualified to respond to the call of the divine and lead an ideal life of holiness.

It is largely in the ethical sphere that the all-consuming quest for holiness manifests itself. According to Jewish tradition, one imitates God and walks in His ways, primarily when one practices loving-kindness and justice.

Obviously, ethical norms can be severed from their religious moorings. In fact, many of the ethical values first formed within the matrix of Judaism have been appropriated even by avowed secularists. But it must not be forgotten that the ethical act itself acquires an entirely different dimension within a religious setting. It is not at all merely a question of whether, as Kant maintains, God is a postulate of ethics. From a religious perspective, the issue is not whether ethics presupposes for its ultimate validation some form of theistic belief or at least "points" to the existence of God. The theocentric orientation of Judaism balks at any conception that "employs" God merely as a postulate of the moral enterprise. It is God who is absolute. He must be *served*, not "used" for our purposes, however worthwhile. Religion definitely is not a handmaiden of ethics.

But though depriving ethics of its autonomous character and "reducing" moral behavior to an aspect of one's total quest for holiness in self-surrender to God, Judaism actually enhances the worth of the individual. Jewish ethics operates not merely with the humanistic notion of the dignity of man. As bearer of the image of the divine, the individual becomes endowed with transcendent worth—a notion that leads to the sacredness of the human personality.

This emphasis upon the sacredness and dignity of the individual makes it impossible for a religious Jew to subscribe to various totalitarian philosophies (quite apart from the fact that these particular political creeds have often been turned into idolatries of demonic character). But while it is possible to reject a variety of political philosophies as incompatible with Judaism, no one particular political ideology can be endorsed without qualifications as *the* expression of Jewish religious ideals. The realization of the inevitable imperfections and limitations that beset all human institutions, however, should not induce a harried retreat into a spiritual ivory tower. Judaism has always frowned upon the kind of "religious egotism" wherein man becomes so preoccupied with his own spiritual perfection that he treats all social responsibilities merely as a means to his personal salvation.

Active involvement in human affairs is expected in a religion that aims for the formation of a truly holy *community* which, in its entirety, bears witness to the kingdom of God. If Jews have played such a prominent role in the civil-rights struggle as well as in so many other humanitarian movements, their "liberalism" cannot be attributed to attitudes engendered by their long history as a harassed minority. What catapulted Jews into the vanguard of the struggle for the advancement of human rights and welfare was the impact of their spiritual legacy which stressed the primacy of the ethicosocial task. Thus it became not a mere desideratum but a religious imperative to lend one's support to those social and political agencies which held out the greatest promise for the promotion of human welfare, especially of the downtrodden and oppressed.

Attempts to "spiritualize" religion so completely as to render it ineffective as an instrument for the transformation of society are entirely foreign to Judaism. The very contrast between the "world" and religion is unacceptable to a faith which does not seek merely to salvage parts of life for "religion" but which claims total commitment of man for the service of God. Not only individuals, but human collectivities (including "sovereign" states!) are summoned to renounce all pretensions to absolute significance before the God who demands love, justice, and concern for the sanctity of the individual.

Because the covenantal obligations of the Jew are so all-embracing, profession of a creed as such never played a significant role. Even the affirmation of the unity of God in the *Shema* was not merely acceptance of a "belief," but, to employ the talmudic phrase, commitment to the yoke of the kingdom of God. Judaism does not lend itself to reduction to essences or abstract, general principles. This is why the minutiae of the Law were spelled out in detail, while even the axioms of belief were sketched only in the vaguest and broadest terms.

Against this background, it is readily understandable why Jewish theology—the little that flourishes today—is not particularly exercised over the so-called "god is dead" issue. For one thing, the belief in the living God, while necessary, is not a sufficient condition for the meaningfulness of the Jewish faith commitment. So far as Jewish theology is concerned, the real issue is not just the feasibility of a theistic position as such—a general philosophical or theological question that can be tackled by thinkers regardless of their particular religious background—but the presuppositions and implications of the belief that God has actually revealed Himself to Israel and called us to His service.

While insisting upon the centrality of observance in the structure of Judaism, I still believe that we cannot altogether ignore the challenge posed by the attrition of faith as such. While I do not wish to minimize the importance of retaining one's Jewish identity and of the performance of at least some *mitzvot* by those who feel that they cannot accept the supernatural premises of the classical Jewish position, it must be borne in mind that Judaism cannot shrug off basic questions involving matters of belief. I totally reject the position of Spinoza and Mendelssohn, who contended that Judaism is nothing but a legal system which regulates conduct but not ideas. After all, a variety of theological presuppositions is indispensable to the halakhic system. While Jewish theology was never explicitly formulated, it is still implicitly contained in the rules of conduct that are prescribed in its "way of life."

Yet there are also immensely practical considerations which dictate more serious attention to the problems posed by the attrition of faith. If the "acids of modernity" (to borrow Walter Lippmann's expression) were to corrode the belief in the living God, the Jew would lose his *raison d'être*. Without a belief in a covenant with God there can be no meaningful Jewish survival. And it is precisely this belief which clashes head-on with the prevailing winds of doctrine such as scientism and naturalism. It must be remembered that it is not science as such, but a pseudofaith, based upon totally unwarranted assumptions that go beyond anything verifiable by scientific procedures, that rules out a priori the possibility of any incursion of the supernatural into the domain of the natural. It is on the basis of this "scientific" article of faith that religious faith in God ceases to be a mystery; it becomes just another problem of psychology. Thus, biblical criticism, dialectical materialism, and naturalism are but a syndrome of the determination to explain *away* the objective validity of all religious faith.

But Judaism must not permit itself to be trapped (a danger that looms especially large in an age of ecumenism) into accepting the basic premise of scientism and allowing religious faith to be relegated to a pragmatically valuable but purely subjective experience (shades of the Freudian "illusion"). Judaism must not renounce its claim that God has actually spoken to man.

It should also be remembered that scientism has reached its nemesis in the nihilism which represents the ultimate and inescapable consequence of its premises. If man were to rely exclusively on purely scientific methods, he would be utterly bereft of any guidance in his quest for standards of value. (It is self-evident that no "ought" can be inferred from what "is.") Confronted by such an intolerable situation, the modern Jew may yet seek a way out from the "absurdity" bred by his pseudofaith and discover that he too is addressed in and through Torah by the living God who summons him to become a builder of His kingdom.